Twentieth
Century China
A History in Documents

Twentieth Century China
A History in Documents

R. Keith Schoppa

OXFORD
UNIVERSITY PRESS

To Beth, for her love, support, and perspective.

General Editors

Board of Advisors

UNIVERSITY PRESS

Oxford   New York
Auckland Bangkok Buenos Aires Cape Town Chennai
Dar es Salaam Delhi Hong Kong Istanbul Karachi Kolkata
Kuala Lumpur Madrid Melbourne Mexico City Mumbai Nairobi
São Paulo Shanghai Singapore Taipei Tokyo Toronto

Copyright © 2004 by R. Keith Schoppa

Published by Oxford University Press, Inc.
198 Madison Avenue, New York, New York 10016
www.oup.com

Oxford is a registered trademark of Oxford University Press

Library of Congress Cataloging-in-Publication Data
Schoppa, R. Keith
Twentieth century China: a history in documents / R. Keith Schoppa.
p. cm. — (Pages from history)
Includes bibliographical references and index.
ISBN 0-19-514745-6 (alk. paper)
1. China-History—20th century-Sources. I. Title. II. Series.
DS773.89.S36 2004
951.05—dc22
2004002804

Printed in the United States of America
On acid-free paper

Contents

What Is a Document?

To the historian, a document is, quite simply, any sort of historical evidence. It is a primary source, the raw material of history. A document may be more than the expected government paperwork, such as a treaty or passport. It is also a letter, diary, will, grocery list, newspaper article, recipe, memoir, oral history, school yearbook, map, chart, architectural plan, poster, musical score, play script, novel, political cartoon, painting, photograph—even an object.

Using primary sources allows us not just to read *about* history, but to read history itself. It allows us to immerse ourselves in the look and feel of an era gone by, to understand its people and their language, whether verbal or visual. And it allows us to take an active, hands-on role in (re)constructing history.

Using primary sources requires us to use our powers of detection to ferret out the relevant facts and to draw conclusions from them; just as Agatha Christie uses the scores in a bridge game to determine the identity of a murderer, the historian uses facts from a variety of sources—some, perhaps, seemingly inconsequential—to build a historical case.

The poet W. H. Auden wrote that history was the study of questions. Primary sources force us to ask questions—and then, by answering them, to construct a narrative or an argument that makes sense to us. Moreover, as we draw on the many sources from "the dust-bin of history," we can endow that narrative with character, personality, and texture—all the elements that make history so endlessly intriguing.

Cartoon
This political cartoon addresses the issue of church and state. It illustrates the Supreme Court's role in balancing the demands of the 1st Amendment of the Constitution and the desires of the religious population.

Illustration
Illustrations from children's books, such as this alphabet from the New England Primer, tell us how children were educated, and also what the religious and moral values of the time were.

The said Indian Nations parties to this treaty, shall be at liberty to fish, and hunt, within the Territory and Lands which they have now ceded to the United States, so long as, they shall demean themselves peaceably.

In Witness whereof Charles Jouett Esquire a Commissioner on the part of the United States, and the Sachems, Chiefs and Warriors of the Indian Nations aforesaid; have hereto set their hands and seals.

Charles Jouett.

Map

A 1788 British map of India shows the region prior to British colonization, an indication of the kingdoms and provinces whose ethnic divisions would resurface later in India's history.

Treaty

A government document such as this 1805 treaty can reveal not only the details of government policy, but information about the people who signed it. Here, the Indians' names were written in English transliteration by U.S. officials; the Indians added pictographs to the right of their names.

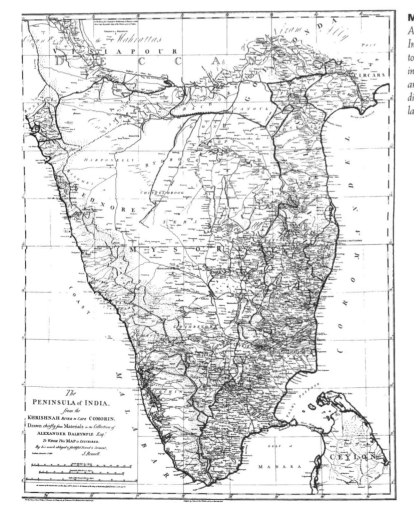

The
PENINSULA of INDIA,
from the
KHRISHNAH RIVER to CAPE COMORIN.
Drawn chiefly from Materials in the Collection of
ALEXANDER DALRYMPLE Esq.
To Whom This MAP is Inscribed,
By his much obliged & faithful Friend & Servant,
J. Rennell.

Literature

The first written version of the Old English epic Beowulf, from the late 10th century, is physical evidence of the transition from oral to written history. Charred by fire, it is also a physical record of the wear and tear of history.

How to Read a Document

To read a document effectively, it is important to understand the context of that document. When did it appear? Who wrote, drew, painted, or photographed it and why? Who were the targeted audiences, and how did the document's originators aim to affect their readers or viewers? The reader must go beyond the date and author of the document to understand its true meaning.

Most of the documents in this book deal with China's twentieth-century revolution and its struggle to establish a modern nation state. Some deal with the lives of ordinary citizens living in the shadow of these revolutionary changes. The authors of the documents have many different viewpoints, because there were many different revolutionary roads to travel. The types of documents in this book are wide ranging; they include poems, personal accounts, posters, advertisements, transcriptions of radio addresses, policy papers, and government documents.

The cartoon and poster on the opposite page both reflect the political turmoil of the time they appeared, but they had entirely different objectives. Political cartoons often use humor, symbolism, irony, or sarcasm to comment on a political situation. The political posters that became very popular in the 1960s and the years after aim to set forward politically correct policy lines and to urge support for them or to attack those who do not follow these policy lines.

Point of View
The "trash" being swept out of China reveals how the West saw China as a whole. Each item of trash is named, pointing out China's superstition, bigotry, and intolerance—as perceived by the West.

Symbolism
The Allied Powers, represented by a broom sweeping the trash out of China, are bringing "civilization," which is written on the broomstick. The Allied Powers have swept away the negative traits that the "more civilized" Western nations see in Chinese culture. The Boxers are at the top of the heap, because their uprising had sparked Western intervention.

Context
The government produced this poster in 1968, during the Cultural Revolution, when the cult of Mao Zedong was at its peak.

Symbolism
Mao appears at the center of the poster as the Red Sun—a name by which he was known at the time—with beams radiating out to the masses of people. The image of the sun, both life-sustainer and dominator, powerfully conveyed to the people the importance of Mao in the Chinese world.

Format
Propaganda posters were important in mass campaigns organized by the government to mobilize the people to participate in various political, economic, military, or cultural programs. They were used to educate, inspire, and, in some cases, criticize people. In reading such posters, it is important to note what is specifically depicted and how.

Title
The poster's title, "Advance victoriously while following Chairman Mao's revolutionary line in literature and the arts," thrusts forth a military theme, consonant with the spirit of the Cultural Revolution.

Introduction

S ome analysts and futurists are predicting that the twenty-first century will be China's century. The once-great civilization that countries around the world looked to with admiration is seemingly primed to reemerge as a leader in the international community of nations. The foundation of its coming success (if these predictions materialize) was its bloody and tragic twentieth century. It was a period of revolutions, from the opening salvos of change fired by its Manchu leaders to the political revolution of China's Nationalist Party in the 1920s, to the political, social, economic, and cultural upheavals of the Communists in the last half of the century.

During China's period of slow decline from the late eighteenth into the early twentieth century and throughout its twentieth-century revolution, one of the most important problems facing individual Chinese and China as a nation was choosing appropriate political, social, cultural, and economic identities as contexts and situations changed. This study of twentieth-century China through various kinds of documentary evidence begins with the turn-of-the-century Boxer uprising, which sets the stage for understanding the choices at stake. It focuses on the dramatic choices of identity with which the revolution of the twentieth century has continually confronted the Chinese and their nation. In many cases these choices have meant life or death.

This is no story of abstract historical forces vying for primacy in the history of a nation. Rather, it is a story of the people—leaders and followers—whose decisions propelled modern Chinese history in the erratic directions it took. It is a dramatic and often violent tale, alternately soaring with hope and plunging into deep despair. The story compels our interest because of its importance for the world today; because it is one of world history's greatest revolutions; and because it provides an extraordinarily interesting study of the processes that an ancient culture undergoes in transforming itself into that which we call "modern."

The theme of historical identities runs like a thread through this story. Identity plays crucial roles in historical processes: actions of

In the midst of modern consumerism, laborers, like beasts of burden, pull heavy loads through city streets as they have done for centuries.

At open-air barber's stalls, picking out ear wax was a service the barber often performed when a customer had his hair cut.

individuals and states depend in large part on how they perceive their identities and how they are perceived by others with whom they must interact. In the first decade of the twentieth century, one driving question of identity was the relationship between the ruling Manchus and the ethnic Han Chinese. The latter contended that China must be controlled by Chinese, not ethnic outsiders. The other crucial change in identity for the people was casting off the label of monarchical subjects and becoming citizens of the republic. This basic political change was followed by an even more wrenching identity crisis during the May Fourth Movement, when traditional cultural identity was tossed on history's trash heap, and China's people and nation were faced with having to construct a new cultural identity.

The revolution of the 1920s gave the Chinese people for the first time the political choice that would remain for most of the rest of the century: identity as a Nationalist Party member with loyalties to Sun Yat-sen and Chiang Kai-shek, or as a Communist Party member with allegiance to Mao Zedong and Deng Xiaoping. From the 1920s through the 1940s, this choice was a critical one as each party experimented with new policies and structures. It was Chiang's Nationalists who officially held the reins of power in Nanjing, but it was Mao's Communists who emerged in the late 1940s to challenge the Nationalists in civil war and seize power in 1949. This struggle for power had as its backdrop, and often-critical intervener, the brutal military aggression of the Japanese.

The Communist victory in the civil war settled, on its face, the issue of political identity for the Chinese nation. But the years of Mao Zedong's leadership saw renewed issues of political identity. Mao was driven by a fierce revolutionary romanticism and an overweening sense of himself as a man of destiny. His years of rule started with amazing success, but quickly spiraled into the illogical radicalism of the Great Leap Forward, the worst famine in world history, and the destructive insanity of the Cultural Revolution. During these years, people's choices about their identities could lead to imprisonment, forced labor, torture, death, or a combination of these. Though the engine behind Mao's policies was both ideological and personal, once again it was the hopes and lives of the Chinese people that were trampled.

The Communist ideological identity of the Mao years, so seemingly confirmed as the new Chinese identity, was overturned, in deed if not in name, during the tenures of his successors, Deng

Xiaoping, Jiang Zemin, and Hu Jintao. Turning to market reforms, and by the end of the century to the privatization of state companies, the Chinese government identified itself with economic liberalization. Though in essence this was the birth of outright capitalism, the government touted it as "socialism with Chinese characteristics." The government identified itself just as clearly with political authoritarianism, clamping down on Democracy Wall in 1979, on the Beijing spring in 1989, and on all dissent in between and after those milestones of protest. At the turn of the twenty-first century, China's identity was not firmly set. Indeed, given the fully operating democracy in the Republic of China on Taiwan and the still-to-be-determined relationship between Taiwan and the mainland, the identity of China was very much up in the air. Furthermore, it was not only the political and economic identities that were unclear, but the moral center of Chinese culture as well, a situation underscored by the rise of religious movements and renewed problems between the Han Chinese and ethnic minorities.

The documents in this book have been selected to elucidate the Chinese twentieth-century experience of seeking new identities amid change and revolution. They are wide-ranging: official reports and statements, eyewitness and participant accounts, articles, cartoons, poetry, songs, and advertisements. Sidebars and photographs help bring the documents alive and add insight and commentary on the documents. As a whole, this book is meant to kindle an interest not only in Chinese history but also in "doing history" in general.

Prologue

The Boxer Catastrophe

They were mostly adolescent gangs who attacked Christian converts, missionaries, and churches. Rising out of drought conditions and anti-foreign feeling in northern China, these so-called Boxers were ragtag groups that terrorized local communities from 1898 to 1900. Had the government been strong and prosperous, as it had been a century earlier, it most certainly could have suppressed them. But China was weak and close to bankruptcy after more than half a century of wars against outside aggressors (Great Britain, France, and Japan) and decades of trying to put down internal rebellions. China was also limited by its status as a semi-colony after Western powers forced a "treaty system" upon it in the mid-nineteenth century—a system that gave various economic and political rights and privileges to Westerners, and in the process cut back on Chinese rights.

In the closing years of the 1890s a new threat arose from Western imperialist nations; they began to demand large chunks of territory to lease for periods of twenty-five to ninety-nine years. "Carving up the Chinese melon," it was called. In its wretched state, China had few options. China's ruler, the Empress Dowager Cixi, apparently at her wit's end, tragically decided that she might use the Boxers as a force against the West. Western missionary and diplomatic demands that China subdue the Boxers thus went nowhere. At last, when the Boxers surrounded the foreign ambassadors' quarters in Beijing and put them under siege in the summer of 1900, eight nations (Japan and seven nations from the West, including the United States) sent a relief expedition to lift the siege. The Boxers melted away into the North China plain and the Empress Dowager fled. But the Westerners stayed for another year.

Foreign troops from the eight-nation Allied Powers temporarily occupy the grounds of the Forbidden City in Beijing in November 1900. Their year-long occupation, marked by killing, destruction, and looting, followed their suppression of the Boxer movement.

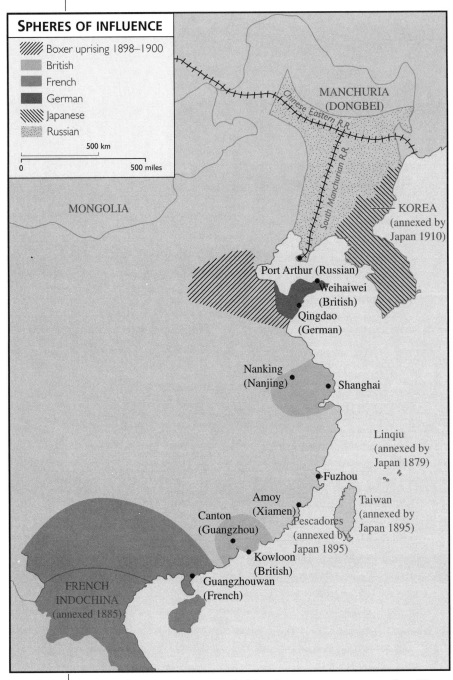

SPHERES OF INFLUENCE

- //// Boxer uprising 1898–1900
- British
- French
- German
- \\\\ Japanese
- Russian

500 km
0   500 miles

MONGOLIA

MANCHURIA
(DONGBEI)

Chinese Eastern R.R.

South Manchurian R.R.

KOREA
(annexed by
Japan 1910)

Port Arthur (Russian)
Weihaiwei
(British)
Qingdao
(German)

Nanking
(Nanjing)   Shanghai

Linqiu
(annexed by
Japan 1879)

Fuzhou

Amoy
(Xiamen)   Taiwan
(annexed by
Japan 1895)

Canton
(Guangzhou)   Pescadores
(annexed by
Japan 1895)

Kowloon
(British)

FRENCH
INDOCHINA
(annexed 1885) Guangzhouwan
(French)

The Western position, led by the missionaries, was that China had to pay for not quelling the Boxers. Forty-five thousand Western and Japanese troops were in China by late 1900. They spent their time burning, raping, looting, and beheading. Missionaries joined in the looting; one, an American missionary named Gilbert Reid, wrote an essay in a leading American magazine rationalizing missionaries' looting of Chinese property:

"To confiscate the property of those who were enemies in war may be theoretically wrong, but precedent had established the right. For those who have known the facts and have passed through a war of awful memory, the matter of loot is one of high ethics."

But the low point came in September 1901, when China was forced to sign the Boxer Protocol, an agreement that punished Chinese who had been linked to the affair and made various political and military demands. The most crushing burden was a huge indemnity—the West would make China pay, literally. The total was 450 million taels (about U.S. $333 million in 1901 dollars). The Protocol specified that China was to pay the indemnity in gold in thirty-nine annual installments. By the end, with interest payments, China would have paid about one billion taels. Mark Twain's punning joke about the punishments and the indemnity had, from a Western point of view, considerable reality: "Taels I win, heads you lose."

For a government that had already been unable to function well for lack of money, the indemnity was crushing. As China entered the twentieth century, it did so degraded, humiliated, and impoverished.

China and the West

In his essay, "To the Person Sitting in Darkness," published in the *North American Review* in 1901, Mark Twain attacked with sarcasm and wit the missionaries who had taken revenge on the Chinese for the Boxer troubles by looting property and then trying to rationalize their looting. Twain recounts the actions of the Rev. Mr. Ament who personally collected indemnities in localities where Ament's own converts had been killed; Ament put the number at 300. For each of these he collected 300 taels, and then reportedly assessed fines that amounted to thirteen times the original indemnity. All of the money, he claimed, would be used for "propagating the Gospel." He argued that missionaries were not vindictive, and that they were doing nothing "that the circumstance did not demand." He suggested that Protestants were less bloodthirsty than Catholics, who not only took money from the Chinese but beheaded Chinese to equal the number of Catholics killed.

Our Reverend Ament is the right man in the right place. What we want of our missionaries out there is, not that they shall merely

It is not bloodthirstiness in missionaries to desire to see further shedding of [Chinese] blood, but an understanding of Chinese character and conditions, and a realization that the policy of general forgiveness means the loss of many valuable native [Christian] and foreign lives.

—The Reverend D. Z. Sheffield on the Boxer aftermath, in a letter to Judson Smith, March 26, 1901

楊村大戰

Foreign soldiers clash with Boxers at the "Great Battle of Yang Village"—as denoted by the title of this woodcut. In the background, Boxers, who carried out their fighting in units of 25 to 100, fire a cannon at a foreign ship.

represent in their acts and persons the grace and gentleness and charity and loving kindness of our religion, but they represent the American spirit. . . .

Our Reverend Ament is justifiably jealous of those enterprising Catholics, who not only get big money for each lost convert, but get the "head for head" besides. But he should soothe himself with the reflection that the entirety of their exactions are for their own pockets, whereas he, less selfishly, devotes only 300 taels per head to that service, and gives the whole vast thirteen repetitions of the property-indemnity to the service of propagating the Gospel. His magnanimity has won him the approval of his nation, and will get him a monument. Let him be content with these rewards. We all hold him dear for manfully defending his fellow missionaries from exaggerated charges which were beginning to distress us, but which his testimony has so considerably modified that we can now contemplate them without noticeable pain. For now we know that, even before the siege, the missionaries were not "generally" out looting, and that, "since the siege," they have acted quite handsomely, except when "circumstances" crowded them. I am arranging for the monument. Subscriptions for it can be sent to the American Board [of Missions]; designs for it can be sent to me. Designs must allegorically set forth the Thirteen reduplications of the Indemnity, and the Object for which they were exacted; as Ornaments, the designs must exhibit 680 heads, so disposed as to give a pleasing and pretty effect; for the Catholics have done nicely, and are entitled to notice in the monument. . . .

We have Mr. Ament's impassioned assurance that the missionaries are not "vindictive." Let us hope and pray that they will never become so, but will remain in the almost morbidly fair and just and gentle temper which is affording so much satisfaction to their brother and champion today.

On September 7, 1901, the eight nations whose soldiers lifted the Boxer siege forced China to sign the Boxer Protocol. Though each of its articles was galling, humiliating, or destructive, by far the most devastating for its long-term effect was the indemnity provided for in Article 6. Article 2B cut at the heart of the Chinese political system, which was based upon official examinations. Articles 1 and 3, here omitted, were apologies for the killings of a German and Japanese diplomat.

Article 2A

. . . the principal authors of the outrages and crimes committed against the foreign Governments and their nationals, are to be condemned to death by execution [or] death by committing suicide. . . .

This judgment was made by an unidentified soldier in the Boxer campaign, recorded in a book published a year after the Western forces entered China.

It is safe to say that where one real Boxer has been killed since the capture of [Beijing], fifty harmless coolies or laborers on the farms, including not a few women and children, have been slain.

A Japanese soldier wipes blood from his sword after decapitating suspected Boxers. Because foreign troops often had no way to differentiate Boxers from non-Boxers, violence and bloodshed was common among non-Boxer populations.

Legations

Ambassadors and their staffs

His Majesty

"His Majesty" refers to the emperor whom the Empress Dowager had placed under house arrest after he became involved with radical reformers in 1898.

Article 2B

. . . the suspension of official examinations for five years in all cities where foreigners were massacred or submitted to cruel treatment.

Article 4

The Chinese Government has agreed to erect an expiatory monument in each of the foreign or international cemeteries which were desecrated and in which the tombs were destroyed.

It has been agreed with the Representatives of the Powers that the legations interested shall settle the details for the erection of these monuments, China bearing all the expenses thereof, estimated at ten thousand taels for the cemeteries at Peking and within its neighborhood, and five thousand taels for the cemeteries in the provinces. . . .

Article 5

China has agreed to prohibit the importation into its territory of arms and ammunition, as well as of materials exclusively used for the manufacture of arms and ammunition. . . .

Article 6

By an Imperial Edict dated the 29th of May, 1901, His Majesty the Emperor of China agreed to pay the Powers an indemnity of four hundred and fifty millions of Haikwan Taels. This sum represents the total amount of the indemnities for States, companies, or societies, [and] private individuals. . . .

Article 7

The Chinese Government has agreed that the quarter occupied by the legations shall be considered as one specially reserved for their use and place under their exclusive control, in which Chinese shall not have the right to reside and which may be made defensible. . . .

Article 8

The Chinese Government has consented to raze the forts of [Dagu] and those which might impede free communication between Peking [Beijing] and the sea; steps have been taken for carrying this out.

Article 9

The Chinese Government has conceded the right to the Powers in the protocol annexed to the letter of the 16th of January, 1901, to occupy certain points, to be determined by an agreement

Groups of Boxers walk through the streets of Tianjin, a city near Beijing, in 1901. This is one of only a handful of known candid photographs of Boxers.

between them, for the maintenance of open communications between the capital and the sea. . . .

Article 10
The Chinese Government has agreed to post and to have published during two years in all district cities the following Imperial Edicts:

a. Edict of the 1st of February, prohibiting forever, under pain of death, membership in any antiforeign society.

b. Edicts of the 13th and 21st February, 29th April, and 19th August, enumerating the punishments inflicted upon the guilty.

c. Edict of the 19th of August, 1901, prohibiting examinations in all cities where foreigners were massacred or subjected to cruel treatment.

d. Edict of February 1st, 1901, declaring all governors-general, governors, and provincial or local officials responsible for order in their respective districts, and that in case of new antiforeign troubles or other infractions of treaties which shall not be immediately repressed and the authors of which shall not be punished, these officials shall be immediately dismissed, without possibility of being given new functions or new honors.

The posting of these edicts is being carried on throughout the Empire.

Article 11
The Chinese Government has agreed to renegotiate the amendments deemed necessary by the foreign Governments to the treaties of commerce and navigation and other subjects concerning commercial relations, with the object of facilitating them.

Article 12
An imperial edict of the 24th of July, 1901, reformed the Office of Foreign Affairs (Zongli Yamen), on the lines indicated by the Powers, that is to say, transformed it into a Ministry of Foreign Affairs, which takes precedence over the six other Ministries of State. . . .

These two political cartoons view the Boxers from the perspective of the West and the Western actions at the time of the Boxers from the perspective of the Chinese. The first, published originally in the *Brooklyn Eagle* in July of 1900 is titled "The Open Door that China Needs." The Western powers (or as the broom puts it, "Civilization") are sweeping out the door those elements seen by the West as bad. It is ironic, given the general reactions of most Westerners to Chinese, that one of the swept-out items is "intolerance."

This cartoon, published in the *Anhui Common Speech Journal* in 1905, is titled "National Humiliation Picture." The Chinese carries a flag proclaiming his readiness to submit to foreign occupation, but the foreign soldier is nevertheless ready to slash the Chinese to death.

Chapter One

An Old World Dies; A New One Is Born

The Boxer catastrophe in 1900 and the Empress Dowager Cixi's subsequent year-and-a-half self-imposed exile in Xi'an, an old imperial capital about 800 miles southwest of Beijing, convinced her of the necessity for reform. The Empress Dowager and her dynasty, known as the Qing, were Manchus from far northeastern China. They had ruled China since 1644. Recognizing that China now faced possible extinction as a state if its leaders did not try to address the horde of problems in front of them, she turned first to education. The court decreed the establishment of a modern school system, and, in one of the most revolutionary acts of any Chinese government in the twentieth century, abolished the civil service examination system. The government instituted military reform, establishing the so-called New Army, trained in modern weapons and techniques and inspired by the spirit of nationalism.

The administration of the national government, existing basically as it had been constructed more than 1,000 years earlier, was totally revamped. Even more revolutionary was the Empress Dowager's political decision to move to a constitutional government, though many scholars believe it was primarily a strategy to maintain the dynasty's power. If she had lived longer, she just might have been able to pull off this revolutionary blitz in the structuring of a new world. But after her death in November 1908, her successors slowed the reforms, in the process stirring up further opposition to the Manchus.

A large part of the Manchus' problems was their ethnic identity: as non-Chinese, they had been in charge of China during its disastrous

The Empress Dowager Cixi stands before one of her thrones. The empress essentially ruled China from 1861 until her death in 1908. For most of that time, she was ultraconservative, but she herself prompted the first modern institutional changes in the first decade of the twentieth century.

nineteenth-century fall from wealth and power. No matter how much the Manchus reformed now, nationalistic Chinese saw them as the root of China's problems. Revolutionary leaders such as Sun Yat-sen, a Western-educated medical doctor, plotted coups and planned for a new Chinese republic. Many, especially in urban areas, joined organizations directed toward both further reform and ousting the Manchus. A rebellion that broke out in central China in October 1911 led to the February 1912 abdication of the Manchu emperor and the end of the Chinese monarchy. With these events, a new, uncharted world came into being.

The Revolutionary Movement

The 1905 abolition of the civil service examination was the most revolutionary act in China's twentieth-century history. Why? First, the examination was the more than millennium-old vehicle that had produced China's political and social leaders. Once it was gone, what would be the source of China's leaders? Perhaps even more important, the civil service examination had provided Chinese leaders with a shared way of looking at life and dealing with problems. All who

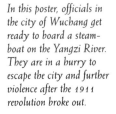

In this poster, officials in the city of Wuchang get ready to board a steam-boat on the Yangzi River. They are in a hurry to escape the city and further violence after the 1911 revolution broke out.

had taken the exam had to study Confucianism, together with the philosophical commentaries that elaborated on and explained it. The examination system had thus been the principal force that carried forward the Chinese way.

In this formal request sent to the court in 1904, key officials urged the abolition of the civil service examination. The court had previously ordered the establishment of a nationwide system of schools that would initially co-exist with the examination system. This petition suggests major problems with putting such a system into place, the foremost being that young men continued to invest in tutorials to pass the examination. If a modern school system was going to work, many saw that the exam system had to go.

Since we received the imperial rescript to improve the management of schools, more than two years have passed. But up to now, schools could not be established in great number in any province because of the embarrassing difficulty of providing funds. Public funds are limited. Everything depends on contributions provided by the population. But the funds cannot be gathered by contributions because the examination system has not yet been discontinued. The literati throughout the empire say that it is not the intention of the court to stress especially the importance of the schools. Thus if the examination system is not transformed and reduced, the people will certainly feel hesitant. . . .

Those entering the schools are depending upon the examination system as a means for backsliding. They are willing neither to turn wholeheartedly to study in the schools nor to observe respectfully the rules of the schools. Furthermore, the papers in the examination system are almost always plagiarized; but study in the schools requires real application. The examination system relies only upon the failure or success of one day; in the schools several years have to be spent in thorough investigation. In the examination system the candidates are selected merely for their polished style; there is no way to test their personal qualities. The schools, however, pay attention to the way of life of the students, and, moreover, the workings of their minds can be clearly shown. A comparison of the examination system and the schools will show clearly which is difficult and which is easy. It is always the inclination of men to evade the difficult and to follow the easy. . . .

But at this time the situation of our country is very dangerous. There can be no rescue without men of ability. Unless schools are established there will be no way to bring forward men of ability to

Literati

Those who passed the Chinese civil service exam

When the Manchus took control of China in the seventeenth century, they ordered that each Chinese man braid his hair in a queue as a sign of subjection. When the Manchus were overthrown in 1912, cutting the queue became a symbol of liberation.

Han

The ethnic Chinese

avert the danger of these times. If we continue thus to follow routine, sitting and wasting years and months while the situation of the country is urgent, how can we subsist? . . .

We think, arguing according to the principle of the matter, that it is necessary to discontinue the examination system at once, so that the management of the schools may improve in quality and funds may be provided.

As part of the educational reforms of the Manchu government, many young Chinese studied in Japan, which had modernized with amazing speed after being "opened" to trade and dealings with the West. By the 1890s some Chinese had come to see Japan as a model, though there was something of a love-hate relationship, given Japan's shocking military defeat of China in 1894–95. That war notwithstanding, by 1906 there were about 13,000 Chinese students in Japanese colleges and military academies. Chinese students began to set up associations based on their native place; students from the province of Zhejiang, for example, formed a Zhejiang Association. In these new organizations they began to raise questions such as: "Why is China so 'backward' when compared to the vibrant, changing Japan?" Increasingly the answer was "the Manchus."

It is therefore not too surprising that the central force in the revolutionary movement, the Revolutionary Alliance, was formed in Tokyo in 1905. Founded by Sun Yat-sen, it was the first to set down a plan for what would happen after the Manchus were ousted. Its manifesto's first two points hold high the banner of nationalism; the third describes the nature of the state; and the last deals with Sun's social and economic ideals. The manifesto ends with a description of the stages of the revolution.

We recall that, since the beginning of our nation, the Chinese have always ruled China; although at times alien peoples have usurped our rule, yet our ancestors were able to drive them out and restore Chinese sovereignty so that they could hand down the nation to posterity. Now the men of Han have raised a righteous (or patriotic) army to exterminate the northern barbarians. This is a . . . great righteous cause, . . . a national revolution. . . . [We] proclaim to the world in utmost sincerity the outline of the present revolution and the fundamental plan for the future administration of the nation.

1. Drive out the Tartars: The Manchus conquered China, and enslaved our Chinese people. Those who opposed them were killed by hundreds of thousands, and our Chinese have been a people without a nation for two hundred and sixty years. The extreme cruelties and tyrannies of the Manchu government have now reached their limit. With the righteous army poised against them, we will overthrow that government, and restore our sovereign rights. . . .

2. Restore China: China is the China of the Chinese. The government of China should be in the hands of the Chinese. After driving out the Tartars we must restore our sovereign state.

3. Establish the Republic: Now our revolution is based on equality, in order to establish a republican government. All our people are equal and enjoy political rights; the president will be publicly chosen by the people of the country. The parliament will be made up of members publicly chosen by the people of the country. A constitution of the Chinese Republic will be enacted, and every person must abide by it. . . .

4. Equalize land ownership: The good fortune of civilization is to be shared equally by all the people of the nation. We should improve our social and economic organization, and assess the value of all the land in the country. Its present price shall be received by the owner, but all increases in [land] value resulting from reform and social improvements after the revolution shall belong to the state, to be shared by all the people, in order to create a socialist state, where each family within the empire can be well supported, each person satisfied, and no one fail to secure employment. . . .

The above four points will be carried out in three steps in due order. Of these three periods, the first is the period in which the Military Government leads the people in eradicating all traditional evils and abuses. The second is the period in which the Military Government gives the power of local self-government to the people while retaining general control over national affairs. The third is the period in which the Military Government is divested of its powers, and the government will by itself manage national affairs under the constitution. It is hoped that our people will proceed in due order and cultivate their free and equal status; the foundation of the Chinese Republic will be entirely based on this.

In the years after 1905, various violent plots were hatched against Manchu officials and carried out in guerrilla fashion. One involved several men and one woman who all were from

Tartars
The Manchus

My voice reechoes from heaven to earth, I tear my lungs to shreds in crying out to my fellow countrymen: Listen! Our China must have a revolution today! If we are to throw off the Manchu yoke, we must have revolution today. We must have revolution if China is to be independent. We must have revolution if China is to take its place as a powerful nation on the globe, if China is to survive for long in the new world of the twentieth century, if China is to be a great country in the world and play the leading role.

—From a manifesto written by eighteen-year-old revolutionary Zou Rong in 1903

Chinese scholars wrote biji (jottings or thoughts), which often were not published until after the writers' deaths, when they were collected and published as part of the "collected works" of the author. Feminist author Qiu Jin jotted her thoughts on the role of women in traditional culture, which were published in 1960.

We, the two hundred million women of China, are the most unfairly treated objects on earth. If we have a decent father, then we will be all right at the time of our birth; but if he is crude by nature, or an unreasonable man, he will immediately start spewing out phrases like "Oh what an ill-omened day, here's another useless one."

the city of Shaoxing in Zhejiang Province, but who did not know one another until they studied together in Japan. The men, led by Xu Xilin, plotted to kill the Manchu governor of neighboring Anhui Province; at the same time, the woman, Qiu Jin, was to rise in rebellion in Shaoxing. The men succeeded in killing the governor, Enming, but were seized immediately and beheaded. Xu's heart was cut out and presented before the governor's corpse. Authorities then became aware of Qiu Jin's plans, and arrested and beheaded her. To rebel and fail was obviously a bloody business. The assassination of Enming frightened all Manchu officials, especially because at the same time, Sun Yat-sen was setting in motion several (in the end, unsuccessful) mini-rebellions in south China. Before his execution, Xu made this statement to authorities, which appeared in a Chinese newspaper in 1907.

The Manchus have enslaved us Han for nearly three hundred years. On the surface they seem to be implementing constitutionalism, but that's only to ensnare people's minds. In reality they are upholding the centralization of authority so as to enhance their power. The Manchus' presumption is that if there is constitutionalism, then revolution will be impossible. . . . If constitutionalism means centralization, the more constitutionalism there is the

Sun Yat-sen, seated in the center, is photographed with members of the Revolutionary Alliance, which he established in Tokyo in 1905.

faster the Han people will die. . . . I have harbored anti-Manchu feelings for more than ten years. Only today have I achieved my goal. My intention was to kill Enming, then to kill Duanfang, Tieliang, and Liangbi, so as to avenge the Han people. . . . You say that the governor was a good official, that he treated me very well. Granted! But since my goal is to oppose the Manchus, I cannot be concerned with whether a particular Manchu official was a good official or a bad official. As for his treating me well, that was the private kindness of an individual person. My killing of the governor, on the other hand, expressed the universal principle of anti-Manchuism.

Not all revolutionary activities were focused on launching uprisings or on terrorist attacks and assassinations. As the first decade of the twentieth century neared its end, street demonstrations in many cities called for the immediate establishment of a constitution with representative assemblies at the national, provincial, and local levels. Before her death, the Empress Dowager had set forth a calendar that envisioned a fully operating constitutional system by 1917. But once provisional provincial assemblies met in 1909, the pressure on the Qing government to telescope the process increased. But the regents of the new emperor made political blunder after political blunder, riling up more and more Chinese. Also rising were fears that imperialist powers were waiting in the wings to snatch parts of China from the fumbling grasp of the Manchus, whose ineffective rule seemed to many to threaten the dismantling of the Chinese nation.

In this memoir, Liu Jingshan, a student at the Shanxi Military Primary School, describes patriotic activities to save China, activities that inevitably took on an anti-Manchu tone. Liu's description indicates the importance of the new school system (initiated by the Manchus) in the growing revolutionary anti-Manchu fervor.

In 1911, when I was eighteen, the rumor was afloat that the Powers were about to divide China, and this naturally accelerated the tendency toward revolution. Patriots among my classmates set up one "save-the-nation" organization after another. . . . We organized a society for martial arts and practiced in preparation for hand-to-hand fighting. In late March [late April in the Gregorian calendar], we asked our classmates to make donations to reprint a "save-the-nation" leaflet for the Revolutionary Alliance. It said that

The man holding a writing brush exhorts, "Awake quickly! Awake quickly!! Let all you brothers rouse your spirits." This cartoon, which appeared on May 16, 1909, in the Shanghai newspaper Minhu Bao [The People's Cry], *suggests that the written word was the powerful key to mobilizing the Chinese people.*

the powers had designated their territories [for seizure]—northern Manchuria, Mongolia, and Xinjiang to Russia; southern Manchuria and Fujian to Japan; Shandong to Germany; the Yangte [Yangzi] basin to Britain, etc., . . . with only [the province of] Zhili left to the Qing empire. The leaflet appealed to the people to rise up and save their country. On Sunday morning, our classmates distributed the leaflets to the street, sent them to colleges and special schools, and mailed them to all the middle and senior primary schools of each prefecture, district, and county. Suddenly, there was massive unrest across the country. College and special-school students held assemblies and planned strikes, creating chaos everywhere.

The reactionary Shanxi authorities held an emergency meeting at the governor's official residence and decided to stop mail, confiscate leaflets, and ban strikes to suppress the revolutionary activities. They criticized and threatened the military students saying that the Revolutionary Party members worked out the plan, spread false rumors, and distributed leaflets to incite people.

Students at various colleges and schools criticized the[se] reactionary Shanxi authorities as traitors because they did not direct or support the patriotic movement of these students, but instead,

The Anti-U.S. Boycott of 1905

One of the earliest examples of mass nationalism was the Chinese boycott of trade with the United States. Long-term reasons included the racist anti-Chinese immigration policies existing from the 1880s; a more immediate cause was the humiliating ill-treatment of Chinese who visited the United States for the 1904 St. Louis World's Fair—required, for example, to wear their passports around their necks.

suppressed and destroyed it. The students turned from opposing the powers to overthrowing the Qing dynasty.

Ending Traditions

The binding of five- or six-year-old girls' feet began as a fad in the Song dynasty (960–1279), mimicking the practices of a court ballerina. The foot was bound tightly with the toes bent (and broken) under the instep, so that the foot would ideally be only about three inches long. This produced a type of walking that seemed seductive to many men, and, in China's patriarchal society, the custom had the added benefit of hobbling women to keep them from gallivanting around. Small feet were considered to be a valuable asset for marriage. In the late nineteenth and early twentieth centuries, reformist societies to abolish foot binding emerged. As one of China's first feminists, Qiu Jin took a strong stand against the custom. Here she muses on the practice and its prime justification.

The bound foot of a Chinese woman was ideally no more than three inches long. Here her tiny shoe lies at the foot of the stool. The foot-binding process disfigured and hobbled a woman for life.

Before many years have passed, without anyone's bothering to ask if it's right or wrong, they take out a pair of snow-white bands and bind them around our feet, tightening them with strips of white cotton; even when we go to bed at night we are not allowed to loosen them the least bit, with the result that the flesh peels away and the bones buckle under. The sole purpose of this is just to ensure that our relatives, friends, and neighbors will say, "At the so-and-so's the girls have small feet."

When military rebellion erupted into revolution in the fall of 1911, it was almost by accident. Revolutionaries, preparing for an uprising in the central Chinese city of Wuchang, made the mistake of dropping glowing cigarette ashes into gunpowder. The explosions gave them away; but they decided to act anyway because they already faced certain death if caught. Largely because much of the city's military force was upriver in Sichuan province putting down a disturbance involving railroad rights' recovery, the rebellion flared into civil war. But because Sun Yat-sen was away on a fundraising trip, leadership fell to a military man who was not even a revolutionary. Nevertheless, the revolutionaries swept to a series of rapid military victories in south and central China.

The court called on longtime civil and military official Yuan Shikai, whom they had dismissed three years earlier. Yuan bided his time to see which side would more likely emerge the victor. He eventually worked to bring the dynasty's abdication. Revolutionary act followed revolutionary act, obliterating the old world and giving birth to a new one. After the Qing court abdicated, they were allowed to continue living in their palace, the Forbidden City. Yuan Shikai became president of the Republic of China. Sun Yat-sen, in contrast, served as the relatively unimportant national director of railroads. The abdication edict, issued by the court on February 12, 1912, marked the end of 2,000 years of imperial rule in China.

The British in China During the Revolution

Revolutionary troops chose to walk beside the railroad tracks between Shanghai and Nanjing rather than ride the British-controlled trains because they feared that destruction of railroad property would bring the British into the civil war with political and economic demands or worse.

According to the imperialist nations, treaty agreements reigned supreme in every circumstance. Thus, when a northern Chinese province was suffering a devastating famine, Britain insisted on continuing to export soybeans, citing a 1906 agreement that forbade Chinese to involve themselves in the trade by halting it or even slowing it down.

As a consequence of the uprising of the Republican Army, to which the different provinces immediately responded, the Empire seethed like a boiling cauldron and the people were plunged into utter misery. Yuan Shikai was, therefore, especially commanded some time ago to dispatch commissioners to confer with the representatives of the Republican Army on the general situation and to discuss matters pertaining to the convening of a National Assembly for the decision of the suitable mode of settlement. . . . Separated as the South and North are by great distances, the unwillingness of either side to yield to the other can result only in the continued interruption of trade and the prolongation of hostilities, for, so long as the form of government is undecided, the Nation can have no peace. It is now evident that the hearts of the majority of the people are in favor of a republican form of government: the provinces of the South were the first to espouse the cause, and the generals of the North have since pledged their support. From the preference of the people's hearts, the Will of Heaven can be discerned. How could We then dare to oppose the will of the millions for the glory of one Family! Therefore, observing the tendencies of the age on one hand and studying the opinions of the people on the other, We and His Majesty the Emperor hereby vest the sovereignty in the People and decide in favor of a republican form of constitutional government. Thus we would gratify on the one hand the desires of the whole nation who, tired of anarchy, are desirous of peace, and on the other hand would follow in the footsteps of the Ancient Sages who regarded the Throne as the sacred trust of the Nation.

Now Yuan Shikai was elected by the provisional parliament to be the Premier. During this period of transference of government from the old to the new, there should be some means of uniting the South and the North. Let Yuan Shikai organize with full powers a provisional republican government and confer with the Republican Army as to the methods of union, thus assuring peace to the people and tranquility to the Empire, and forming to one Great Republic of China by the union as heretofore, of the five peoples, namely, Manchus, Chinese, Mongols, Mohammedans, and Tibetans together with their territory in its integrity. We and His Majesty the Emperor, thus enabled to live in retirement, free from responsibilities and cares, . . . shall enjoy without interruption the courteous treatment of the Nation and see with Our own eyes the consummation of an illustrious government. Is not this highly advisable.

The Will of Heaven

Since the beginning of the imperial system, the emperor was thought to hold power through a mandate from Heaven, an impersonal force in the universe. So long as he ruled with benevolence for the people, he could continue to rule. But if he was perceived as failing to do so—and that reality would produce natural disasters—then the people who spoke for Heaven could overthrow the emperor and give the mandate to someone else. That idea is clearly expressed in the abdication announcement.

Chapter Two

The Slide into Chaos

The early republic was a period of hope and optimism that the new China, born out of the demise of the Manchus, would be able to develop into a full-fledged republic. The first elections for a national assembly in the winter of 1912–13 only propelled those hopes: the party of Sun Yat-sen, the Guomindang, or Nationalist Party, won and controlled 45 percent of both houses in the assembly. But Sun was not the country's president. That position had gone to Yuan Shikai, the general who had engineered the Manchu abdication, despite the fact that Yuan was not in the least sympathetic to republicanism. Most historians today believe that the revolutionaries committed themselves to Yuan in order to shorten the warfare, because many felt that an extended period of civil war would only bring in foreigners with more greedy demands and efforts to seize even greater control.

The euphoria following the Guomindang assembly victory was brief. In March 1913, Song Jiaoren, the thirty-year-old revolutionary pegged to become prime minister, was shot dead at the Shanghai train station. President Yuan Shikai was implicated in the killing. Then Yuan largely ignored the National Assembly when it met in April. In despair, the Guomindang and its allies began a new revolt, sometimes called the "second revolution," this time against Yuan and his regime. Yuan and his army crushed the revolt handily. In November, Yuan outlawed the Guomindang, and in February 1914 he abolished all parliamentary bodies.

It is clear that whatever Yuan's hopes were for the new China, they did not include republican institutions. For Yuan, the key to making a new China lay in a strongly centralized government that would be able to direct and control the whole process. From 1914 to 1916, he set out to become emperor and to reestablish the imperial system. But the

Yuan Shikai, the founder of the modern Chinese military, is dressed in military garb. Such a splendid uniform was apparently not enough for him—he attempted to become emperor late in his life.

Get rid of the idea that China has had a revolution and is a republic; that point is just where we have been deceived in the United States. China is at present the rotten crumbling remnant of the old bureaucracy that surrounded the corruption of the Manchus and that made them possible.

—John Dewey, in a letter to his children, June 2, 1919

Chinese were not willing to support such a backward step. In the face of another rebellion, this one larger than that of 1913, Yuan backpedaled. In June 1916 he died suddenly of natural causes.

Ironically, his death proved to be a greater disaster than his life. While he lived, he had firm control over the military forces. Many officers owed personal loyalty to Yuan, for they had been cadets under his leadership at the key military academy in the last years of the Qing. With his death, many of them became contenders for the presidency of the country. The years from 1916 to 1928 were marked by bloody struggles between Yuan's former generals to win the capital and thereby national power. Known as warlords, these men terrorized much of China, unmercifully taxed the areas they controlled, ravaged many areas of their wealth and property, and—through large-scale military campaigns—killed thousands and perhaps hundreds of thousands of people. The hopes of the early republic were dashed: instead of a "new," modernizing China, the country found itself sliding with increasing speed down a channel of self-demolition.

The Presidency of Yuan Shikai

Yuan believed that parliamentary bodies at the county, provincial, and national level created a situation where there was no central direction, and that each body would go off on its own and forget the needs of the nation. To Yuan's way of thinking, such political messiness would undercut rather than help the construction of a new China. Although in this inaugural address, given to the Council of Government in December 1913, Yuan mouthed the words republicans liked to hear, he gave these words a different meaning.

Nowadays, the word "equality" is in all men's mouths, but equality only means that all men are equal in the sight of the law. It does not imply that distinctions of rank are to be obliterated and that each man may be a rule unto himself in negation of the law. . . . "Liberty" is another beautiful modern expression, but it is limited to the bounds of the law, within which men are free. Such a thing as unrestricted liberty does not exist. Those who have advocated equality and liberty without enquiring whether sanction was extended to a reign of license knew perfectly well that such things must not be: they made use of stately catchwords as a rallying cry for furthering rebellion. . . . Again, "republic" is an elegant expression, but what foreigners understand by this term is merely the universal right to a voice in the country and not that the whole nation must needs interfere in the conduct of government. What possible result save the direst confusion could ensue from such interference? As to the term "popular rights," it comprises the right of representation and the suffrage, besides the supreme privilege of electing the president: it must not be understood to include the conduct of administration.

In the aftermath of Yuan's destruction of the republic, and as he was moving toward taking more power for himself, World War I exploded in Europe. For China, the war posed a tremendous threat: what if the European nations with holdings in China used China as a battleground? To forestall that possibility, China declared its neutrality. In the end it made little difference because Japan was asked by its ally Great Britain to seize German-held territories in Asia and the Pacific. Japan did just that, moving quickly into the German sphere of interest in Shandong province and into German-held Pacific islands. By autumn 1914, Japan had finished its active involvement in the war and could focus on ways of gaining an advantage in China while the European powers were out of the picture.

The Temple of Heaven, constructed in 1420, is in the southern part of Beijing. In imperial times, the emperor offered sacrifices to Heaven at the winter solstice to ensure a good harvest. Yuan Shikai performed rituals here as he moved to reestablish the monarchy in 1915–16.

In mid-January 1915, Japan presented to President Yuan a list of twenty-one demands that would substantially increase Japan's economic and political power in China. Indeed, one group of demands (Group 5), if accepted, would have reduced Chinese power so severely that it would have made China a protectorate of Japan, giving Japan considerable political and economic authority. In the end, Japan issued an ultimatum for China to sign the demands, with the stipulation that demands in Group 5 would be negotiated later. Yuan agreed to the other demands on May 8, 1915, a date that in subsequent years came to be commemorated as National Humiliation Day. The nature of the demands reveals both the depths of Japan's continental interest and the height of Japanese arrogance.

Group 1

The Japanese Government and the Chinese Government being desirous of maintaining the general peace in Eastern Asia and further strengthening the friendly relations and good neighborhood existing between the two nations agree to the following articles:

Article 1: The Chinese Government engages to give full assent to all matters upon which the Japanese Government may hereafter agree with the German Government relating to the disposition of all rights, interests, and concessions which Germany, by virtue of treaties or otherwise, possesses in relation to the Province of Shantung (Shandong).

Article 2: The Chinese Government engages that within the Province of Shantung and along its coast, no territory or island will be ceded or leased to a third Power under any pretext.

Article 3: The Chinese Government consents to Japan's building a railway from Chefoo [Yantai] or Lungkow [Longzhou] to join the Kiaochow-Chinanfu [Jiazhou-Jinanfu] Railway.

Article 4: The Chinese Government engages, in interest of trade and for the residence of foreigners, to open by herself as soon as possible certain important cities and towns in the Province of Shantung as Commercial Ports. What places shall be opened are to be jointly decided upon in a separate agreement.

Group 2

The Japanese Government and the Chinese Government, since the Chinese Government has always acknowledged the special position enjoyed by Japan in South Manchuria and Eastern Inner Mongolia, agree to the following articles:

Article 1: The two Contracting Parties mutually agree that the term of lease of Port Arthur and Dalny [Dalien, on the Liaodong peninsula between China and northern Korea] and the term of lease of the South Manchurian Railway and the Antung-Mukden [Andtong-Shenyang] Railway shall be extended to the period of ninety-nine years.

Article 2: Japanese subjects in South Manchuria and Eastern Inner Mongolia shall have the right to lease or own land required either for erecting suitable buildings for trade and manufacturing or for farming.

Article 3: Japanese subjects shall be free to reside and travel in South Manchuria and Eastern Inner Mongolia and to engage in business and in manufacture of any kind whatsoever.

Article 4: The Chinese Government agrees to grant Japanese subjects the right of opening mines in South Manchuria and Eastern Inner Mongolia. . . .

Article 5: The Chinese Government agrees that in respect of the (two) cases mentioned herein below the Japanese Government's consent shall first be obtained before action is taken:

(a) Whenever permission is granted to the subject of a third Power to build a railway or to make a loan with a third Power for the purpose of building a railway in South Manchuria and Eastern Inner Mongolia.

(b) Whenever a loan is to be made with a third Power the local taxes of South Manchuria and Eastern Inner Mongolia will be pledged as security.

Article 6: The Chinese Government agrees that if the Chinese Government employs political, financial, or military advisers or instructors in South Manchuria or Eastern Inner Mongolia, the Japanese Government shall be first consulted.

Article 7: The Chinese Government agrees that the control and management of the Kirin-Changchun [Jilin-Changqun] Railway shall be handed over to the Japanese Government for a term of ninety-nine years dating from the signing of this agreement.

Group 3

The Japanese Government and the Chinese Government, seeing that Japanese financiers and the Hanyehping [Hanyeping] Company have close relations with each other at present and desiring that the common interests if the two nations shall be advanced, agree to the following articles:

Article 1: The two Contracting Parties mutually agree that when the opportune moment arrives the Hanyehping Company

In February 1922, warlord Wu Peifu brutally broke a strike of railway workers in Henan Province, killing thirty-five and injuring many more. This poster portrays the warlord as a two-headed tiger ridden by imperialists. Getting rid of warlords and imperialists became the chief goal of revolutionaries in the 1920s.

shall be made a joint concern of the two nations; and they further agree that, without the previous consent of Japan, China shall not by her own act dispose of the rights and property of whatsoever nature of the said Company nor cause the said Company to dispose freely of the same.

Article 2: The Chinese Government agrees that all mines in the neighborhood of those owned by the Hanyehping Company shall not be permitted, without the consent of the said Company, to be worked by other persons outside of the said Company; and further agrees that if it is desired to carry out any undertaking which, it is apprehended, may directly or indirectly affect the interests of the said Company, the consent of the said Company shall first be obtained.

Group 4

The Japanese Government and the Chinese Government with the object of effectively preserving the territorial integrity of China agree to the following special article: The Chinese Government engages not to cede or lease to a third Power any harbor or bay or island along the coast of China.

Group 5

Article 1: The Chinese Central Government shall employ influential Japanese as advisers in political, financial, and military affairs.

Article 2: Japanese hospitals, churches, and schools in the interior of China shall be granted the right of owning land.

Article 3: Inasmuch as the Japanese Government and the Chinese Government have had many cases of disputes between Japanese and Chinese police which caused no little misunderstanding, it is for this reason necessary that the police departments of important places (in China) shall be jointly administered by Japanese and Chinese. . . .

Article 4: China shall purchase from Japan a fixed amount of munitions of war (say 50 percent or more of what is needed by the Chinese Government) or there shall be established in China a Sino-Japanese jointly worked arsenal. . . .

Article 5: China agrees to grant to Japan the right of constructing a railway connecting Wuchang with Kiu-kiang [Jiujiang] and Nanchang, another line between Nanchang and Hangchow, [Hangzhou] and another between Nanchang and Chao-chow [Chaozhou].

Article 6: If China needs foreign capital to work mines, build railways and construct harbor-works (including dockyards) in the Province of Fukien [Fujian], Japan shall be first consulted.

Article 7: China agrees that Japanese subjects shall have the right of missionary propaganda in China.

Warlords

Using war to further their own power, and outrageous levels of taxation to become rich, warlords were the scourges of the areas they controlled. The warlord Zhang Zongzhang, based in Shandong Province, was one of the most thuggish of them all. Zhang, whose army included a unit of several thousand boys whose average age was ten, was known for his propensity for "opening melons," a euphemism for splitting skulls, and for hanging human heads on telegraph poles as a show of his power. Lin Yutang, one of China's most popular writers, wrote this satirical description after Zhang's death; it is masterful in its understatement and in its "damning with faint praise."

He was six feet tall, a towering giant, with a pair of squint eyes and a pair of abnormally massive hands. He was direct, forceful, terribly efficient at times: obstinate and gifted with moderate intelligence. He was patriotic according to his lights. . . . He could drink, and he was awfully fond of "dog-meat," and he could swear all he wanted to and as much as he wanted to, irrespective of his

Attributes of the Dog-Meat General and His Rule

Rumor had it that Zhang had his three "don't knows": he did not know how much money he had, how many troops he had, or how many women he had in his harem.

Not long after Zhang became governor, two phrases were heard all over the cities: "Cut apart to catch light" and "listen to the telephone." The former referred to the human heads which were treated like watermelons, cut in halves to bask in the sun; the latter referred to the same, except the heads were hung from telephone poles, and from afar they seemed to be listening on the telephone. At the same time, at the train stations along the Jiaoji and Jinpu lines, people started to hear the strange expression, "My head is my passport; my ass is my ticket." This was because people were being regularly kicked, beaten up, abused in vile language, and spat in the face by soldiers.

—Writer Gong Yao in a 1936 article titled "On Zhang Zongzhang Whose Corruption and Brutality is a Calamity for the Nation and its People," in *Yijing* [Unorthodox classic]

official superiors and inferiors. He made no pretence to being a gentleman, and didn't affect to send nice-sounding circular telegrams, like the rest of [the warlords]. He was ruthlessly honest, and this honesty made him much loved by all his close associates. . . . If he made orgies he didn't try to conceal them from his friends and foes. If he coveted his subordinate's wife he told him openly, and wrote no psalm of repentance about it like King David. And he always played square. If he took his subordinate's wife he made her husband the chief of police of [a major city]. And he took good care of other people's morals. He forbade girl students from entering parks in Jinan, and protected them from the men-gorillas who stood at every corner and nook to devour them. And he was pious, and he kept a harem. . . . He was very fond of his executioner, and he was thoroughly devoted to his mother.

Once he appointed a man magistrate in a certain district in Shandong, and another day he appointed another man to the same office and started a quarrel. Both claimed that they had been personally appointed by General Dog-meat. It was agreed, therefore, that they should go and see the General to clear up the difficulty. When they arrived it was evening, and General Zhang was in bed in the midst of his orgies. "Come in," he said, with his usual candor.

The two magistrates then explained that they had both been appointed by him to the same district.

"You fools!" he said, "can't you settle such a little thing between yourselves, but must come to bother me about it?"

. . . like all Chinese robbers, he was an honest man.

Not all warlords shared Zhang Zongchang's thuggish glorying in violence and licentiousness. Indeed, several warlords probably had the capability to become the leader of the Chinese nation or at least a significant positive leader on the national stage. For example, there was Wu Peifu. He had passed the lowest-level examination under the imperial civil service system and throughout his life he maintained a deep love for traditional Chinese culture. He saw himself as a student not only of the Confucian classics but also of the Buddhist canon. He joined these humane interests with a military career, having graduated from Yuan Shikai's Baoding Military Academy. During the warlord wars, he headed one of the central warlord coalitions.

In this poem, Wu speaks of Japan's increasingly threatening actions in Manchuria, a role that was made possible by its

Despite his violent crushing of the 1922 railroad workers strike, Wu Peifu had a reputation as a student of both Confucianism and Buddhism and had a fervent love of traditional Chinese culture.

military victories over China in 1894–95 and over Russia in 1904–5 and most recently by China's agreeing to the Twenty-One Demands. This poem's conclusion makes clear Wu's commitment to Buddhism.

Ascend the Penglai Pavilion
Turning north to Manchuria
In the Gulf of Chihli, a great storm is gathering!
Recalling a couple of years before,
In Kirin, Heilungkiang, Liaoning, Shenyang, people
   were peacefully living.
Bamboo fences lined the foot of the Chang Pai Mountain,
Cities stood serenely by the Heilungkiang. Now, Japanese
   pirates are roaming, and
A storm is gathering.

Ever since the Sino-Japanese War,
Our territory has shrunken.
After the Russo-Japanese War,
Our national sovereignty has fallen.
The country beautiful as ever,
Yet, barbarians, scattered all over.
When can I lead my picked trained army,
Wage a battle to recover the territory?
Then, I will return, to go up the Peng Mountain
And say my prayers to the Buddha.

Penglai

Penglai is a city on the northern coast of the province of Shandong; Wu looks north from there directly across the Gulf of Chihli [Zhili] to Manchuria.

Kirin [Jilin], Heilungkiang [Heilongjiang], and Liaoning

Kirin [Jilin], Heilungkiang [Heilongjiang], and Liaoning are the provinces that make up Manchuria; Shenyang is a city in Manchuria, sometimes referred to before 1949 by its old Manchu name of Mukden.

Along with civilian casualties of the warlord wars, the most obvious victims of the warlord period were the soldiers who made up the warlords' armies. Men joined the armies to make a living—though most made very little. Troops took what they needed as they moved through areas. National regulations specified that men enlisting in the armed forces had to be between nineteen and twenty-six, yet the case of Zhang Zongzhang shows that at least some warlords were willing to take much younger men and even boys. Battle deaths in more than 140 wars fought between 1916 and 1928 were high, with a large percentage of the wounded dying because of lack of medical care.

The revolutionary tract from which these words of a soldier are taken was seized by military authorities in August 1920. It reveals, among other things, how shallow

The Economic Scourge of Warlordism

The —-ese Army stationed in eastern Sichuan boasted twenty thousand rifles and was a force of some thirty thousand strong—counting all the officers and subs, foot soldiers, cooks, porters, and other flunkies, *and* the assorted dependents, legal and otherwise. But, when it came time to close the register and sign for the provincial pay subsidy at the end of the month, there were only forty thousand yuan in it for them. To make up the rest of their support they had to rely on duty from opium coming into the province and the county government's taxes on households doing the planting and inhaling, respectively. There were the land tax, the indolence tax on farmers too lazy to plant opium, the assessment on opium poppies—and on opium lamps—plus all the various and sundry taxes on brothels and anyone in the flesh trade. Yet these sources of provisions had run particularly dry, leaving pay in arrears of outlays, till all the expenses had to be gouged from peasants. . . .

—Writer Shen Congwen, in his 1935 essay "Staff Adviser," *Wenxue*

and relatively meaningless the force of nationalism was at the time, and how lower classes believed that the elite's talk of the nation or country was simply a wedge used to pry money away from the masses.

Brothers, when we went into the army to be soldiers, was it for love of our country, or was it to make a living? I believe we all went in to make a living; no one would say it was for love of country. What does that mean? Brothers, just think, we all have families, but if you start to talk about "country," which piece of land belongs to us poor people? Which particular event has anything to do with us poor people? The people who are marshals or high officers can run the areas under their control, they can levy taxes on the people under their rule, they can requisition grain and other supplies. They can also take the name of "country," or of a province, and then take the things which ordinary people produce to make a living and pawn them or sell them to foreigners, get together some money and have a wild time with the young gentlemen, the young ladies and the older ladies. They use the country as their money tree, as their amulet; they use the people of the country as their slaves, their chickens, their dogs, their cows or their horses. If they don't use the word "country" then they cannot sell the products that the people make, or seize the people's food and clothing, so they are always patriotic with their mouths open, patriotic with their mouths shut.

But we brothers, unless we are eating at home and don't have to spend any money, wherever we go outside, whoever we see, we always have to pay when we eat, and we have to pay for our clothes. Where is our "country"? If we were not in the army, we would still have our families, but in the army we haven't even got our own family. And if as soldiers we go into battle, we may not even have our lives anymore. Once when I went up to the front, I saw lots of dead bodies lying around haphazardly by the roadside. There was no one to bury them. The bodies were covered in blood from head to foot; the stench was terrible. When I looked at their insignia I saw that they were all our brothers. I used to think that when soldiers died in battle it was a glorious and magnificent death, but when I saw that they had lost their arms or legs, that their brains had been dashed out or their stomachs had burst open, then the courage and the daring that our officers usually manage to plant in our stomachs faded away. Not only did it fade away, but I felt that all the training we had received in the regiment had oppressed and duped us.

Our bodies were born of our parents and we were raised by them; we were given a lot of kindness by our families, and we should love them. The country is another thing—what does it have to offer us? It can't be seen, it can't be heard, it doesn't respond to our calls. It is nothing but a few rogues who want to bully and oppress us, and to dupe us, and are afraid that we may see that the country is only one individual, or one family, which we should not believe in. They create a country out of thin air, and raise it to a great height; they say that it has the right of life or death over people, and that people have the duty to serve it. Unless things are like this, they claim, there can be no peace on earth, and the people will have no one to protect them. The laws, the orders, the obedience, the rewards, the resistance, the violations, the beatings, the executions—all these pretexts are their private creations: they get us brothers to help them in the guise of the Chinese character "country." . . .

A marshal gets several million yuan a year; a provincial warlord gets several hundred thousand; a division commander gets eight hundred ounces of silver per month, not including the expenses of his office. A brigade commander gets four hundred ounces, a regimental commander three hundred, a battalion commander two hundred, and a company commander fifty. The platoon commander gets twenty-four, the quartermaster twenty. But people like us, the junior privates, make at most 4.8 ounces, and the senior privates 5.2. When you deduct living expenses from these four or five ounces, there isn't enough left for pocket money, so how can we talk of sending money to our families? . . . When we are dead we get no more than fourteen dollars and twenty cents—ten dollars for the coffin, four for a shroud, and a few cents for paper. If they put it kindly, they say we died in the firing line; if they put it nastily, they say we deserted in the face of the enemy. Is this injustice or not?

Yuan

The basic unit of currency in China after 1912; the tael was the basic unit in imperial China and was an ounce of silver

Paper

In funeral rituals paper money was burned for the deceased to use in the afterlife.

One of the tragedies of the warlord period was the dependence of most warlords on money from opium sales and taxes levied on land, sales, services, trade, businesses, and entertainment. In the late Qing and under the presidency of Yuan Shikai, opium production had been largely suppressed. But warlords encouraged production because opium was such a desired commodity. In some areas warlords demanded that farmers stop growing other cash crops and cultivate opium poppies instead. In other areas, warlords placed such high taxes on area farmers that the only way they could pay them was by growing opium, which sold at high prices.

Warlords often demanded that farmers cultivate opium poppies in order to produce the greatest revenue possible. This policy increased opium smoking among the Chinese people.

Huang Shaoxiong, a member of the Guangxi warlord clique in the 1920s, served as governor of the province; he describes in this account of the opium trade, which was published in a collection of his works in 1986, how warlord governments came to depend on the drug. Opium money permitted government actions that otherwise would not have been possible. It provided the means for solidi-fying "connections" between warlords. In the case of Guangxi, which imported most of its opium from neighboring provinces, it affected inter-province relationships, for Guangxi's dependence on opium from those provinces meant that it had to maintain peace with them.

After the New Guangxi Clique unified the province I became governor. I fully understood the benefits of opium and paid particular attention to controlling, unifying, and opening the trade. We used the label of opium suppression, but our real goal was to bring opium profits to the government. This was in 1926, so you could say we were the first to openly put opium revenues in government accounts, but later Nanjing and the other provincial governments would follow us.

How much did Guangxi make from opium per year? . . . during the rule [of a former governor] over half of the income was from opium. . . . According to the Guangxi Government Record, total income for 1932 was 31,000,000 dollars, of which opium income was 15,880,000 dollars. At a rate of 500 dollars per thousand ounces this would mean that over 30,000,000 ounces of opium moved through Guangxi. . . .

In 1926 Li Zongren took his 7th Army on the Northern Expedition, . . . and I became the most powerful person in the military and government of Guangxi. Liu Rifu,[a military leader], in order to win my favor and consolidate his own position, sent me a telegraph saying that he had seized 700,000 ounces of smuggled opium, which he was presenting to the provincial government. At this point I was looking for money to finance the [provincial] bank with, and the report was a godsend. Where did these 700,000 ounces of opium come from? To this day I'm not entirely clear. If a garrison caught an opium gang with "smuggled opium" they could confiscate it, and this often happened. Liu Rifu often sent me opium he had confiscated as a way of currying favor, and this was the extent of opium suppression at the time. Liu Rifu gave the opium to me so I would not dismiss him. . . . I converted the 700,000 ounces of opium into 700,000 dollars cash, which became the capital of the Bank of Guangxi.

All this opium money of course had a great effect on Guangxi's social and economic life and on the government of the province. Regardless of whether it was the Old Guangxi Clique or the New, no Guangxi government could afford bad relations with Yunnan and Guizhou, as these were the sources of our opium. Although Yunnan troops invaded us twice, it was always Guangxi that sent representatives to Yunnan to try to smooth things out, as they had other options for shipping their opium.

The hole of an opium pipe is as small as a needle, but you can put a water buffalo in it and you can also smoke hundreds of mu of land through it.

—Popular saying about the economic impact of opium

Chapter Three

Forming a New Culture

The May Fourth Movement

Though warlords' actions created often-catastrophic consequences, the most momentous problem China faced in the first decade or so of the republic was how to put together a new culture. It was a necessary project because most of China's traditional Confucian ideology and its central political and social institutions had suffered mortal wounds when the civil service examination was abolished in 1905 and the monarchy was overthrown in 1912. In addition, there were widespread demands throughout Chinese society to throw off the Confucian stranglehold that still remained on family relationships. In these relationships, being male and being older had always trumped being female and being young. Many times these traditional hierarchical relationships produced a great unhappiness—and sometimes tragedy—for individuals. The years after 1915 saw many Chinese youth rebelling against the old ways and struggling to replace them with something new. Their actions were part of what is known as the May Fourth Movement, named for a student demonstration in Beijing on May 4, 1919.

That day, about three thousand students from thirteen colleges and universities gathered at the Gate of Heavenly Peace in front of the Forbidden City—the old imperial palace—to protest the Allied powers' decision at the Versailles Conference that allowed Japan to continue to hold Shandong Province. During World War I, Japan had seized the territory, which had been occupied by Germany. It was symbolically important for Chinese because it was the birthplace of Confucius. After the demonstration, the students marched to the home of one of three officials who had been accused of pro-Japanese action. They torched the house. The protesters caught another of the offending officials and

Demonstrators carry signs denouncing the Chinese government ministers who collaborated with the Japanese and were therefore considered traitors. Known as the May Fourth Incident, this demonstration took place at the Gate of Heavenly Peace, just outside Beijing's Forbidden City, on May 4, 1919.

beat him. More than thirty students were arrested. But that was only the beginning of the trouble. Further demonstrations were called to protest the student arrests.

Protests spread around the country, becoming most forceful in Shanghai, China's economic capital. There, in early June, students, teachers, industrial workers, merchants, businessmen, urban professionals, even the city's organized crime machine launched a general strike. Because of Shanghai's economic centrality to the nation, a long strike with everything shut down could have caused governmental collapse. The goal of the protests was to apply enough pressure on the Chinese delegation at Versailles that it would not sign the peace treaty. In early July word came that the delegates had indeed refused to sign it. Direct political action and pressure had carried the day.

Though the May Fourth Incident and its aftermath were political, the May Fourth Movement that bracketed the incident was a social, literary, and cultural revolution of great importance for the new China. There was no central direction of this movement. Instead, many leaders and participants acted in different social and political arenas and on various levels in society. The dates usually given for the movement are 1915, when the most significant journal of the day, *New Youth*, was first published, to 1924, when political issues began to overshadow other concerns. One important laboratory for working to form a new culture was Beijing University, whose chancellor assembled a faculty with a wide range of intellectual allegiances—from Marxism to Anarchism to Christianity to Confucianism. The hope was that out of the contending ideas a new China might be created.

A crucial aspect of the movement was its commitment to language reform. Up until this time, Chinese was written not as people spoke it (in the vernacular) but in a complex and difficult literary language that only scholars could read. The May Fourth cry was that a new culture must have a new living language; and practically speaking, a new nation had to have a literate population, which would be an impossibility if language reform did not happen.

Over the course of the May Fourth Movement, its goals and directions changed. From the beginning until about 1919, the movement emphasized breaking traditional family constraints and stressed the self-realization of the individual. It was the only period in the entire twentieth century when and personal freedoms and the individual were so openly championed. Then, after the May 1919 demonstration, the movement veered off this course in a new direction that emphasized reforming the nation and ending its plight inflicted by the hands of outside imperialists and inside warlords. This new emphasis rapidly swallowed up the focus on the individual.

Political Activity

Students distributed this "Manifesto of All the Students of Beijing" at the Gate of Heavenly Peace on May 4, 1919.

Japan's demand for the possession of Qingdao and other rights in Shandong is now going to be acceded to in the Paris Peace Conference. Her diplomacy has secured a great victory; and ours has led to a great failure. The loss of Shandong means the destruction of the integrity of China's territory. Once the integrity of her territory has been destroyed, China will soon be annihilated. Accordingly, we students today are making a demonstration march to the Allied legations, asking the Allies to support justice. We earnestly hope that all agricultural, industrial, commercial, and other groups of the whole nation will rise and hold citizens' meetings to strive to secure our sovereignty in foreign affairs and to get rid of the traitors at home. This is the last chance for China in her life and death struggle. Today we swear two solemn oaths with all our countrymen: (1) China's territory may be conquered, but it cannot be given away; (2) the Chinese people may be massacred, but they will not surrender.

Our country is about to be annihilated. Up, brethren!

A Cultural Revolution

Many women suffered greatly in the old family system. In a society that valued males (who could take care of their parents in old age), the birth of a girl (who would grow up to marry and leave her parents), was often an unwanted event. In poor areas where food was often in short supply, infant girls were sometimes killed. In most areas of China, at about the age of five or six, girls had their feet bound, a centuries-old practice that supposedly increased their marriageability, but left them hobbled for life. When girls were married, they left their birth families to go to their husband's family, perhaps never to return to their parents' home. A girl was generally not married to anyone she knew or loved, but to someone selected by her family or a matchmaker. Once in her

The May Fourth Incident in Perspective

The patriotic movement had actually a deeper meaning than mere patriotism. The taste of colonialism in its full bitterness had never come home to the Chinese until then, even though we had already had the experience of several decades of foreign exploitation behind us. The sharp pain of imperialistic oppression then reached the marrow of our bone, and it awakened us from the nightmares of impractical democratic reforms. The issue of the former German possessions in Shandong, which started the uproar of the student movement, could not be separated from the larger problem.

—Qu Qiubai, a writer and political leader who headed the Communist Party briefly in the late 1920s

During the May Fourth Movement, feminism became an increasingly common theme in the writings of both reformers and revolutionaries. Here young women in Beijing—having, like most younger women, dispensed with foot binding—take an excursion to the city's Central Park.

In this 1918 essay, "My Views on Chastity," Lu Xun challenges the traditional social views on chastity for women.

First of all, is chastity a virtue? Virtues should be universal, required of all, within the reach of all, and beneficial to others as well as oneself. Only then are they worth having. But in addition to the fact that all men are excluded from what goes by the name of chastity today, not even all women are eligible for his honor. Hence it cannot be counted a virtue, or held up as an example. . . . When a rough man swoops down on one of the weaker sex (women are still weak as things stand today), if her father, brothers, husband, and neighbors fail her too, her best course is to die. She may, of course, die after being defiled; or she may not die at all. Later on, her father, brothers, husband, and neighbors will get together with the writers, scholars, and moralists; and no whit abashed by their own cowardice and incompetence, nor concerned how to punish the criminal, will start wagging their tongues. Is she dead or not? Was she raped or not? How gratifying if she has died, how shocking if she has not! So they create all these glorious women martyrs on the one hand and these wantons universally condemned on the other. If we think this over soberly, we can see that, far from being praiseworthy, it is absolutely inhuman.

husband's home, she was under the autocratic rule of her mother-in-law. If her husband (or fiancé) died, there was great social pressure for her to remain unmarried and chaste for the rest of her life. Little wonder that the female suicide rate in China among young women was the highest for that age group in the world.

In the May Fourth period, women emerged as politically assertive, participating in demonstrations, attending schools in much greater numbers, and unbinding their feet—a psychologically, if not physically, healing action. Traditionally, Chinese women did not attend schools, but generally began to do so in the first decade of the twentieth century. In this 1949 memoir, Deng Yingchao, the wife of important post-1949 governmental premier and foreign minister Zhou Enlai, reflects on her role in the May Fourth activities when she was sixteen and seventeen years old.

At the beginning we, as female students, did not enjoy the same freedom of movement as our male counterparts, insofar as our speaking tours were concerned. According to the feudal custom of China, women were not supposed to make speeches in the street; we, therefore, had to do our work indoors. We gave speeches in such places as libraries and participated in scheduled debates, all inside a hall or room. The audience was large and responsive in each of these meetings, as we emphasized the duty of everyone to save our country and the necessity of punishing those who sold our country out to the enemy. Many speakers broke down when they spoke of the sufferings of the Koreans under Japanese rule, the beatings of the Peking [Beijing] students by the secret police, and our inherent right to assemble for patriotic purposes. . . .

Besides making speeches, we also conducted house-to-house visits which often took us to more remote areas of the city and also to the slums. Some of the families we visited received us warmly, while others slammed their doors in our faces before we could utter a single word. In the latter cases we simply moved on to the next house instead of being discouraged. I recall on our way home from a speaking tour in the western suburb of Tientsin [Tianjin], the clouds suddenly burst and each of us, drenched in a heavy thunderstorm, looked like a wetted-down chicken.

In addition to our speaking tours and house-to-house visits, we also paid great attention to the use of written words as a means of spreading patriotic sentiments. The Association of Tientsin Students published a journal which started as a half-weekly but became a daily shortly afterwards. It had . . . a circulation of 20,000—quite an achievement at that time. In case you are interested, the editor-in-chief was none other than comrade Chou En-lai [Zhou Enlai]. The Association of Patriotic Women in Tientsin, being smaller in membership, published a weekly.

Deng then goes on to describe a specific political clash between student protestors and the police.

On October 10, 1919, the various patriotic organizations in Tientsin sponsored an all-citizen congress, in which the participants would demand the punishment of such traitors as Ts'ao Ju-lin [Cao Rulin], Lu Tsung-yu [Lu Zongyu], and Chang Tsung-hsiang [Zhang Zongxiang], the boycott of Japanese goods, and the exercise of such inalienable rights as those of free speech and demonstrations. Before the congress was called into session, we received information that Yang Yi-teh [Yang Yide] (nicknamed Gangster Yang), the police commissioner of Tientsin, was ready to use force to dissolve the congress if it were held and disperse any crowd gathered for the purpose of staging a demonstration. Instead of being intimidated, we made plans to cope with the armed police. We surrounded the speaker's platform with three different groups of people: the citizens' representatives were placed next to the platform to form the innermost layer and were protected from the outside by the well-organized male students, while we female students were lined up further outside. As soon as the police began to march toward us, we female students would be the first to break through the encirclement. We all carried placards made of hardy bamboo, which could be effectively used as a weapon when occasion called for such a transformation. We were ready for all the eventualities before the meeting began.

As had been expected, the police, with fixed bayonets, quickly moved in to surround us as soon as the meeting began. Surprisingly, they did not interfere with our meeting which went on according to schedule. Not until the meeting was over and the march began did they clash with us. Steadily they closed in, as our vanguards proceeded to march forward.

"Policemen should be patriots too!"

"Patriotic police don't beat up patriotic students!"

We shouted loudly, trying desperately to convert brutal police into compassionate patriots. But the police refused to be converted as they hit us with rifle butts and systematically broke the eye-glasses of many students. In retaliation we hit them with bamboo

Plays of Norwegian dramatist Henrik Ibsen had been translated into Chinese. Ibsen's A Doll's House *(translated into Chinese as* Nora*) dealt with the plight of Nora in an unhappy marriage and, in a larger sense, with female liberation from male domination. This essay, "What Happens after Nora Leaves Home?," is based on a talk Lu Xun gave at the Beijing Women's Normal College on December 26, 1923.*

Nora originally lives contentedly in a so-called happy home, but then she wakes up to the fact that she is simply a puppet of her husband's and her children are her puppets. So she leaves home. . . . What happens after Nora leaves home? . . .

[T]he crucial thing for Nora is money or—to give it a more high-sounding name—economic resources. Of course money cannot buy freedom, but freedom can be sold for money. Human beings have one great drawback, which is that they often get hungry. To remedy this drawback and to avoid being puppets, the most important thing in society today seems to be economic rights. First there must be a fair sharing out between men and women in the family; secondly, men and women must have equal rights in society.

placards and knocked hats from their heads. When they bent down to pick up their hats, we pushed forward so as to continue our march.

Nevertheless, the police were much stronger and also better equipped than we female students, and we were losing the battle fast. At this critical point, fortunately, the automobile team of propaganda arrived and quickly attacked the police from the rear. Driving their automobiles forward, these male students were soon able to breach a big hole in the police ranks. We female students followed the automobiles through the breach and, a few minutes later, freed ourselves from the police encirclement. We marched through the city streets until we finally arrived at the police headquarters. We demanded to see Commissioner Yang and protested against his brutality toward the students. Not until dawn the next day did we finally disperse and go home.

Angered by the October Tenth Incident . . . we female students in Tientsin decided that no longer did we wish to honor the feudal custom of China and that we, female students in Tientsin, had as much right to speak in the street as our male counterparts. The very next day we began to make speeches in the street. From street to street and before one audience after another, we condemned Commissioner Yang for having committed brutality against the students.

Chen Duxiu studied in both France and Japan. In 1915, he founded and edited the most influential journal in twentieth-century China, *New Youth*. It was in the vanguard of the May Fourth Movement. The following editorial appeared in the inaugural year of the journal. It is Chen's charge to youth to change their approach to life in order to change Chinese society.

Youth is like early spring, like the rising sun, like trees and grass in bud, like a newly sharpened blade. It is the most valuable period of life. The function of youth in society is the same as that of a fresh and vital cell in a human body. In the processes of metabolism, the old and the rotten are incessantly eliminated to be replaced by the fresh and living. . . . [I] place my plea before the young and vital youth, in the hope that they will achieve self-awareness. . . . As for your understanding what is right and wrong, in order that you may make your choice, I carefully propose the following six principles, and hope you will give them your calm consideration.

(1) Be independent, not servile. Emancipation means freeing oneself from the bondage of slavery and achieving a completely independent and free personality. I have hands and feet, and I can earn my own living. I have a mouth and a tongue, and I can voice my own likes and dislikes. I have a mind, and I can determine my own beliefs. . . . [T]here is definitely no reason why one should blindly follow others. . . . [It should be clear that] loyalty, filial piety, chastity, and righteousness are a slavish morality.

(2) Be progressive, not conservative. Now our country still has not awakened from its long dream, and isolates itself by going down the old rut. . . . All our traditional ethics, law, scholarship, rites and customs are survivals of feudalism. . . . Revering only the history of the twenty-four dynasties, and making no plans for progress and improvement, our people will be turned out of this twentieth-century world, and be lodged in the dark ditches fit only for slaves, cattle, and horses. . . . Whatever cannot skillfully change itself and progress along with the world will find itself eliminated by natural selection because of failure to adapt to the environment.

(3) Be aggressive, not retiring. It is our natural obligation in life to advance in spite of numerous difficulties.

(4) Be cosmopolitan, not isolationist. If at this point one still raises a particularistic theory of history and of national circumstances and hopes thereby to resist the current, then this still indicates the spirit of an isolationist country and a lack of knowledge of the world. When its citizens lack knowledge of the world, how can a nation expect to survive in it?

(5) Be utilitarian, not formalistic. Though a thing is of gold or jade, if it is of no practical use, then it is of less value than coarse cloth, grain, manure, or dirt. That which brings no benefit to the practical life of an individual or of society is all empty formalism and the stuff of cheats. And even though it were bequeathed to us by our ancestors, taught by the sages, advocated by the government and worshipped by society, the stuff of cheats is still not worth one cent.

(6) Be scientific, not imaginative. To explain truth by science means proving everything with fact. Although the process is slower than that of imagination and arbitrary decision, yet every step is taken on firm ground; it is different from those imaginative flights which eventually cannot advance even one inch. The amount of truth in the universe is boundless, and the fertile areas in the realm of science awaiting the pioneer are immense! Youth, take up the task.

Chen Duxiu, founder of the important journal New Youth, *served as dean of the School of Letters at Beijing University. He was also a founder and the first head of the Chinese Communist Party.*

Lu Xun, who is generally recognized as China's greatest twentieth-century author, first set out to become a doctor, a career he thought that would be most helpful for China. In 1902 he went to Japan, where he studied Japanese for two years. In 1904 he entered the Sendai Provincial Medical School. Two years later he had the experience that opens this preface to his short-story collection *Call to Arms,* published in 1922. He makes clear the reason for his career switch from medicine to writing.

I do not know what advanced methods are now used to teach microbiology, but at that time lantern slides were used to show the microbes; and if the lecture were ended early, the instructor might show slides of natural scenery or news to fill up the time. This was during the Russo-Japanese War, so there were many war films, and I had to join in the clapping and cheering in the lecture hall along with the other students. It was a long time since I had seen any compatriots, but one day I saw a film showing some Chinese, one of whom was bound, while many others stood around him. They were all strong fellows but appeared completely apathetic. According to the commentary the one with his hands bound was a spy working for the Russians, who was to have his head cut off by the Japanese military as a warning to others, while the Chinese beside him had come to enjoy the spectacle.

Before the term was over I had left for Tokyo, because after this film I felt that medical science was not so important after all. The people of a weak and backward country, however strong and healthy they may be, can only serve to be made examples of, or to witness such futile spectacles; and it doesn't really matter how many of them die of illness. The most important thing, therefore, was to change their spirit, and since at that time I felt literature was the best means to this end, I determined to promote a literary movement.

Lu then describes how the first effort to start a literary magazine failed.

Only later did I feel the futility of it all; at that time I did not really understand anything. Later I felt if a man's proposals met with approval, it should encourage him; if they met with opposition, it should make him fight back; but the real tragedy for him was to lift up his voice among the living and meet with no response, neither

Chinese Characters Romanized

There are various ways to put Chinese characters into the Roman alphabet. In the nineteenth century the most common romanizations were Wade-Giles and the old post office romanization. Today the common romanization is called *pinyin.* In the personal name of Lu, "Hsun" is the Wade-Giles romanization, while "Xun" is *pinyin.* In names of cities, the old form is usually the post office romanization where, for example, the current Beijing and Tianjin were written Peking and Tientsin respectively.

approval nor opposition, just as if he were left helpless in a bound-less desert.

And this feeling of loneliness grew day by day, coiling about my soul like a huge poisonous snake. Conversations with an edi-tor of *New Youth* revealed that about the journal there seemed to have been no reaction, favorable or otherwise, and I guessed they must be feeling lonely. However I said:

"Imagine an iron house without windows, absolutely inde-structible, with many people fast asleep inside who will soon die of suffocation. But you know since they will die in their sleep, they will not feel the pain of death. Now if you cry aloud to wake a few of the lighter sleepers, making those unfortunate few suffer the agony of irrevocable death, do you think you are doing them a good turn?"

"But if a few awake, you can't say there is no hope of destroy-ing the iron house."

True, in spite of my own conviction, I could not blot out hope, for hope lies in the future. . . . From that time onwards, I could not stop writing. . . .

Leaders of the May Fourth Movement's attack on "Confucius and sons" targeted filial piety as a value to be tossed into history's trash bin. Filial piety was the obligation that chil-dren had to look after their parents' every need and to be obedient and respectful at all times. For many teenagers and young adults who grew up in the traditional Chinese family system, filial piety simply became a tool by which the older generation restrained and limited the younger generation's freedom of action.

This 1929 sketch from *Zhenshang suibi* [Sketches Written in Bed] by Zhang Yiping, known generally for his humorous prose, shows what kinds of "acts of rebellion" became com-mon in the war on the family system.

The thoughts of Chinese youth underwent the most drastic change about the time of the May Fourth Movement. At the time, most of them protested in an uproar against the family system, the old religions, the old morality, and the old customs, in an effort to break up all traditional institutions. I was then studying in a sum-mer school in Nanjing. I knew a young man who abandoned his own name and substituted the title "He-you-I." Later when I went to Beijing, I met at the gate of the School of Letters of Beijing

On Expressing an Opinion

I dreamed I was in the classroom of a primary school preparing to write an essay, and asked the teacher how to express an opinion.

"That's hard!" Glancing sideways at me over his glasses, he said: "Let me tell you a story—

"When a son is born to a family, the whole household is delighted. When he is one month old they carry him out to display him to the guests—usually expecting some compliments, of course.

One says: 'This child will be rich.' He is heartily thanked.

One says: 'This child will be an official.' Some compliments are paid him in return.

One says: 'This child will die.' He is thor-oughly beaten by the whole family.

"That the child will die is inevitable, while to say that he will be rich or a high official may be a lie. Yet the lie is rewarded, whereas the statement of the inevitable gains a beating. You . . ."

"I don't want to tell lies, sir, neither do I want to be beaten. So what should I say?"

"In that case, say: 'Aha! Just look at this child! My word. . . Did you ever! Oho! Hehe! He, hehehe!'"

—Prose poem by Lu Xun, 1925

Oppose Filial Piety

Shi Cuntong was a young intellectual from Zhejiang province during the May Fourth Movement. He is most well-known for his essay, "Oppose Filial Piety," which appeared in the May Fourth journal *The Zhejiang New Tide* in 1919. He was upset about his father's treatment of him and his mother. The essay argued that filial piety was the same as "the virtue required of a slave" and that when parents "invoke the imperatives of filial piety these days [it is a] demand [for] absolute obedience from the younger generation."

Vladimir Lenin, the leader of the 1917 Russian Revolution, preached that the backward state of such countries as China stemmed directly from the imperialism of the West. The caption of the poster reads: "Long live the movement of the propertyless class."

University a friend of mine accompanied by a young girl with her hair cut short. "May I ask your family name?" I asked her. She stared at me and screamed, "I don't have any family name!" There were also people who wrote letters to their fathers, saying, "From a certain date, I will not recognize you as my father. We are all friends, and equal." [Zhang] Tiemin was among those who had denied their fathers; but when his father died in 1921, he wrote a very touching poem to explain his grievous mourning for him.

The Russian Model

Many students and intellectuals were disheartened over China's plight and doubtful that any meaningful and widespread positive change was likely to occur. The hopes of some, at least, were buoyed by the Communist victory in Russia in the fall of 1917. It was the Bolshevik party that led the revolution in Russia. Might it not also succeed in China?

To many in the May Fourth generation, the watchword of the day was "science." And Marxism and Leninism indeed were seen as scientific. Karl Marx, the foremost theoretician of communism, explained how and why history moved through different stages until communism was reached; Vladimir Lenin, who led the Bolshevik party in Russia, explained why the imperialist powers needed colonies, how imperialism was related to capitalism. The appeal of the thoughts and program of Marx and Lenin (often called Marxism-Leninism) to many idealistic Chinese was its "scientific" explanations that shed light on China's predicament. Also appealing was the fact that communist ideology had already succeeded in Russia.

Li Dazhao was a librarian at Beijing University who, along with *New Youth* editor Chen Duxiu, championed Marxism-Leninism. Their support of the doctrine spread among students, leading to the formation of Marxist study groups and eventually to the founding of the Communist Party. Li's essay, "The Victory of Bolshevism," in celebration of the first anniversary of the Bolshevik victory, appeared in the journal *New Youth* in 1918.

[The ending of World War I] is the victory of humanitarianism, of pacifism; it is the victory of justice and liberty; it is the victory of democracy; it is the victory of socialism; it is the victory of

Bolshevism; it is the victory of the red flag; it is the victory of the labor class of the world; and it is the victory of the twentieth century's new tide. . . .

At the end of the war there were a number of short-lived efforts in Europe to establish Bolshevik-like regimes. Li comments on them.

The pattern of the revolutions generally develops along the same line as that in Russia. The red flag flies everywhere, the soviets are established one after another. Call it revolution entirely *à la Russe,* or call it twentieth century revolution. Such mighty rolling tides are indeed beyond the power of the present capitalist governments to prevent or to stop, for the mass movement of the twentieth century combines the whole of mankind into one great mass. The efforts of each individual within this great mass, following the example of some of them, will then be concentrated and become a great, irresistible social force. Whenever a disturbance in this worldwide social force occurs among the people, it will produce repercussions all over the earth, like storm clouds gathering before the wind and valleys echoing the mountains. In the course of such a world mass movement, all those dregs of history which can impede the progress of the new movement—such as emperors, nobles, warlords, bureaucrats, militarism, capitalism—will certainly be destroyed as though struck by a thunderbolt. Encountering this irresistible tide, these things will be swept away one by one. . . . Henceforth, all that one sees around him will be the triumphant banner of Bolshevism, and all that one hears around him will be Bolshevism's song of victory. The bell has rung for humanitarianism! The dawn of freedom has arrived! See the world of tomorrow: it assuredly will belong to the red flag! . . . The revolution in Russia is but the first fallen leaf warning the world of the approach of autumn. Although the word "Bolshevism" was created by the Russians, the spirit it embodies can be regarded as that of a common awakening in the heart of each individual among mankind of the twentieth century. The victory of Bolshevism, therefore, is the victory of the spirit of common awakening in the heart of each individual among mankind in the twentieth century.

Soviet
Ruling council

á la Russe
French for "in the Russian manner"

Chapter Four

Which Way Do We Go?

Revolution in the 1920s

As the May Fourth Movement veered in the direction of solving national problems rather than individual ones, the twin evils of the nation seemed to many to be the continuing threat of imperialism and the ongoing scourge of the warlords. The political model of the Soviet Union was most appealing to those who wanted rapid change. It had also become the darling of Chinese nationalists, for the Soviet Union had renounced its claims to special privileges in China, the only major foreign power to do so at this time. Agents of the Communist International (Comintern), the organization founded by the Soviet government and charged with inciting revolution around the world, began to meet with interested Chinese in early 1920. By that summer a Communist cell group had formed in Shanghai. The Chinese Communist Party (CCP) was officially formed in July 1921.

The best-known nationalist of the past two decades had been Sun Yat-sen. In the late 1910s he had tried to form an alliance with a rather progressive warlord in Guangdong Province, but these efforts had been unsuccessful. Sun was now open to receiving help from wherever he could get it. It is also likely that the idea of a tightly organized vanguard party loyal to its leader struck a chord with Sun as an important strategy for realizing his goals. Sun met with representatives of the Comintern each year from 1920 to 1922. The Comintern was interested in an alliance with Sun's Nationalist Party because it was well aware that the numbers of Communists alone were insufficient to

Sun Yat-sen, whom many Chinese saw as the "father of the country" after his death, is pictured between two national flags in this souvenir poster of the Northern Expedition. The characters above his head read "The revolution is not yet completed; you comrades must continue to make efforts." Chiang Kai-shek, on horseback, is pictured below with his troops.

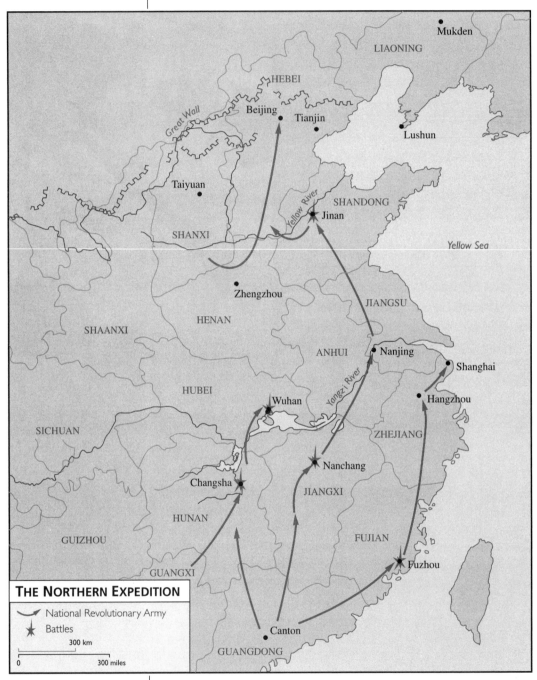

THE NORTHERN EXPEDITION

⌒ National Revolutionary Army
★ Battles

300 km

0   300 miles

ignite a revolution. According to an agreement between Sun and Soviet representatives in early 1923, the Soviet Union would provide advice and specific direction to Sun to restructure his Nationalist Party and to set up a party army. In the fall of 1923, the Comintern sent long-time Communist agent Michael Borodin to direct the changes.

The two parties, the CCP and the Nationalist Party, were linked by what was known as the "bloc within," that is, CCP members could join the Nationalist Party as individuals. This relationship was a Comintern tactic. After the political revolution—the overthrow of the warlords and the casting out of the imperialists—was successful, the CCP believed it could toss out the Nationalist Party, in the words of Soviet leader Joseph Stalin, "like a squeezed-out lemon." Then the Communists would move on to the economic and social revolution. The Nationalists thought of the revolution as being simply the action against the warlords and imperialists. Once they were gone and a proper Republican regime was established, the revolution would be over. With such widely divergent goals, the relationship between these two parties was at best uneasy and usually tense.

But the two parties were able to coexist and, in some cases, to work effectively together until Sun died suddenly of liver cancer in March 1925. He had been the glue that held the unlikely coalition together; when he died, it began to unravel, a process that was speeded by an explosion of nationalism following an episode that underlined for Chinese the dangers of foreign imperialism. On May 30 in Shanghai, British officers fired on a student demonstration in the aftermath of protests over the killing of a worker by a Japanese guard. Eleven Chinese were killed. In June, British troops in Canton [Guangzhou] killed another fifty-two demonstrators. A white-hot nationalistic rage swept the country, providing a favorable context for the start of the revolution. But it also brought to the fore the question of which way to go.

Conservatives in the Nationalist Party believed that the bloc within should be ended and that Borodin's power had to be limited. Growing increasingly powerful in that party was Chiang Kai-shek, who had become commandant at the party's new military academy at Whampoa, near Canton. In the summer of 1926 Chiang launched the Northern Expedition in an effort to defeat the warlords and unite the country. There were two major prongs of the military campaign, one moving directly north to the metropolis of Wuhan on the Yangzi River and the other (which Chiang himself led) northeast to Shanghai. When the CCP and liberal members of the Nationalists, accompanying the Wuhan campaign, reached that city, they undertook a host of radical reforms. Although Chiang was originally something of a centrist in the party, these events began to push him to the right. After Chiang took Shanghai in April 1927, he launched a bloody purge of the Communists that spread over the nation during the next year and a half. The CCP lay in ruins as Chiang established a new national regime at Nanjing in 1928.

A Growing Consumer Culture

By the middle of the 1920s, many cities, especially those with foreign settlements, sported a rapidly developing consumer culture. Indeed, many historians have called this period the twentieth century's "golden age" for Chinese entrepreneurs and businessmen. Newspapers and journals advertised new products and discussed new fashions, changing lifestyles, and personal hygiene. The following advertisements come from the _Shenbao,_ an important Shanghai newspaper.

This advertisement for electric fans, a "luxury" consumer item, makes a customary pitch to potential purchasers. The ad reads "constructed on the premises," a clear statement to purchasers that they are buying a Chinese-made product.

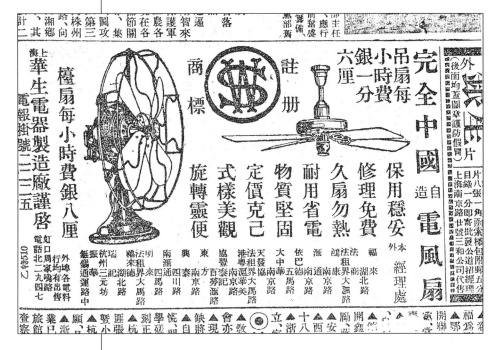

This ad for Colgate toothpaste points to the presence of Western products in Shanghai and their allure to Chinese consumers. The Colgate ad focuses on the importance of clean teeth and fragrant breath for sex appeal (or, as the ad puts it literally, "in the relations between men and women").

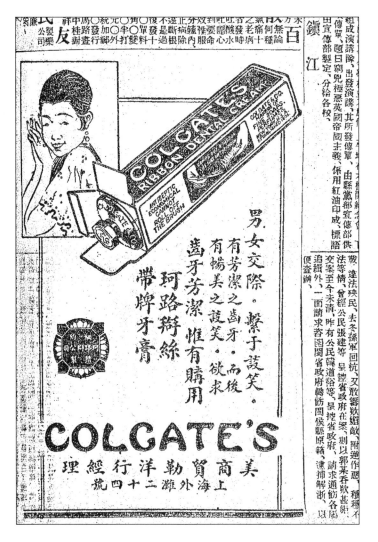

The Legacy of Sun Yat-sen

The Three Principles of the People are the basic ideology of the Nationalist Party. They were written by Sun Yat-sen and later espoused by Chiang Kai-shek when he became head of the party. Sun strongly condemns imperialism for its harmful effects. He compares political values East and West and notes which specific aspects of democracy he espouses. He parts company with the Marxists in his understanding of China's problem ("grinding poverty," he says, in contrast to the Marxists, who say "income disparity") and in his sense about how history moves ("man's continuous struggle for existence" versus "class struggle"). This description comes from a series of lectures Sun gave in 1924.

The Haves and Have-Nots

Both sides of the road are filled with handsome cars, quietly waiting for their masters' bidding after playing tennis or when leaving supper clubs . . . to return home. . . . The electric lights come on. . . . Evening meals begin. In the kitchens, the sounds of basins, pots, bowls, bells; dining rooms with the sound of music, wine glasses being clinked; on the floor the light and urgent footsteps of the "boy." Now and again the happy laughter on the veranda, the sounds of the lute in the music room, the sounds of singing, the bubbling sound of water being poured into glasses—rising and falling in cadence—extravagant joy and rejoicing.

—Journalist and revolutionary Shen Dingyi describing life in the French Concession in 1920

In contrast to the elegance of life in the French Concession was the grinding poverty of peasant life, described here by revolutionary Wang Guansan in Zeren, a short-lived journal, in December 1922.

The inside of all thatched-roof farm homes were the same: black rafters, gray walls, a dirt floor, a kitchen table, a bench, farm implements, and amulets from the local temple. There was generally nothing on the walls; rather more well off families might have several advertisements for brands of incense stuck on the wall. "The floors were covered with chicken shit; and people walked through it with their bare feet." Amid such conditions, the popular saying in the area: "Nothing to eat, nothing to wear—those things still go to the little king [the name farmers in the area gave to landlords]."

Nationalism

In view of the ruthless exploitation of China by foreign powers, China is in fact a subcolony, a status that is much worse than that of a colony. . . . China has concluded unequal treaties with many countries all of whom, because of the existence of these treaties, are China's masters. In fact China has become a colony of all those countries to whom the Chinese are merely slaves. Which one is better, to be slaves to one country or to be slaves to many countries? . . . Today our urgent task is to restore our lost nationalism and to use the combined force of our 400 million people to avenge the wrongs of the world. . . . Only when imperialism is eliminated can there be peace for all mankind. To achieve this goal, we should first rejuvenate Chinese nationalism and restore China's position as a sovereign state.

Democracy

There is a difference between the European and Chinese concept of freedom. While the Europeans struggle for personal freedom, we struggle for national freedom. As far as we are concerned, personal freedom should never be too excessive. In fact, in order to win national freedom, we should not hesitate to sacrifice our personal freedom. . . . The revolutionaries in Europe and America are fond of saying that men are born equal, and this concept of the natural equality of men was incorporated into such documents as the Declaration of Independence during the American Revolution. . . . But is it really true that men are born equal? No stretch of land is completely level; nor are two flowers exactly identical. Since there is no such equality in the sphere of nature, how can there be equality among men? True equality . . . has nothing to do with equality in achievement; it merely means that all people in a democratic society should enjoy the same political rights.

Among the popular rights in a democracy the foremost is the right to vote . . . ; besides the right to vote for officials, the people should also have the right to recall them.

Insofar as the enactment of legislation is concerned, the people should have the right of initiative as well as the right of referendum. Only when the people have these four rights (election, recall, initiative, and referendum) can they be said to have direct control over their government or to enjoy full democracy. . . .

People's Livelihood

The purpose of social progress cannot be more than the realization of the utmost good for the largest number of people in the society, and such realization lies in the harmonization, rather than conflict, between different economic interests . . . the law of social progress is man's continuous struggle for existence rather than class struggle as enunciated by Karl Marx.

What is the basic fact about China? It is the grinding poverty of the Chinese people. A privileged class of the extremely wealthy does not exist in China; instead there is such a thing as universal poverty. The so-called disparity in wealth is really a disparity between the poor and the extremely poor, since all Chinese are undeniably poor.

Different countries have different ways of solving their land problem. . . . The true solution of our land problem is to make sure that farmers own the land which they till; land ownership by tillers is in fact the final goal of the principle of people's livelihood. . . . According to our investigation, a landlord usually receives 60 percent of the crops as rent, leaving only 40 percent to be retained by the tillers. How can a situation be more unfair? . . .

To solve the problem of people's livelihood, we should [also] have the political power to protect our native industry so that it will not be encroached upon by foreign powers. Enchained by unequal treaties, China today not only cannot protect her own industry but is also forced to protect foreign industry at her own expense. . . . In short, we must adopt the political means to abolish the unequal treaties so that we can control our own customs.

On March 11, 1925, the day before he died, Sun signed a political testament that had been drafted by left-wing Guomindang leader Wang Jingwei. In the testament Sun enjoins his followers to carry on in the path of revolution he set forth in his writings. It was distributed to the press immediately after Sun died.

For forty years, I have devoted myself to the cause of the national revolution, the objective of which is to restore to China its liberty and a rank equal [to that of other nations]. The experience of those forty years has convinced me that if we wish to attain that objective, we must rouse the popular masses and unite with the peoples of the world that treat us on an equal footing, so as to pursue the common fight. Today, the revolution has not yet triumphed. May all our comrades, guided by my writings, The Plan for National Reconstruction, The Fundamentals of National Reconstruction, The People's Three Principles, and the Congress Manifesto, continue the struggle for this victory. And, above all, it is also necessary as soon as possible to implement the plans that I

Sun Yat-sen, lifetime revolutionary, was eager to accept help for the revolution from whoever was willing to give it. On his deathbed, he asked for continued assistance from the Soviet Union, whose agents were responsible for reconstructing the Nationalist Party in the 1920s and for helping to build a Nationalist Party army.

have recently proposed for setting up a national convention and for abrogating the unequal treaties. Those are my instructions.

In contrast to the testament, Sun's letter of farewell may only have been read to him. It was drafted by another left-wing leader and approved by Borodin. Among subsequent leaders of the party, the political testament was respected, while the farewell letter was looked on more dubiously, especially as the Guomindang pulled farther and farther away from the Communist Party. The farewell is directed at the Central Committee in the Soviet Union and was first published in the Soviet newspaper *Pravda*.

I am leaving behind me a party which I hoped would be associated with you in the historic work of completely liberating China and other exploited countries from this imperialist system. . . . I have therefore enjoined the Kuomintang [Guomindang] to carry on the work of the national revolutionary movement. . . . To this end I have charged the party to keep in constant touch with you; and I look with confidence to the continuance of the support that your Government has heretofore extended to my country.

In bidding farewell to you, dear comrades, I wish to express my fervent hope that the day may soon dawn when the USSR will greet, as a friend and ally, a strong and independent China and the two allies may together advance to victory in the great struggle for the liberation of the oppressed peoples of the world.

Revolution

Mao Zedong came from a relatively well-to-do, though far from rich peasant family in Hunan Province. In 1918, he graduated from Hunan's First Normal School, a teacher-training college. In late 1918 and early 1919, he took courses at Beijing University and worked at the library under the early Marxist convert, Li Dazhao. He became a founding member of the Chinese Communist Party in 1921; he also became a member of the Nationalist Party through the "bloc within" option. During the middle of the 1920s, he headed the Nationalist Party's Peasant Movement Training Institute and became active in organizing peasant associations to look after the needs and concerns of peasants.

In this 1927 report to the Central Committee of the CCP about the peasant movement in the central province of

Hunan, Mao notes the tremendous potential power of peasants to make revolution. In his stress upon the peasants, he moves away from the traditional Marxist-Leninist position that the urban working class would lead the revolution. His language countenancing violence and terror reveals a man ready to use whatever means were necessary for revolution.

The Importance of the Peasant Problem

During my recent visit to Hunan, I made a first-hand investigation of conditions in the five districts of Xiangtan, Xiangxiang, Hengshan, Liling, and Changsha. In the thirty-two days from January 4 to February 5, I called together fact-finding conferences in villages and county seats, which were attended by experienced peasants and by comrades working in the peasant movement, and I listened attentively to their reports and collected a great deal of material.

The present upsurge of the peasant movement is a colossal event. In a very short time, in China's central, southern, and northern provinces, several hundred million peasants will rise like a mighty storm, like a hurricane, a force so swift and violent that no power, however great, will be able to hold it back. They will smash all the shackles that bind them and rush forward along the road to liberation. They will sweep all the imperialists, warlords, corrupt officials, local tyrants, and evil gentry into their graves.

Down with the Local Tyrants and Evil Gentry!

All Power to the Peasant Associations!

The main targets of attack by the peasants are the local tyrants, the evil gentry, and the lawless landlords, but in passing they also hit out against patriarchal ideas and institutions, against the corrupt officials in the cities and against bad practices and customs in the rural areas. In force and momentum the attack is tempestuous; those who bow before it survive and those who resist perish. As a result, the privileges which the feudal landlords enjoyed for thousands of years are being shattered to pieces. Every bit of the dignity and prestige built up by the landlords is being swept into the dust. With the collapse of the power of the landlords, the peasant associations have now become the sole organs of authority and the popular slogan "All power to the peasant associations" has become a reality.

"It's Terrible!" or "It's Fine!"

The peasants' revolt disturbed the gentry's sweet dreams. When the news from the countryside reached the cities, it caused an immediate

A smiling Mao Zedong had held Communist leadership positions from the very founding of the party. The chief antagonist of Chiang Kai-shek, he became the leader of the party for good in 1935.

uproar among the gentry. Soon after my arrival in Changsha, I met all sorts of people and picked up a good deal of gossip. From the middle social strata upwards to the Guomindang right-wingers, there was not a single person who did not sum up the whole business in the phrase, "It's terrible!" . . . But, as already mentioned, the fact is that the great peasant masses have risen to fulfill their historic mission and that the forces of rural democracy have risen to overthrow the forces of rural feudalism. . . . This is a marvelous feat never before achieved, not just in forty, but in thousands of years. It's fine. It is not "terrible" at all. . . . What the peasants are doing is absolutely right; what they are doing is fine! "It's fine!"

Feudalism

The old regime, in the jargon of the Marxists

The last section of the report contains one of Mao's most reiterated definitions of revolution. He first tells us what it is not and then bluntly tells us what it is.

The Question of "Going too Far"
Then there is another section of people who say, "Yes, peasant associations are necessary, but they are going rather too far." This is the opinion of the middle-of-the-roaders. But what is the actual situation? True, the peasants are in a sense "unruly" in the countryside. . . . At the slightest provocation they make arrests, crown the arrested with tall paper hats, and parade them through the villages, saying, "You dirty landlords, now you know who we are." Doing whatever they like and turning everything upside down, they have created a kind of terror in the countryside. This is what some people call "going too far," or "exceeding the proper limits in righting a wrong," or "really too much."

Such talk may seem plausible, but in fact it is wrong. . . . A revolution is not a dinner party, or writing an essay, or painting a picture, or doing embroidery; it cannot be so refined, so leisurely and gentle, so temperate, kind, courteous, restrained, and magnanimous. A revolution is an insurrection, an act of violence by which one class overthrows another. A rural revolution is a revolution by which the peasantry overthrows the power of the feudal landlord class.

Both sides in the struggle to control China in the late 1920s used indiscriminate violence in striking at the other. A Japanese reporter wrote this account of the bloody ending of the Canton Commune, an ill-fated 1927 Communist effort to seize power in the city of Canton (Guangzhou). The commune lasted only two days, and Chiang's "White [meaning

not communist] Terror" resulted in the killing of as many as 4,000 people.

In order to learn more about the massacre of Communists after their uprising had failed, I boarded the SS *Fushun* in Hong Kong at 11 p.m., December 13 and headed for Canton . . . not until 11 a.m. the next day did we begin to see the skyline of Canton. As the ship came close to the harbor, we saw flames shooting skyward in different parts of the city. The fire had in fact continued for three consecutive days. . . .

The city was still under martial law, and communications with the outside world were completely cut off. Anti-Communist soldiers, each of whom wore a white handkerchief on his head, were posted at every street corner. When questioned, one of the soldiers informed me that many Communists were still in hiding in this part of the city and that a house-to-house search was being conducted to smoke them out. . . .

Eventually I reached the Western Garden. This area, with its fine stores, had been the most prosperous section of the city; now it is a total ruin. Not a single store had been spared from the pillage: its façade, decorated with golden inscriptions, had been broken into pieces, and the glass windows, behind which once were displayed the merchants' precious wares, had all been smashed. . . . Beyond the Western Garden was the place where the Communists had made their last stand. They were all wiped out, of course, having been subjected to a ferocious attack by Lu Fulin's troops. All the buildings had been razed to the ground, and one saw dead bodies everywhere, in the river as well as in the nearby streets. . . .

A large crowd gathered next to one of the remaining walls that had been too stubborn to collapse, and from the crowd I heard the cries: "Kill those bandits!" and "Kill those Communists!" I pushed myself through the crowd and suddenly realized that I was about to witness an execution. Five hapless men, with their hands bound behind them, were sitting on a pile of rubble, and three soldiers, holding pistols, were standing right behind them. One of the soldiers, who seemed to be the man in command, pronounced the expected sentence. "Look at what you Communists did to the city," he said. "I am sentencing all of you to die." Hardly had he completed this statement before several shots burst out. The prisoners slumped in a heap.

The heaviest fighting seemed to have taken place between Ch'angt'I [Changti] and the building that housed the Department of Finance. Wherever I looked, I saw dead bodies. Blood continued to ooze from these bodies, and streams of blood could be found in many streets. The blood eventually reached a drain and disappeared. In one place I saw a large puddle of blood with smashed brains and sliced intestines in it; apparently the bodies had just been moved away. Nearby were the scattered rocks, wooden knives, and bamboo spears that seemed to have been the workers' weapons in fighting the better-equipped enemy. Though the fire had been put out, there was still smoke here and there. The smoke, mixed with the intolerable odor caused by the decomposition of human flesh, made one feel like vomiting. . . .

Arriving at the city park, I saw three trucks piled high with dead bodies. . . .

As the sun descended slowly toward the west and as the park became darker and darker, birds of different sizes flew across the sky to the forest. Shots continued to be heard in the distance. With each shot there was another Communist or alleged Communist leaving this earth.

The following description of terror coming from the Communist side is an eyewitness account of a man, surnamed Su (first name unknown), who survived the Communist occupation of the city of Ji'an [Jian] in Jiangxi Province. He told his story to the *Central Daily News,* the Nationalist Party newspaper in Nanjing; it was published on December 12, 1930.

For three days after the fall of Ji'an on October 4, 1930, the peasants, goaded on by the Communists, actively sought out what they regarded as their class enemies. Some of the so-called enemies were killed on the spot, while others were brought to the city for trial. On October 8 the Counterrevolutionary Extermination Headquarters issued a new order which said in effect that from then on only the Red Guards, upon the recommendation of peasant or worker associations, had the authority to arrest the so-called counterrevolutionaries and that only the Counterrevolutionary Extermination Headquarters could try and sentence the arrested persons. From then on three or four hundred persons were sentenced to death and executed each day.

If the arrested person happened to be an intellectual, the chairman of the Counterrevolutionary Extermination Committee would conduct the inquiry himself. "Are you a member of the Kuomintang [Guomindang]. . . ?" he would ask. If the answer was "Yes," the arrested person would be immediately sentenced to death without further inquiry. If the answer was "No" and yet, in the meantime, someone else stated that the accused, despite the denial, was indeed a member of the Kuomintang . . . , the arrested person would also be sentenced to death. One student of the Fifth Middle School was interrogated by Zhu De [the commander of the Red Army] personally, and this student, when questioned about the organization of the Anti-Bolshevik League, said flatly that he did not know anything about this league. "All you counterrevolutionaries are traitors," Zhu De pounded the table and shouted. As a result of this remark, all the students at the Fifth Middle School were declared counterrevolutionaries and sentenced to death, if unfortunately they fell into Communist hands.

In the case of an arrested person whose class status could not be easily identified, his captors would observe his mannerism or examine his hands or feet. If his manners were judged to have been too elegant or if his hands and feet did not have calluses on them, he would be declared a counterrevolutionary and sentenced to death. Needless to say, all the former or present officials, members of the gentry, or anyone who owned some land or capital— all the people, according to the Communists, were ipso facto counterrevolutionaries and therefore deserved to die. In some cases, all members of their families, including women and children, were also slaughtered. "To kill the grass," the Communists explained, "we must destroy the roots." For the forty-five days when Ji'an was occupied by the Communists, the total number of people killed by the Communists exceeded 10,000. . . .

Chapter Five

The Nanjing Decade

The years from 1928 to 1937 are often called the Nanjing Decade because this was the period when Chiang Kai-shek's regime made its capital at Nanjing, almost 200 miles inland up the Yangzi River from Shanghai. Chiang's government faced huge problems. Most important was reconstruction after the long nightmare of the warlord period. But the new government had to go far beyond reconstructing China. If the nation was to survive and function in the modern world, it had to build modern transportation and communications networks, as well as a solid industrial base. It had to deal somehow with the imperialists whose ousting had been one of the goals of the Northern Expedition, the military campaign to unite China. It had to deal effectively with the Nationalist Party and establish a government that would be seen as quite a few cuts above the warlord regimes. And it had to deal with warlords who remained after Chiang had co-opted them during the Northern Expedition.

These were all tall orders—especially for a regime that did not have enough money. But even if it had had enough money, the times seemed to be against Chiang and his success. From March 1929 to October 1934, Chiang's forces were at war or on war's brink for forty-five of fifty-eight months—78 percent of the time. These wars were fought against warlords rearing their ugly heads, against party members challenging Chiang's rule, against a reborn Communist Party, and, most seriously, against the Japanese invasion of Manchuria and Japan's continuing aggression on Chinese territory.

Japanese aggression was serious for several reasons. First, Japan's appetite for Chinese territory seemed ravenous and insatiable. After seizing Manchuria and provinces in Inner Mongolia, Japan looked

Streetside food stalls were—and still are—commonplace in China. Vendors sold inexpensive noodles and other Chinese "fast food," such as roasted sweet potatoes and chestnuts and stinky tofu.

greedily at territory south of the Great Wall, making continual demands on the Nanjing government. To many Chinese (and doubtless to the Japanese as well), Chiang looked like a toothless tiger. He would not fight the Japanese, he said, because though they were like a disease, it was only a skin disease. It was the renewed Communist threat that he saw as the serious internal disease; that "illness" had to be eradicated before it killed the patient. Obsessed with the Communists, he undertook five "extermination" campaigns, from December 1930 to October 1934, against the Communist base in Jiangxi Province. Primarily because of Chiang's poor strategy, all of them failed until the fifth campaign.

A second serious outgrowth of Japan's aggression was domestic unrest. Most Chinese could not understand how Chiang, who had come to power as a strong nationalist, could allow China to be eaten alive by Japan. Student protests became commonplace; some newspapers became critical of Chiang's failure to act to deter Japan's moves. Chiang reacted by repressing the protests, raiding student dormitories before dawn and sending arrested students to prison, and having his secret police assassinate dissident intellectuals. Chiang tried to make it appear that he was taking the "high road" when he announced his New Life Movement in 1934. This movement was an effort to infuse into his regime the old-time morality of Confucianism and marry it to modern fascism, but it did not draw many supporters and failed miserably.

Given the military and political turmoil, the lack of funds, and Chiang's retreat into reactionary policies, it is surprising that Chiang was able to make headway on any of the outstanding problems that had to be dealt with. But there were some successes. Through negotiations with foreign powers, Chiang's government was able to begin to dismantle the unequal treaty system, gaining control over China's tariff and reducing the number of foreign concession areas. Through the continuing fighting, he was able to bring almost two-thirds of the country under his control by 1937. He made progress in road-building and railroad development, expanding the rail mileage from 1,220 in 1928 to 2,300 in 1937. But progress in these areas was minimal. By 1937, China, with its population of 400 to 500 million, had the same number of miles of paved highways as Spain, but fewer miles of railroads than Illinois.

The Nanjing Decade ended in full-scale war with Japan. In late 1936 Zhang Xueliang, Chiang's top military leader, had had enough of Chiang's appeasement of the Japanese and kidnapped Chiang. Chiang had ordered Zhang to blockade the Communists to keep

The Unequal Treaty System

From 1842 to 1860, foreign imperialists took advantage of China's weakness to force on China an "unequal treaty system"—unequal because the foreigners received privileges and the Chinese got nothing in return. One aspect of the treaties under this system was that foreigners got the "right" to set up concession areas (sections in cities called treaty ports) where foreign law, military, police, and businessmen were in charge. Another aspect of the treaty system was that foreigners would set the level of China's tariffs. This meant that China could not raise its tariffs to keep out unwanted foreign goods.

them enclosed; but Zhang, who questioned why Chinese were continuing to fight Chinese, had called off the blockade. When Chiang went to find out what was going on, Zhang kidnapped him and held him until he agreed to join the Communists in a united front against the Japanese. Therefore, when fighting broke out in northern China in July 1937, Chiang was committed to following through on his united-front pledge. Born in war, Chiang's Nanjing regime died in war.

Social Currents

The New Life Movement was an effort by Chiang and the Nanjing government to combat the appeal and success of the Communist movement by offering a new ideological focus. Strangely, that new focus was on warmed-over past traditions. The movement attempted to resurrect Confucius and Confucian values. Chiang's government installed as its hero Zeng Guofan, a traditional Confucian who had been in the leadership that defeated the dangerous Taiping Rebellion, which led to millions of deaths between 1851 and 1864. At a time when Chiang feared Communism, it made perfect sense to champion and use as a model someone who had defeated another ideological threat.

The movement began on February 19, 1934, with much fanfare. In the end, though its anniversary was celebrated through World War II, it accomplished little. Because of her husband's leadership in the movement, Madame Chiang would be expected to have a positive take on the effort. This article was published in English by *China Weekly Review Press* in 1935.

China, like almost every other nation during the past few years, has felt the tremendously enervating effects of world depression. Each nation, according to its lights, has sought to find a way out of stagnation into normalcy. Italy has its fascism, Germany its Nazism, the Soviet Union its first and second five-year plans, and America its New Deal. The primary aim of each is to solve the economic problems involved and to bring material prosperity to the people. China, like the rest of the nations, is confronted with a similar problem, added to which is the necessity of rescuing the people from the cumulative miseries of poverty, ignorance, and superstition, combined with the after effects of communistic

The urbane Madame Chiang Kai-shek helped lighten up her husband's frequent dour arrogance. A Christian, and fluent in English, she was much admired by American journalists and political leaders.

Madame Chiang Kai-shek, a Thumbnail Sketch

Madame Chiang Kai-shek (nee, Soong Meiling) was the daughter of a Chinese businessman. She graduated from Wellesley College in Massachusetts. A Methodist, she extracted from Chiang Kai-shek a promise to convert to Christianity after their marriage in 1927; Chiang was baptized a Christian in 1930. Her next older sister married Sun Yat-sen; her oldest sister married H. H. Kung, who became an important financial figure in Chiang Kai-shek's government.

Government-Issued Rules for the New Life

Clothing should be clean and tidy. Buttons should be well buttoned.

Sit upright.

Do not throw food on the ground.

Do not write on walls.

Be punctual for appointments.

Help your neighbor if a fire breaks out.

Do not laugh when others have funerals.

Do not scold, swear at, or hit others.

Stay in line at the station when buying tickets.

Say good morning to others every morning.

Do not gamble or visit prostitutes.

Salute the national flag when it is raised and brought down.

Be filial to your parents and love your brothers and sisters.

Be loyal to your friends.

Go to bed early and rise early.

Keep your face clean.

Comb your hair.

Do not eat snacks.

Do not smoke.

Keep bathrooms clean.

Exterminate flies.

Exterminate mosquitoes.

Exterminate rats.

Do not urinate as you please.

Get vaccinated.

Restaurants, hotels, and teahouses should be clean.

—List by the New Life Promotion Society of Nanchang, *What Must Be Known about New Life*, 1935

orgies and natural calamities, and last but not least, the grave consequences of external aggression.

To this end, what is known as the New Life movement has been launched, to strike at the very roots of the several evils. . . .

The idea of the New Life movement became crystallized in the mind of Generalissimo Chiang Kai-shek during the anticommunist campaign. He realized that military occupation of recovered territory was not enough; that it must be followed up by social and economic reconstruction in the divested areas; and that, to be effective, a national consciousness and spirit of mutual cooperation must be aroused. He saw that the immediate need was the development of the vitality of the spirit of the people, which seemed to have been crushed. He contemplated the perspective of history in light of existing conditions about him; he realized how much depended upon the people's consciousness of their heritage from the past and conviction came to him that the four great virtues of old China, *Li, I* [*yi*], *Lien* [*lian*], and *Chih* [*zhi*] constituted a remedy that could rescue the country from stagnation and ruin, because at the time when those principles were practiced, China was indeed a great nation. He decided then and there to base a New Life movement upon them, to try to recover what had been lost by forgetfulness of this source of China's greatness. . . .

Madame Chiang then defines these values. *Li* is defined as "courtesy"; *I* is translated as "duty or service" to oneself and others; *Lien* becomes "honesty" as well as "a clear demarcation between what is public and what is private"; and *Chih* is defined as "high-mindedness and honor."

Some people have criticized the New Life movement on the ground that, since there is not sufficient food for everyone in the land, it is useless to talk about or seek spiritual regeneration. We reject the argument by pointing out the very fact that, if everyone from the highest official to the lowest wheel-barrow-man would conscientiously practice these principles in everyday life, there would be food for all. If we have the right conception of *Li*, we recognize not outward pomp but the sterling native qualities in our fellow men. If we practice *I*, we feel an obligation not to hold wealth and enjoy it wastefully while our fellow countrymen may be on the verge of starvation or suffering from sickness or other misfortunes. Again with *Lien*: if officials recognize the rights of people under them, they do not try to benefit themselves at the expense of people just because the latter are too powerless and ignorant to fight in their own defense. And if *Chih* is a reality, no one is shameless or stoops to mean or underhanded deeds. . . .

[T]he Generalissimo, before the end of the spring school season, called a meeting of all the middle-school students in Nanchang. He spoke at length to them of the conditions in the country at large and particularly in their own districts. He pointed out to them the necessity of recognizing the sacrifices their parents were making to give them educations and the fact that such sacrifices entailed a proportionate responsibility on the part of the students to repay the community for what they were receiving. . . .

As a direct result of this talk the students pledged themselves to return to their homes to take an active part in giving a practical impetus to the principles of the New Life movement. Some pledged themselves to open up kindergartens for the village children; others, to teach night classes for the adults; others to lecture on hygiene and sanitation; and still others, to make fly swatters and to rid their communities of breeding places of insects which carry malarial infections. The reports have just arrived, and these show that the students take their work seriously.

Out of all this is emerging a new citizen, a contented farmer and artisan, on the one hand, and, on the other, a teacher with new ideals, born of the contentment he is producing. . . .

One Day in China

Editors of the Shanghai newspaper *Shenbao* decided to initiate a project that would capture snapshot accounts of life in China. They solicited descriptions of what people were doing and the kind of lives they were living on May 21, 1936. They produced rich portraits of the lives of the common people. This sketch by Kang Yimin of the city of Wuxi in Jiangsu province describes road construction.

Village men and women with carrying poles made of mulberry branches on their shoulders or with baskets made of mulberry branches in their hands, trotted along the footpaths separating the fields. . . .

Suddenly the sound of a gong floated up and down the streets. . . .

Reverence for Ancestors

Ancestors played a chief role in family life. Relatives of important longtime ancestors of the male family line as well as deceased parents and grandparents would place commemorative tablets on altars in homes. They were remembered with rituals involving incense and the offering of sacrifices of crops or food on birth and death days. It was the responsibility of the present generation to venerate the ancestors and to have offspring so that the ancestral line was carried on.

A woman uses wooden tongs to put food in a bird cage at a bird market. Birds and grasshoppers were two favorite pets sold at animal markets throughout China.

Shouts erupted from the village, "Go build the road! Go build the road!" After that, a group of peasants carrying hoes and rakes went to the wheat field, through which a line had been drawn with gray powder.

A peasant who had arrived late spoke to the person who sounded the gong: "Qian Erguan, all you watch-group heads and ten-household heads must really be pleased. You have only to use your mouth to make assignment after assignment, and the real work gets done without your touching a thing. . . ."

"Old He," the person who sounded the gong said as he walked along, "Don't talk like that! These days it isn't easy to manage public works projects in this remote and poor village. . . ."

In the end it is we common people who suffer a bitter fate. We conscientiously, diligently planted a crop of wheat and eagerly waited for it to ripen so it could be taken to market and converted into cash for household expenditures. Who would have expected that just as the green plants were about to form kernels, it was though they were suddenly struck by a disease that transformed them from green wheat plants into weeds and required that they be pulled up by the roots. . . ."

"Township Head, go ahead and do your own thing," said Wang Xiangji, with sweat pouring from his forehead, as he tightened his fists and rolled up his sleeves. "I haven't broken any law. Whoever wants to take my ancestors' graves and build a road through them, I'll fight that person to the death."

"I've told you before." The township head seemed impatient. "You are using your mouth and tongue for nothing. These are public affairs being done in the public spirit, and not only graves but even houses where people live are being torn down. What's the use of your fighting to the death against me!"

"I'm not afraid of my house being torn down, but it won't be easy to touch my ancestors' graves!" Wang Xiangji saw that having argued half a day with the township head hadn't scored him half a point and he turned to the people to plead his case: "Everyone one of you here think about it. Who doesn't have ancestors? Who doesn't want sons and grandsons? . . . .

"Xiangji." Qian Erguan, seeing no end to this scene, made his way out of the circle of people and sought to become the mediator. . . . "I wonder whether we can ask the township head to go to the higher-ups, clear matters up a bit, and get a few more days so that Xiangji can choose a good and auspicious day to dig up the coffins. Otherwise, violating the earth and making members of a family suffer some kind of disaster isn't fair either."

A very different contribution to the newspaper's collection is this account of the experiences of a man imprisoned and tortured after being suspected as a Communist. The letter was submitted to the newspaper by a friend of the man from Sichuan Province. He used a pseudonym, an indication that he feared that authorities might try to strike out at him for releasing this information.

I was very surprised [to receive a letter]. The letter was from my good friend Xi. My friend Xi was arrested last year as a suspected Communist, and seven full months have passed since then. He got out of prison yesterday and is going to the countryside right away to rest, so he can't come visit me and instead has written me this letter. The letter is as follows—

Dear Tian:

This letter I am writing to you will without a doubt surprise you. My friend, let me tell you that yesterday at seven o'clock in the morning I was released from prison, without any explanation.

I went into prison without knowing what was happening and I came out or prison without knowing what was happening. I don't know whether I should feel sad or happy! . . .

On being arrested, Xi was tortured to confess that he was a Communist, because another prisoner had named him as one.

The fact of the matter was that I had absolutely nothing to say, but he was not the least bit willing to listen to any explanation. Several men lifted me up in the air and left me hanging here, in order to force me to admit that I was a Communist and to make me reveal the names of other party members. My friend, imagine being so tired that you thought you were going to die swinging on a swing, but instead I was swinging in the air held by a rope which was hanging from the rafters and was tied to my thumb. This was no fun! While hanging in the air, I sobbed to the point where no more tears would flow. Crying out and screaming were of no avail. I thought I was dead and lost consciousness. . . . There was no way out. All I could do was to sell myself. I blurted out, "Yes—yes—yes—yes—" again and again, hoping that the suffering would stop at least temporarily. Huh! That string of yes's was quite effective. The rope went slack, and I dropped to the ground.

Xi goes on to recount that he was brought face to face with his accuser, but the accuser did not recant. Xi is eventually imprisoned and subject to all sorts of tortures.

Now I've returned to this world to live again as a human being again. . . .

My friend! What I have reported to you is really only one ten-thousandth of the story because some parts I can't bear to write, some I don't dare write, some I won't write for fear of depressing you, and some you wouldn't believe. . . . For this one case, seventy or eighty people were unjustly arrested. I heard that all of them will be eventually released. . . .

Political and Military Realities

Chiang Kai-shek's illness metaphor—Japan is a disease of the skin, while the Communists are a disease of the heart—comes from a speech he delivered to senior officers on May 8, 1933, in Nanchang, the capital of Jiangxi Province, where

military campaigns were being waged against the Communists. Here Chiang speaks of the two enemies, the Communists and the Japanese. The Nationalist regime's fourth military campaign against the Communists had ended in failure two months before this address; Chiang would not launch another effort until the fall. Two months before this speech, Japan had seized the province of Rehe, in eastern Inner Mongolia. The month of the speech, Japan had forced the Tanggu Truce down China's throat. This "truce" created a zone in northern China that was the size of the state of Connecticut, where Chinese could not maintain military troops.

Most of you have been in Jiangxi fighting the Communist bandits for three years: some of you have been here only one year. During this difficult, bloody struggle, more than ten thousand of our brave men have perished, including colonels and generals. Yet, despite this enormous sacrifice, the Communist bandits have not been exterminated and the country remains ununified. Taking advantage of this situation, the Japanese imperialists have continued to advance and persist in their aggression.

Today we are facing dangers from within as well as without. Domestically the brutal, violent bandits are burning and killing every day, and across the sea come the Japanese imperialists who take over one piece of territory after another. These imperialists will not be satisfied until they exterminate China as a nation.

Why do the Japanese imperialists choose this particular time to attack us?

They, like other imperialists, relish other people's misfortunes and bully those who are too weak to resist. They attack us because we have this bandit rebellion that prevents our country from being unified. In other words, it is this internal rebellion that invites aggression from abroad. We have no hope at all to resist this aggression as long as the bandits persist in their violent activities and as long as China remains ununified. To resist aggression at this time would mean the subjection of China to simultaneous attacks by both the Communist bandits and the Japanese imperialists. Attacked from within as well as without, China would certainly be defeated. In the name of saving our country by resisting Japanese aggression, we might send her to an early end.

The only way of saving our country, from an objective and strategic point of view, is to follow an ancient adage that "internal pacification must take precedence over external war." When the country is pacified and the goal of unification has been achieved,

The cry of the National Revolutionary Army at the time of the Northern Expedition— overthrow imperialism—is now a crime.

—Statement by leader of the National Salvation Movement, opponents of Chiang's appeasement policy, in February 1936

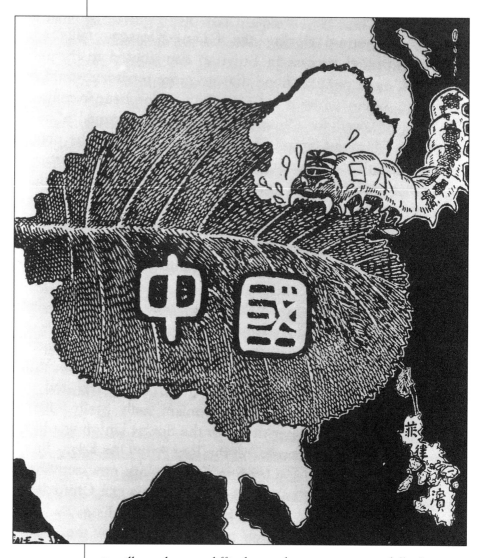

Japan as aggressor, represented by the hungry silkworm, eats through the mulberry leaf, which symbolizes China in this 1936 cartoon. Silk production was important in both China and Japan, making this cartoon especially appropriate.

it will not be too difficult a task to resist successfully Japanese aggression. The total population of Japan is only 60 million, and the total number of men she can put on the battlefield will not exceed 6 million, as compared to the total number of 400 million for China and a much larger number of men we can arm. In terms of natural resources, territorial size, historical heritage, and individual creativity, Japan is also inferior to China. Under normal circumstances she cannot and will not succeed in her aggression against us. It is the Communist bandits and the internal difficulties they have created that give the Japanese imperialists their golden opportunity.

In 1928 our country could have been unified had the Communists bandits not renewed their disruptive activities in

Jiangxi and elsewhere. They have not only prevented China from being unified but also caused the deterioration of the economy and the waste of natural resources. The Japanese enemy, taking advantage of this situation, has launched one aggression after another.

After the September Eighteenth Incident, Japan occupied Manchuria. She then attacked Shanghai and invaded Rehe. The intensification of foreign aggression has provided the Communist bandits with the opportunity of rest and regrouping, thus strengthening themselves. Foreign aggressors and domestic rebels thus work hand in hand. Had there been no bandit rebellions, there would not have been Japanese aggression. Once we recognize this relationship between cause and effect, it is clear that to resist Japanese aggression from abroad, we must first exterminate the Communist bandits at home.

The Japanese aggression comes from without and can be compared to a disease of the skin, while the bandit rebellion, working from within, is really a disease of the heart. We must cure a disease of the heart before proceeding with the cure of a disease of the skin, because the heart disease, if not cured, will kill the patient, while the skin disease will not. Once the Communist bandits are exterminated and the country is pacified, I firmly believe that the Japanese imperialists will not dare attack China again. If they do, they will be destroyed. Therefore, as revolutionary soldiers, we must have the right sense of priority, namely, the precedence of internal pacification over external war.

Once we realize how important this sense of priority is, we will not envy the glamour that is associated with the resistance to Japanese aggression. We must know that only by crushing the bandit rebellion can we carry out the Three Principles of the People and thus assure our country's everlasting existence. I cannot find any task more honorable than this one.

One of the strangest episodes in twentieth-century China occurred in December 1936 at the ancient capital of Xi'an, in Shaanxi Province. There General Zhang Xueliang kidnapped Generalissimo Chiang Kai-shek. The group of kidnappers, which included other military officers, held Chiang for two weeks. Chiang almost certainly gained his release by agreeing to join the Communists in a united front. He took his captor, Zhang, with him on his return to Nanjing, where he was greeted with a huge, supportive demonstration. Zhang remained under house arrest until 1990.

September Eighteenth Incident

On this day in 1931, the Japanese military blew up a stretch of Japanese-controlled railroad track on the South Manchurian Railway. They blamed it on the Chinese and used it as a pretext for a military campaign that led to the Japanese seizure of Manchuria.

These views of the kidnapping come from Chiang Kai-shek's 1956 book, *The Soviet Union in China*.

. . . the Communists had launched a nationwide offensive of peace propaganda, the primary target of which was the northeastern Army, commanded by Chang Hsueh-liang [Zhang Xueliang] and stationed in Shensi [Shaanxi]. Shortly afterward both Chang Hsueh-liang and Yang Hu-ch'eng [Yang Hucheng] had become conspiratorially involved with them. Such propaganda lines as "resist Japan and do not fight the Communists" were widely circulated, and there was positive evidence that Chang and Yang had established direct contact with the Communist headquarters. Under the protection of these two men, the Communists and their sympathizers, such as members of the Third Party [a liberal alternative to the conservative Nationalists and the radical Communists] and the China Salvation Association, propagandized openly in Sian [Xi'an].

If this situation deteriorated further, I thought, a rebellion would invariably materialize. To reverse the trend and to stabilize the situation, I went to Sian. I planned to call a meeting of all the generals toward the end of that year and clarify for them the government's policy regarding the extirpation of the Communists and the resistance to Japan. I would warn them that they should by no means be enticed and led astray by the Communist propaganda, the so-called cessation of hostilities and unity against Japan.

On December 12, Chang Hsueh-liang and Yang Hu-ch'eng, by the use of force, succeeded in kidnapping me. I knew even then that these two men had been deceived and used by the Communists to the point that they had unwittingly dealt a fatal blow to the security of the nation. When Chang Hsueh-liang came to see me, I said to him, in simple and clear language, that he must repent and redeem his crime by immediately returning me to Nanking [Nanjing] for the sake of the security of the nation as well as the sake of his own future. "Do not fall into the trap of these demonic Communists," I scolded him loudly; "and it is not yet too late to wake up."

Under the circumstances Chang Hsueh-liang did not dare present to me his so-called eight conditions that had been prepared in advance. Instead, he said that the situation was much more complicated than I thought and that he wanted me to suppress my anger before he would describe it in detail. I scolded him again, saying that he was not allowed to mention any political matter in front of me.

China Salvation Association

An organization that condemned Japanese aggression and demanded that Chiang's government take a stand against it

Not until the third day of my captivity did Chang Hsueh-liang, in a pleading tone, describe for me his so-called eight conditions. He said that he would personally escort me to Nanking if I endorsed them. I replied that whatever his requests were, they could not be discussed in Sian where he himself was pressured and threatened by the Communists. I knew then that even if Chang himself did wake up to face his mistake, the Communist bandits, who were behind him, would prefer my death rather than my release if I did not accept their conditions. I decided that I would exchange my life for my principle if necessary, and absolutely refused to discuss any political matters with these traitors. . . .

On December 22, Madame Chiang suddenly arrived at Sian. The moment I saw her, I said to her as follows: "For the past ten days these traitors have used all kinds of methods to pressure me to endorse their conditions. Your decision to come here to share the ordeal with me is motivated by your love of the country and nothing else. If any of these traitors ever approaches you and asks you to use your influence to persuade me to change my mind, you must absolutely refuse. We should die rather than agree to their conditions." She replied that she valued my integrity more highly than my life and that she would never try to persuade me to do anything against my wishes. She would live and die together with me, she added.

Three days later, on the afternoon of Christmas Day, we were released unconditionally and returned to Nanking.

Only after the conclusion of this world-shaking event did I learn about its true nature. The most unexpected was the discovery that Chang Hsueh-liang had been the primary motivator, though Yang Hu-ch'eng first advanced the kidnapping idea. Another discovery was that neither of the two had consulted with the Communists before the kidnapping. . . .

Chiang Kai-shek made his capital Nanjing, on the Yangzi River in east-central China. His rule from 1928 to 1949 was marked by continual wars and violent social turbulence.

Zhang Xueliang, the kidnapper, gave this speech to his senior staff on December 13, 1936, the day after the kidnapping. In it, he explains why he undertook the kidnapping.

I have not come to work in the office for more than a month and consequently have not had an opportunity to speak with you. The reason I have not attended to my official duties is my dissatisfaction with them—namely, I no longer want to fight the Communists. At a time when the nation is in peril at the hands of a foreign aggressor [Japan], we, instead of facing our real enemy, choose to fight among ourselves. This grieves me greatly.

I presume that by now all of you have heard about yesterday's events. Let me explain for you the rationale for my action.

Prior to yesterday's events I had repeatedly expressed to the Generalissimo [Chiang] my belief that we must stop the civil war and form a united front to face Japan. Unfortunately I was not able to change his mind. He said I was wrong; yet he gave me no guidance as to why I was wrong.

As his view and mine became irreconcilable and as this dispute must be put to an end, I decided that there were only three courses of action open to me. First, I could resign. Second, I could continue my persuasion in the hope that someday he would be convinced of the correctness of my proposals. Third, I could do what I did yesterday—namely, use force to drive home a point.

I could have easily taken the first course of action and returned to the Northeast [Manchuria] to fight the enemy on my own had it not been for the fact that Japan was as much an enemy to me personally as she was to the nation, that I shouldered great responsibility for the state, and that, finally, all of my subordinates shared my opinion with regard to Japan. It was extremely doubtful, however, that my resignation could bring about the same result as choice number three hopefully would.

As for the second course of action, I have pursued it consistently for the past month. I searched for every approach and used every argument to convince the Generalissimo of the correctness of my views. My motive was pure; my intention was selfless. I journeyed twice to Loyang to see him; and, to convince him of the purity of my motives, I did not bring my bodyguards with me. But I failed in my persuasion. I was his second in command; yet he not only refused my proposals but also would not allow me to complete my presentation. He only listened to those who agreed with him.

As the first and second courses of action could not and would not yield any result, the only choice open to me was the third. Let me explain the immediate causes that finally prompted me to take action.

First, seven leaders of the patriotic movement were arrested in Shanghai. What crimes did they commit? Well, according to Shen Chun-yu, an old professor who was one of the arrested, their crime was patriotism. Once when I spoke on behalf of the seven arrested, the Generalissimo's response was: "Of all the people in the nation only you look at this matter differently." Second, on December 9 when the students in Sian planned a massive

CHIANG KAI-SHEK IS PRISONER OF MUTINOUS SHENSI TROOPS, DEMANDING WAR ON JAPAN

Tokyo Sees Danger in Chinese Rebellion; Officials Anxiously Await Next Move by Foe

By The Associated Press

TOKYO, Sunday, Dec. 13.—The seizing of Generalissimo Chiang Kai-shek by anti-Japanese rebels in China is considered here to have thrown the whole Far Eastern situation into confusion, the outcome of which it is impossible to foresee. Official quarters said the Japanese Government was most gravely concerned about immediate developments and possible future consequences of General Chang Hsueh-liang's rebellion. Official comment, however, was withheld until the situation becomes clearer.

Coming so soon after the recent conflict on the borders of Suiyuan and Chahar Provinces, in which Chinese troops loyal to General Chiang repulsed Mongol and Manchukuoan irregulars aided by Japanese military, the virtual kidnapping of the Chinese generalissimo by his subordinate shocked Tokyo.

Recently General Chiang has been trying—hitherto successfully—to re-establish Nanking's authority in the Northwest. An

MANCHURIAN IN REVOLT

Chang Hsueh-liang for Return of Communists to Nanking Regime.

LOST TERRITORY SOUGHT

Generalissimo Seized in Midst of Preparations to Discipline Those Friendly With Reds.

The New York Times coverage of the kidnapping of Chiang Kai-shek notes correctly that the mutiny of troops in Shensi (Shaanxi) Province resulted from the desire of the army and the general population to stand against Japanese aggression.

demonstration for patriotism, Governor Shao Li-tzu [Shao Lizi] and I did our utmost to persuade them not to proceed with the implementation of their plan. We suggested that any opinion they wished to express could be done in writing. When they insisted on carrying out the demonstration, we said that under no circumstances would they be allowed to demonstrate before the Generalissimo's headquarters in Linkuan. Had the police not opened fire and thus aroused public anger, I doubt very much that the students would have gone to Linkuan in the first place. I went there to talk with them; eventually I was able to persuade them to return to the city. Instead of a word of approval or appreciation, the Generalissimo accused me of having failed to use more effective means to suppress the students. His accusation convinced me that he would never change his policy toward Japan. . . .

In taking the action that we did yesterday, personal considerations—glory or shame, life or death—never entered our minds. We did this for our country and our people. . . .

Chapter Six

Communist Resurgence

The Communist movement was wounded in the aftermath of Chiang Kai-shek's White Terror, but not mortally as first thought. In 1928–29, the Chinese Communist Party (CCP) got a new lease on life in the southeastern province of Jiangxi through the leadership of longtime CCP member Mao Zedong and his chief military commander and founder of the Red Army, Zhu De. Unlike the first version of the Communist movement, which had focused in proper Marxist fashion on the proletariat or the urban working class, the revived Communist movement centered on peasants in the Chinese countryside. While the CCP headquarters remained underground in Shanghai, Mao and Zhu expanded their control of rural counties until they were able to announce the establishment in November 1931 of the Chinese Soviet Republic, often called the Jiangxi Soviet because it was located primarily in Jiangxi Province. In January 1933, the party headquarters, finally recognizing that the party's center of gravity had shifted to the countryside, relocated to Jiangxi.

In the Jiangxi Soviet, the centerpiece of the Communist effort became land reform, specifically, confiscating land from landlords and rich peasants and redistributing it to those peasants who traditionally held little or no land. Though the name "rich peasant" seems to be contradictory, a rich peasant was the economic upper crust of the stratum of peasants. He might own a little land, but he also rented land, which differentiated him from the landlord stratum. Land reform pitted class against class in often-violent struggle. Eventually the CCP had to call off the revolution this was producing, because it was antagonizing too many in the general population. To facilitate more gender equality among the people, the CCP also announced a new marriage law that made divorce easy and that forbade arranged marriage and marriage through purchase or sale.

Mao Zedong (right) stands beside rival Zhang Guotao in front of party headquarters in Yan'an. Zhang left the Communist Party in 1938 and sought the protection of the government of Chiang Kai-shek. When the Communists won the civil war in 1949, Zhang fled to Hong Kong.

Beginning in December 1930, even before the formal establishment of the Jiangxi Soviet, Chiang Kai-shek undertook massive military campaigns from his capital in Nanjing to defeat the reborn Communist effort. He launched five so-called "extermination campaigns" against the Communist base. In the first four, Chiang overextended his troops and the Communists were able to cut supply lines and launch successful counterattacks. All four failed. In the last campaign, begun in October 1933, the Nationalist forces moved slowly, built roads to make supply easier, constructed blockhouses as they advanced, and worked to mobilize the population in the areas that they had seized.

As Chiang's forces tightened the noose around the base, the Communists realized that they had to retreat. In October 1934, some 86,000 people fled from the base to the southwest. Chased by Chiang's army for much of the roughly 370-day trek, which has become known as the Long March, Communist forces were faced with immense obstacles—forbidding and often deadly terrain, hostile local populations, and uncertainty about their destination. When they eventually arrived in the impoverished town of Yan'an in a parched and barren area of Shaanxi Province, there were only about 8,000 soldiers still alive. But the experience proved pivotal in the Communist rise to power. For, it is said, those who survived the Long March were filled with a sense of destiny, that they had a duty to succeed in the revolution, if only to make up for the thousands who had died along the way. Indeed, from 1949 until 1997 the CCP and China would be led by survivors of the Long March.

After late 1935, when the CCP was based at Yan'an, Chiang agreed to join them in a united front to fight the Japanese. The united front worked for a time, but had fallen apart by January 1941, when Chiang's forces attacked Communist troops in east-central China in the New Fourth Army Incident. During the Sino-Japanese war, which lasted from 1937 to 1945, the Communists, under the increasingly powerful Mao Zedong, fought the Japanese in north China and, in the process, mobilized and won over huge portions of the population in areas where they worked.

Mao began to write essays that became the canon for the party. He and the party leadership experimented with new policies that would become significant after they gained control of China in 1949. Their "mass line" approach was an effort to undo centuries of Chinese bureaucratic "top-down" governance by calling for greater reliance on the masses (or "bottom-up" governance).

As huge numbers of people with wide-ranging beliefs and allegiances fled from areas occupied by the Japanese to join the Communist Party, CCP leadership instituted "rectification" campaigns to ensure the proper "redness" (ideological correctness) of the party. These campaigns included self-criticisms by party cadres or officials, struggle sessions where groups would criticize the accused cadre openly and severely, and—if the cadre was still unrepentant—apply psychological pressure against the accused. Mao said he used these "re-education" tactics against dissenters rather than killing them, as Stalin did in the Soviet Union, because, as he put it, when one cuts off people's heads they do not grow back as cabbages would. But some critics noted that the process of re-education was really "thought control," and—if psychological pressures were applied—even "brainwashing."

Finally, the party took on the task of dealing with intellectuals and writers who tended to have individualistic and idealistic viewpoints that often clashed with party goals and approaches. In May 1942, at a forum on art and literature, the party came down hard on any idea of art for art's sake. Art and literature existed solely to serve the people, and the people were defined as the peasants, working classes, and soldiers. Those writers and thinkers who transgressed this line quickly became the objects of attack and were punished by being sent to the countryside or even killed. This was the beginning of a policy of dealing with intellectual critics of the party that would continue into the twenty-first century.

The Jiangxi Soviet and its Demise

In 1932, Jiangxi Soviet leaders announced the first Chinese Communist attempt at land reform, an effort that would become the heart of the Communist social revolution of the 1940s and 1950s. This law brought forth the difficult and tricky problem of placing peasants into categories—rich, middle, and poor—so that decisions could be made about who was to have land taken from them, who was to receive land, and how much they would lose or receive. A major issue here was where the line should be drawn between rich peasant and middle peasant, for rich peasants generally had land taken from them while middle peasants received land. In essence, the law raised the violent head of class struggle. Indeed, this law tore the social fabric so deeply and gave rise to so much violence that the CCP called a halt to it.

Rural Population in Xunwu County, Jiangxi Province, 1930

Mao conducted a survey in Xunwu county in 1929 and 1930. He hoped to be able to analyze how rural society was constructed so that he might have a better idea of how to plan for revolution. Though Xunwu was not a typical county (there is no such thing), these statistics provide one example of the numbers in specific categories in one county where CCP leaders undertook land redistribution. Those groups receiving rent did so "in kind"—that is, in rice—and not in cash.

Group	Percent of County Population
Large landlords (*receive rent of more than 33.25 tons of rice*)	0.045
Middle landlords (*receive rent of between 13.3 and 33.25 tons of rice*)	0.4
Small landlords (*receive rent of less than 13.3 tons of rice*)	3.0
Rich peasants (*have surplus grain and capital to make loans*)	4.0
Middle peasants (*have enough to eat and do not receive loans*)	18.255
Poor peasants (*have insufficient grain and receive loans*)	70.0
Manual workers (*craftsmen, boatmen, porters*)	3.0
Hired hands (*permanent and day laborers*)	0.3
Loafers (*no occupation or property*)	1.0

Laws 7 and 10 below give evidence of tactics some elites adopted in order to escape the redistribution. It is striking that already in this first land law, the Communist authorities tended to see class as hereditary: sons and daughters of gentry (traditionally, those men who received civil service examination degrees under the old system), landlords, and counterrevolutionary rich peasants were treated as their parents were.

A. Whose Land Should Be Confiscated?

1. Land (including land rented to tenants), houses, and all other forms of property, including household items, that belonged to members of the gentry and landlords are to be confiscated.

2. Land, houses, and all other forms of property, including household items, that belong to family shrines, Buddhist or Daoist temples, clan or social organizations are to be confiscated.

3. Land owned by rich peasants should be confiscated.

B. Who Should Receive Land?

1. The amount of land to be distributed is the same for all tenant farmers and poor peasants. Whether the land of the middle peasant should be redistributed so as to assure that they have the same amount as that of the tenant farmers and poor peasants depends upon the decision to be made by the middle peasants themselves. . . .

2. The relatives of a farm laborer shall receive land. He himself should also receive land if he is unemployed. (By unemployment is meant the lack of employment for most of the year. It does not include temporary employment that lasts only a short period of time.)

3. Independent artisans . . . , physicians, and teachers are to receive land if they have been unemployed for six months or longer.

4. Shop owners and their relatives shall not receive any land.

5. Rich peasants will receive poor land in accordance with the size of their respective households as well as the number of able-bodied workers in them.

6. Beginning with the operation of this statute, members of the gentry, landlords and members of counter-revolutionary organizations will not be entitled to land distribution.

7. There are cases in which members of the gentry, landlords, and counterrevolutionary rich peasants have adopted the method of "invitation marriage" by marrying their wives and daughters to

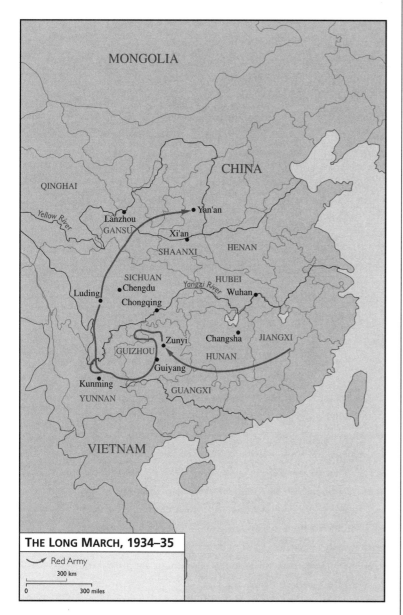

THE LONG MARCH, 1934–35

Red Army
300 km
0   300 miles

farm laborers, tenant farmers, poor or middle peasants for the sole purpose of preserving their properties. The properties in question, including houses, shall be confiscated by the government forthwith. However, the farm laborers, tenant farmers, poor and middle peasants who have been thus married will receive their fair share when the confiscated properties . . . are redistributed.

8. As for the adopted sons or daughters of members of the gentry, landlords, and those rich peasants who have in the past been members of counterrevolutionary organizations, they are not entitled to land distribution. . . .

9. As for Buddhist monks and nuns, Taoist priests, magicians and sorcerers, fortunetellers, geomancers, and other feudal remnants as well as Protestant ministers and Catholic priests, they are not entitled to land distribution. . . .

10. Beginning with the operation of this statute, the sons and daughters of the members of the gentry or landlords are no longer entitled to land distribution even though they have been adopted by poor laborers or peasants as their own children.

11. Members of the gentry landlords, and those rich peasants who have in the past assumed the leadership in opposing land distribution of their own accord, together with all of their relatives, are not entitled to land distribution.

12. Rural merchants who, prior to the revolution, had been able to support their families through trade and commerce are not entitled to land distribution.

13. Unemployed peddlers are entitled to land distribution.

14. A woman can dispose of her land the way she wishes when she is married.

American journalist Edgar Snow's 1937 book, *Red Star over China* presented to the West the first clear picture of the Communist movement and relations in the mid-1930s between the Nationalist Party and the CCP. Especially significant was Snow's depiction of Mao Zedong and the Long March, the 6,000-mile trek over steep snow-covered mountains, through swampy marshlands, and into areas still inhabited by aboriginal tribes who decapitated their enemies and kept their heads as trophies. Snow's account was enormously positive about the Communist effort; he remained a strong supporter of the Communist regime until his death in the early 1970s.

In the Grasslands there was no human habitation (houses) for ten days. Almost perpetual rain falls over this swampland, and it is possible to cross its center only by a maze of narrow footholds known to the native mountaineers who led the Reds. More animals were lost, and more men. Many foundered in the weird sea of wet grass, and dropped from sight into the depth of the swamp, beyond reach of their comrades. There was no firewood; they were obliged to eat their green wheat and vegetables raw. There were even no trees for shelter, and the lightly equipped Reds carried no tents. At night they huddled under bushes tied together,

which gave but scant protection against the rain. But from this trial, too, they emerged triumphant—more so, at least, than the White troops, who pursued them, lost their way, and turned back, with only a fraction of their number intact.

The Red Army now reached the Kansu [Gansu] border. Several battles still lay ahead, the loss of any one of which might have meant decisive defeat. More Nanking [Nanjing], Tungbei [Dong-bei], and Moslem troops had been mobilized in southern Kansu to stop their march, but they managed to break through all these blockades, and in the process annexed hundreds of horses from the Moslem cavalry, which people had confidently predicted would finish them once and for all. Footsore, weary, and at the limit of human endurance, they finally entered northern Shensi [Shaanxi], just below the Great Wall. On October 20, 1935, a year after its departure from Kiangsi [Jiangxi], the vanguard of the First Front Army connected with the 25th, 26th, and 27th Red Armies, which had already established a small base of Soviet power in Shensi in 1933. Numbering less than 20,000 survivors now, they sat down to realize the significance of their achievement.

The statistical recapitulation of the Long March is impressive. It shows that there was an average of almost a skirmish a day, somewhere on the line, while altogether fifteen whole days were devoted to major pitched battles. Out of a total of 368 days en route, 235 were consumed in marches by day, and 18 in marches by night. Of the 100 days of halts—many of which were devoted to skirmishes—56 days were spent in north-western Szechwan

This sketch by a participant on the Long March shows the Red Army as it crosses the Luding Bridge, high over the Datong River, in May 1935. The Nationalists had removed the bridge's planks and placed a blockhouse at the far end. Twenty Red Army volunteers crossed the bridge on the chains, took the block-house, and restored the planks, making it possible for the whole army to cross.

[Sichuan], leaving only 44 days of rest over a distance of about 5,000 [sic] miles, or an average of one halt for every 114 miles of marching. The mean daily stage covered was 71 *li*, or nearly 24 miles—a phenomenal pace for a great army and its transport to *average* over some of the most hazardous terrain on earth.

Altogether the Reds crossed 18 mountain ranges, five of which were perennially snow-capped, and they crossed 24 rivers. They passed through 12 different provinces, occupied 62 cities, and broke through enveloping armies of ten different provincial war-lords, besides defeating, eluding, or outmaneuvering the various forces of Central Government troops sent against them. They entered and successfully crossed six different aboriginal districts, and penetrated areas through which no Chinese army had gone for scores of years.

However one may feel about the Reds and what they represent politically (and here there is plenty of room for argument!), it is impossible to deny recognition of their Long March—the Ch'ang Cheng [Changzheng], as they call it—as one of the great exploits of military history. . . .

While the Red Army's March to the North-west was unquestionably a strategic retreat, it can hardly be called a major disaster, for the Reds finally reached their objective with their nucleus still intact, and their morale and political will evidently as strong as ever. The Reds themselves declared, and apparently believed, that they were advancing towards the anti-Japanese front, and this was a psychological factor of great importance. It helped them turn what might have been a demoralized retreat into a spirited march of victory.

Literature and Dissent

In May 1942 the Communist Party staged an important meeting called the Yan'an Forum on Art and Literature on the functions of art and literature in the new China. In this speech given at the meeting, Mao announced the party's position that art and literature should serve the revolutionary cause and "the people"—defined as workers, peasants, and soldiers. The guidelines he introduced remained the standards for judging literature and the arts until the 1990s, when restrictions began to loosen in some areas. They would also place the Communist Party in the position of being antagonistic to art and literature and to the intellectuals who produced them.

The first problem is: For whom are our art and literature intended?

This problem, as a matter of fact, was solved long ago by Marxists, and especially by Lenin. As far back as 1905, Lenin emphatically pointed out that our art and literature should "serve the millions and millions of working people."

. . . Who then are the people? The overwhelming majority, constituting more than 90 percent of our total population, are the workers, peasants, soldiers, and the urban petty bourgeoisie. . . . Our art and literature should be intended for these four kinds of people. To serve them, we must take the standpoint of the proletariat instead of that of the petty bourgeoisie. Today writers and artists who cling to their individualistic petty-bourgeois standpoint cannot truly serve the mass of revolutionary workers, peasants, and soldiers, but will be interested mainly in the small number of petty-bourgeois intellectuals. . . .

A complete solution of this problem will require a long time, maybe eight or ten years. But, no matter how long it takes, we must find the solution, and it must be unequivocal and complete. Our artists and writers must fulfill this task; they must gradually shift their standpoint over to the side of the workers, peasants, and soldiers, to the side of the proletariat, by going into their midst and plunging into the actual struggle and by studying Marxism and society. Only in this way can we have art and literature that are genuinely for the workers, peasants, and soldiers, and genuinely proletarian. . . .

. . . In the world today all culture, all art and literature belong to definite classes and follow definite political lines. There is in fact no such thing as art for art's sake, art which stands above classes or art that runs parallel to or remains independent of politics. Proletarian art and literature are part of the whole cause of the proletarian revolution, in the words of Lenin, "cog and wheel" of a single mechanism. Therefore, the Party's artistic and literary activity occupies a definite and assigned position in the Party's total revolutionary work and is subordinated to the prescribed revolutionary task of the Party in a given revolutionary period.

Writer and party intellectual Wang Shiwei dared to criticize the party leadership for having a privileged lifestyle as compared to the lifestyle of the rank and file. This essay appeared in February 1942 in a journal published by the Yan'an Literary Resistance Association. Because of this and another essay, the party put Wang on trial in May and June 1942 in struggle meetings, where he was verbally accused

Wang Shiwei's articles are impregnated with a gloomy spirit. Reading them gives me the feeling of entering the temple of a spirit that protects the town. His style is mediocre. . . . He depicts Yan'an as dark and sinister; he pits artists against statesmen, old cadres against the young and stirs them up. His viewpoint is reactionary, and his remedies poisonous. This "individual" does not deserve to be described as "human" let alone as a "comrade."

—Poet Ai Qing, commenting on Wang Shiwei's "Wild Lily," at struggle meetings against Wang Shiwei, June 28 and 29, 1942

and browbeaten. In Wang's case, Mao's adage about cabbage heads and not killing dissenters went unheeded: the party executed him in 1947.

During the New Year holiday I was walking home in the dark one evening from a friend's place. Ahead of me were two women comrades talking in animated whispers. We were some way apart so I quietly moved closer to hear what they were saying.

"He keeps on talking about other people's petty-bourgeois egalitarianism; but the truth is that he thinks he is something special. He always looks after his own interests. As for the comrades underneath him, he doesn't care whether they are sick or well, he doesn't even care if they die, he hardly gives a damn! . . .

"Crows are black wherever they are. Even Comrade XXX acts like that."

"You're right! All this bullshit about loving your own class. They don't even show ordinary human sympathy! You often see people pretending to smile and be friendly, but it's all on the surface, it doesn't mean anything. And if you offend them, they glare at you, pull their rank and start lecturing you."

"It's not only the big shots who act that way, the small fry are just the same. Our section leader XXX crawls when he's talking to his superiors, but he behaves very arrogantly towards us. Often comrades have been ill and he hasn't even dropped in to see how they are. But when an eagle stole one of his chickens, you should have seen the fuss he made! After that, every time he saw an eagle he'd start screaming and throwing clods of earth at it—the self-seeking bastard!"

There was a long silence. In one way, I admired the comrade's sharp tongue. But I also felt depressed.

"It's sad that so many comrades are falling ill. Nobody wants people like that to visit them when they fall ill, they just make you feel worse. Their tone of voice, their whole attitude they don't make you feel they care about you."

"Right. They don't care about others, and others don't care about them. If they did mass work, they'd be bound to fail."

. . .

I [now] intend to . . . discuss the question of equality and the ranking system. . . .

Those who say that a system of ranks is reasonable use roughly the following arguments: (1) they base themselves on the principle of "from each according to their ability, to each according to

Comrade XXX

A person the author wishes to keep anonymous.

Yan'an was situated in an area of desperate poverty. Because building materials were not generally available in this arid region of bald mountains, Long Marchers dug into the sides of hills and mountains to construct cave residences, such as this one, where Mao resided.

their worth," which means that those with more responsibilities should consume more; (2) in the near future the three-thirds government intends to carry out a new salary system, and naturally there will be pay differentials; and (3) the Soviet Union also has a system of ranks.

In my opinion all these arguments are open to debate. As for (1), we are still in the midst of revolution, with all its hardships and difficulties: all of us, despite fatigue, are laboring to surmount the present crisis, and many comrades have ruined their precious health. Because of this it does not yet seem the right time for anyone, no matter who, to start talking about "to each according to their worth." On the contrary, all the more reason why those with greater responsibilities should show themselves willing to share weal and woe with the rank and file. (This is a national virtue that should be encouraged.) In so doing, they would win the profound love of the lower ranks. Only then would it be possible to create ironlike unity. It goes without saying that it is not only reasonable but necessary that those with big responsibilities who need special treatment for their health should get such treatment. The same goes for those with positions of medium responsibility. As for (2), the pay system if the three-thirds government should also avoid

Three-thirds government

The tripartite system under which the Communists nominally shared power with the "petit bourgeoisie and the enlightened gentry" in the areas under their control excessive differentials; it is right that non-party officials should get slightly better treatment, but those officials who are Party members should uphold our excellent traditions of frugal struggle so that we are in a position to mobilize even more non-party people to join and cooperate with us. As for (3), excuse my rudeness, but I would beg those "great masters" who can't open their mouths without talking about "Ancient Greece" to hold their tongues.

I am not an egalitarian, but to divide clothing into three and food into five grades is neither necessary nor rational, especially with regard to clothes. (I myself am graded as "cadres clothes and private kitchen," so this is not just a case of sour grapes.) All such problems should be resolved on the basis of need and reason. At present there is no noodle soup for sick comrades to eat and young students only get two meals of thin congee a day (when they are asked whether they have had enough to eat, Party members are expected to lead the rest in a chorus of "Yes, we're full"). Relatively healthy "big shots" get far more than they need to eat and drink, with the result that their subordinates look upon them as a race apart, and not only do not love them, but even . . . this makes me most uneasy. But perhaps it is a "petty bourgeois emotion" to always be talking about "love" and "warmth"? I await your verdict.

Congee

A type of porridge

One of twentieth-century China's most renowned female authors, Ding Ling began writing short stories about feminine themes and individual personal fulfillment during the May Fourth period. She went to Yan'an during the war to help the Communist cause. Though she did not share Wang Shiwei's grim fate, her insistence on the rights of women at Yan'an in this 1942 essay, "Thoughts on March 8 (International Women's Day)," which appeared in the newspaper *Jiefang Ribao* [Liberation Daily], prompted the party to attack her as "narrowly feminist." The Yan'an leaders considered feminist issues divisive and antithetical to nation building. Ding avoided further persecution at the time by caving in to party pressure, even joining in the attacks on Wang Shiwei. But in the People's Republic, established in 1949, she did not fare so well: she was exiled to far northern China from 1957 to 1979 because of her writings.

When will it no longer be necessary to attach special weight to the word "woman" and to raise it specially?

Each year this day comes round. Every year on this day meetings are held all over the world where women muster their forces.

Even though things have not been as lively these last two years in Yan'an as they were in previous years, it appears that at least a few people are busy at work here. . . .

I myself am a woman, so I understand the failings of women better than others. But I also have a deeper understanding of what they suffer. Women are incapable of transcending the age they live in, of being perfect, or of being hard as steel. They are capable of resisting all the temptations of society or all the silent oppression they suffer here in Yan'an. They each have their own past written in blood and tears, they have experienced great emotions—in elation as in depression, in the lone battle of life or in the humdrum stream of life. This is even truer of the women comrades who come to Yan'an, so I have much sympathy for those fallen and classed as criminals. What's more, I hope that men, especially those in top positions, and women themselves will consider women's mistakes in their social context. It would be better if there were less empty theorizing and more talk about real problems, so that theory and practice are not divorced, and if each Communist Party member were more responsible for his own moral conduct.

Chinese women cheer Madame Chiang Kai-shek at an International Women's Day celebration on March 8, in the Nationalists' wartime capital of Chongqing. Women in Yan'an also participated in celebrations that day, though male Communists resisted, claiming that feminist concerns detracted from nationalistic goals.

Chapter Seven

China At War

The Fight Against Japan

The fighting that erupted at the Marco Polo Bridge outside Beijing on July 7, 1937, sparked eight years of war. Early August saw the Japanese strike at Shanghai and begin their drive up the Yangzi River. Chiang Kai-shek and his government fled up that river, stopping first at Wuhan and eventually making it through the Yangzi River gorges to the city of Chongqing. There, in a city that had not yet been brought into the modern world, he would remain until the end of the war. The provinces of Sichuan (in which Chongqing lies) and Yunnan to its southwest became known as Free China—unoccupied by Japan or Communists.

The Japanese war effort included terror and biological and chemical warfare. The most notorious event was the so-called Rape of Nanjing, Chiang's former capital, where in December 1937 and January 1938 Japanese troops were given free rein by their commanders. As a result, the Japanese killed (bayoneted, buried alive, burned alive, shot, and drowned) as many as 300,000 Chinese and raped thousands of women. In the north, the Communists launched the large Hundred Regiments Campaign (actually there were 104 regiments participating) in the second half of 1940. The Japanese responded with a campaign of terror, the Three-All Campaign—"kill all, burn all, loot all." Japanese forces also used poison gas and dropped bubonic plague–infected materials, usually fleas mixed with rice and grain chaff, on a number of Chinese cities.

The Nationalists and Communists formed an uneasy united front to fight the Japanese. The Communist Eighth Route Army in the north was generally independent of Chiang's control. The New Fourth Route Army in China's east-central region tried to make joint

Japanese troops march into Beijing, which fell on July 28, 1937, three weeks after the beginning of open fighting.

action between Nationalists and Communists work. The difficult relationship broke down entirely, however, when Chiang's forces attacked Communist units in January 1941.

The Japanese conquered the most territory on China's eastern seaboard, which included the majority of China's industry and much of its best farmland. In those occupied areas, the Japanese found Chinese who would collaborate with them. In the early days of the war, there were two collaborationist governments, one in Beijing, the other in Nanjing. From March 1940 on, there was the national collaborationist government at Nanjing led by former radical Nationalist Party leader Wang Jingwei. Collaborators worked with the Japanese for a variety of reasons, some because

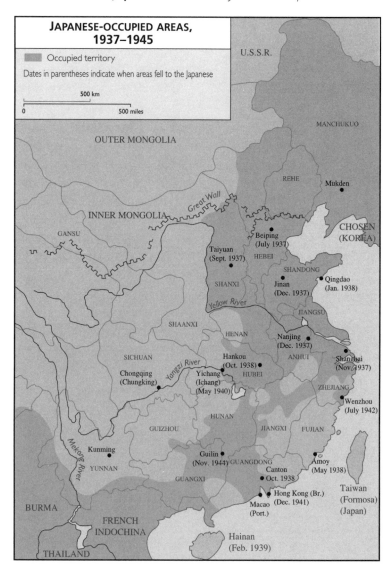

JAPANESE-OCCUPIED AREAS, 1937–1945

Occupied territory

Dates in parentheses indicate when areas fell to the Japanese

500 km

0   500 miles

U.S.S.R.

OUTER MONGOLIA

MANCHUKUO

REHE   Mukden

INNER MONGOLIA   Great Wall

GANSU

CHOSEN (KOREA)

Beiping (July 1937)

Taiyuan (Sept. 1937)   HEBEI

SHANXI   SHANDONG

Jinan (Dec. 1937)   Qingdao (Jan. 1938)

SHAANXI   JIANGSU

HENAN   Nanjing (Dec. 1937)

SICHUAN   Hankou (Oct. 1938)   ANHUI   Shanghai (Nov. 1937)

Chongqing (Chungking)   Yangzi River   Yichang (Ichang) (May 1940)   HUBEI

ZHEJIANG

Yellow River

Wenzhou (July 1942)

HUNAN

GUIZHOU   JIANGXI   FUJIAN

Kunming   Guilin (Nov. 1944)   GUANGDONG   Amoy (May 1938)

Mekong River

YUNNAN   Canton Oct. 1938

GUANGXI   Taiwan (Formosa) (Japan)

Hong Kong (Br.) (Dec. 1941)

BURMA   Macao (Port.)

FRENCH INDOCHINA   Hainan (Feb. 1939)

THAILAND

they thought it was the best way to save China and others simply for what they could get out of it. But collaborators on the national level were tried after the war for treason; many were jailed and executed.

When the Japanese bombed U.S. naval ships at Pearl Harbor, Hawaii, in December 1941, China became an ally of the United States. The United States sent as much aid to China as it could, hoping that Chiang could bolster his army enough to be able to take back eastern China, which could then be used as a launching pad for U.S. bombers to fly over Japan. But many things hampered the effort. Victory over Hitler in Europe was a higher priority for the Americans than the war in the Pacific. Further, when the Japanese cut off the Burma Road in early 1942, they closed the last land route to Free China. From that point on, everything that reached Chiang, his army, and his government had to be flown in by airlift. By that time, the United States had given up its eastern China strategy for an "island hopping" campaign to reach Pacific islands from which Japan could be attacked.

One U.S. fear about postwar East Asia was that a totally defeated Japan and a China still torn between Nationalists and Communists would leave the area easy target for the Soviet Union. Because of this concern, as the war's end neared, the United States devoted considerable time to trying to bring the Nationalists and Communists together. But the unexpectedly rapid end of the war after the United States dropped the atomic bombs on Hiroshima and Nagasaki on August 6 and 9, respectively, left the Communists and Nationalists at odds.

An estimated twenty million Chinese died during the war. Countless more were wounded; even more became refugees. For China, it was the worst possible nightmare. For Japan it created a legacy of distrust and suspicion in China and all of East and Southeast Asia.

Chiang Kai-shek and other Chinese officers examine a map to plan the details of their next military campaign.

Japan's "New Order in Asia"

On November 3, 1938, Japan's Prime Minister Konoye Fumimaro announced in this document, which first appeared in Tokyo, a "New Order in East Asia." Japan argued that it was working to destroy the old Western imperialist control and that it would establish an East Asia for the East Asians. At the end of the war, Konoye committed suicide after being named a war criminal.

Inspired by His majesty's power and might, the land and sea forces of the Empire of Japan have now captured the cities of Canton and Wuhan and pacified many important regions in China. . . . [W]e shall proceed with our effort in the establishment of a New Order that guarantees permanent peace in all of East Asia. The establishment of a New Order in East Asia is the final goal of our military operations.

By the establishment of a New Order in East Asia we mean mutual assistance and cooperation between Japan, China, and Manchukuo in political, economic, and cultural matters. Eventually a new form of internationalism will prevail between these three countries in the sense that we shall build a common defense, create a new culture, and cooperate fully in economic matters. An East Asia thus stabilized will contribute materially to world progress. China's willingness to shoulder her share of the responsibility in establishing this New Order is what the Empire of Japan actively seeks. All Chinese must understand the constructive nature of this New Order, given the present situation in East Asia. What the Empire of Japan can and will do for China is certainly more beneficial than any aid offered by her traditional allies.

Chiang Kai-shek wrote this attack on the "New Order in East Asia" in December 1936. It was first published in *The Works of President Chiang* in 1968.

Our war of resistance has now entered a new stage. . . .

Our determination to continue the war and the national unity behind this determination have prompted the enemy to employ all kinds of intimidation and enticement, in addition to outright military pressure, to weaken our will. Beginning on November 3 when the government of Japan issued a so-called declaration, its premier, as well as its army, navy, and diplomatic spokesmen, have made absurd and contradictory statements. The purpose of these statements is not only to deceive Japanese people at home and foreign powers abroad but also to confuse, stupefy, and intimidate the Chinese people. . . .

. . . [A]s for the establishment of a so-called New Order in East Asia, it has been the most vainglorious, most conceited of the Japanese slogans shouted so far. . . . Eventually, said Japan's foreign minister, China will rise from her semi-colonial status and all of East Asia will be "stabilized." In a speech delivered on December 14, Premier Konoye said: "The ultimate purpose involving the settlement of the China Incident is not only military victory for

Manchukuo

The new name for Manchuria by the Japanese. It means the country or land of the Manchus.

The China Incident

The Japanese name for the war

Japan but also the resurrection of China and the establishment of a New Order in East Asia. . . ."

What does Konoye mean by a "resurrected China"? He means a slavish China to be dominated by Japan for eternity. His so-called New Order is based upon close collaboration between a master called Japan, a puppet called Manchukuo, and a slave called China, and the puppet and the slave will dance to the tune of their imperial master Japan. In the name of forestalling a Communist deluge, Japan in fact wants to establish her military domination of China. In the name of promoting Oriental civilization, Japan in fact wants to terminate China's cultural heritage. In the name of eliminating economic barriers and preventing Europe or America from establishing hegemony in the Pacific, Japan in fact wants to control the economic life of China. It does not require much intelligence to recognize Japan's diabolic intention behind this façade called New Order in East Asia. In short, the purpose of establishing this New Order is to replace the normal relationship between nations under international law by the creation of a master-and-slave relationship between Japan and China, so that Japan will be in a position not only to dominate the Pacific but also to conquer, eventually, the world.

Chinese Collaboration

Wang Jingwei's political career probably zigzagged the most of any leader in twentieth-century China. He began his career as one of Sun Yat-sen's closest protégés and as editor of Sun's revolutionary newspaper, the *Min Bao* [People's Daily]. In 1910 he was arrested for plotting an assassination of the Chinese regent for the young emperor. Though such an act might ordinarily have brought a death sentence, the Manchu regime released him in 1911, perhaps as a gesture to quiet revolutionary forces.

Wang emerged in the 1920s as the leader of the liberal wing of the Nationalist Party, closely allied with the Communist Party. Many political leaders thought he would be the natural successor to Sun Yat-sen. But Chiang Kai-shek's rise to power forced Wang into the opposition; indeed, into the early 1930s he was involved in efforts to overthrow Chiang. Still, his collaboration with the Japanese is quite surprising. He gave this radio address in Tokyo on June 24, 1941. He died of natural causes in 1944 and was thus spared what almost certainly would have been a show trial and execution.

To Those Who Fight

In a dark
And cold night
The Japanese robbers
Came,
And from our
Hands,
From our
Bosoms
Seized our innocent comrades
And locked them behind a fence of violence.
Their bodies
Showed
Angry scars,
Their hearts
Throbbed
In grief and hatred,
They shivered
In Dairen, in the camps
Of the Manchurian wilderness,
Waiting for the drunken,
And meat-gorged brutes,
Wielding their swords
To tease
These abandoned
Lives
And their hungry
Blood . . .

A glorious name—
The people!
O our people,
Stood at the Marco Polo Bridge,
Facing the buffeting winds,
Blowing their bugle of assault.
O our people,
You have stood up
Like a giant,
On this immense land.

—Poet Tian Jian, writing in Wuchang, February 24, 1937

Refugees stream out of Shanghai in the wake of the Japanese invasion in August 1937. Tens of millions of Chinese fled for their lives. During the first months of the invasion, the Japanese indeed appeared to be a military juggernaut, but by mid-1938 momentum slowed, as the war became a stalemate.

I am deeply moved as I speak to you today in Tokyo, the capital of your great country. I studied in your country thirty-eight years ago. My stay then was short, and due particularly to my limited abilities I could not master your language and learning. However, if, fortunately, I know something, I owe it to my old teachers and classmates. I can never forget what they have done for me. To have been able to come to your great country again and meet you, the people of Japan, is like meeting my old teachers and classmates and I am filled with the warm feeling. . . .

When the slogan of "the construction of a new order in East Asia" was heard in your country, our people found a gleam of hope in the darkness. . . . The significance of the construction of a new order in East Asia lies, on the one hand, in endeavoring to eliminate from East Asia the evils of Western economic imperialism and, on the other, in checking the rising tide of Communism which has been threatening our prosperity for these twenty years. Japan was the only country in the East who could shoulder the responsibility for such undertakings single-handedly. Although we have Dr. Sun

Yat-sen's Pan-Asianism, his followers and compatriots have failed to make united efforts for the attainment of that ideal.

There may be causes for the recent unfortunate conflict between our twocountries. If, however, we examine ourselves as to why we have failed in our efforts to purge the country of the evils of Western economic imperialism and to check the rise of Communism, thereby leaving the country to deteriorate into a semi-colonial status and the people in the deepest distress, we cannot but blame ourselves. When we heard of the slogan of the construction of a new order in East Asia put forth by Japan, we immediately opened our eyes to the fact that it was not time for quarreling among ourselves, and realized that we should revert to our essential character founded upon the moral principles of the East, breaking down the old order consisting of a chain of pressures brought to bear upon us by economic imperialism and Communism, and establish a new order based on independence, freedom, co-existence, and co-prosperity. . . .

The most important significance lies in the fact that Japan will give aid to China in providing such conditions as are necessary for her development into a modern State if China will participate with determination and sincerity in the construction of a new order in East Asia. . . .

All our people will unite with you, I am sure, for the performance of the high task to which the peoples of East Asia are called. My friends, no one knows what new developments may take place tomorrow in the international situation.

Whatever happens, the attitude of our two countries to reconstruct East Asia in the friendly relationship of co-existence and co-prosperity will be forever unchangeable.

In conclusion, let me wish you health and prosperity. Banzai for the Empire of Japan! Banzai for the Republic of China!

War Crimes

Much of the distrust and suspicion of Japan in the last half of the twentieth century in East and Southeast Asia stemmed from its brutally aggressive actions in the war in China and the Pacific. After that war an international judicial tribunal held in Tokyo under the auspices of the Allied powers, but primarily the United States, found Japan guilty of numerous war crimes, the most notorious of which was the Rape of

Pan-Asianism

The belief that Asian countries would do well to work together against a common enemy, the imperialist West

On the train I discovered I was being followed by a Chinese-traitor [collaborator] plainclothes detective. He sat next to me and, posing as an ordinary passenger, periodically looked over and spoke to me. At first we chatted casually about everyday matters, but then we gradually shifted to the situation in China proper and recent student movements. He blabbed on and on throughout the whole trip. I disliked him very much but I had to pretend to be interested. When the train arrived in Yingkou, I was immediately grabbed by the [Japanese] military police, who took me to the . . . Police Station. . . .

My interrogator was typical of the "people from the friendly power" [that is, the Japanese—in a phrase coined by the Japanese]. He spoke beautiful Chinese, asking questions more or less similar to the ones that the detective had asked on the . . . train. But this time I had to write down in detail my native place, my address, and the names of my ancestors for three generations. In the end, his face became serious and he said to me: "You are a student. We have universities in Manzhouguo [Manchukuo] and they are free of charge. Why must you go to China to study? Hey, it's all right if you go to China as long as you report monthly on the situation concerning the Chinese student movement. Otherwise, I will consider you a member of the group that opposes Manzhouguo and resists [Japan].

—A letter written by Meng Wei, a college student in Manchuria, 1936

Nanjing. Japan's use of biological and chemical weapons also marked it as an international outlaw. This report is from the verdict issued by the Military Tribunal for the Trial of War Criminals on March 10, 1947.

[On December 15], 2,000 of the city's police force, having been captured by the Japanese army, were marched toward an area . . . where they were systematically machine-gunned. Those who were wounded were subsequently buried alive. . . .

[On the next day], 5,000 refugees who had gathered in the Overseas Chinese Reception Center . . . were systematically machine-gunned and their bodies thrown into the river.

On December 14, Yao [Jialong], a native of Nanjing, . . . was ordered to watch the performance when Japanese soldiers took turns raping his wife. When his eight-year-old son and three-year-old daughter pleaded for mercy on behalf of their mother, the rapers picked them up with their bayonets and roasted them to death over a camp fire.

[Between] December 13 [and] 17, a large number of Japanese troops took turns raping a young [girl] in the street outside

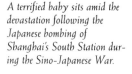

A terrified baby sits amid the devastation following the Japanese bombing of Shanghai's South Station during the Sino-Japanese War.

Zhonghua Gate; and when a group of Buddhist monks passed by, they were ordered to rape this girl too. After the monks had refused to comply with this order, the Japanese cut off their penises, an act which caused the monks to bleed to death.

For many years people assumed that the Japanese use of biological and chemical weapons had been isolated in the north. However, recent studies have shown that the Japanese used these criminal tactics in central and eastern China as well. This 1994 report comes from a history written by county scholars of Quzhou city, located in Zhejiang Province, on China's east coast.

Beginning in 1938, the 731 biological unit of the Kwantung Army began to manufacture biological weapons, cultivating plague, cholera, and typhoid. They experimented on more than 3,000 Chinese who died. In October 1940, the Japanese air force dropped plague-infected material on Quzhou, Ningbo, Dongyang, Yiwu, and Lanqi counties in the province of Zhejiang and several sites outside of the province.

According to the report of the Zhejiang Provincial Public Health Office, at 6:30 a.m. on October 4, a single plane entered the air space over the city [of Quzhou], flying low and fast. As the air raid siren was sounded in the area of Zhaijia Lane, the plane dropped a mixture of wheat, wheat chaff, millet, and fleas. At the time, witnesses thought this was very strange. A resident of Zhaijia Lane, one Xu Jingshan, who worked at the Pucheng Paper Store, gathered some of the grain and fleas and sent it to the county health department for examination. That body forwarded it on to the provincial health bureau. Its report stated that it had cultured the germs but that there were absolutely no bacilli that could cause illness.

Nevertheless, on November 11, an 8-year old girl, Wu Shiying, became ill and died. Examination showed that it was the plague . . . . By the end of the year, twenty-two people living on five contiguous streets had contracted plague and all but one had died. In 1941 in the city, 281 became infected and 274 died—a death rate of 97.5 percent. In 1941, the Japanese used night bombing of the city; residents were forced to leave the city, helping to spread plague into the surrounding countryside.

In 1941, there were seventeen households where everyone died, thirty-nine households where two died, and twenty households

Kwantung Army

Japan's military force in Manchuria

where three died. In the period when the plague spread, businesses stopped operating, schools closed, and much transport halted. Passenger and freight traffic passing through the city was undependable. Life was difficult.

War Years, a Western View

In 1937 two publishing companies, Random House in New York and Faber and Faber in London, commissioned the authors W. H. Auden and Christopher Isherwood "to write a travel book about the East." They wrote, "The choice of itinerary was left to our own discretion. The outbreak of the Sino-Japanese War in August decided us to go to China." What follows, from the book _Journey to a War,_ is an account of their experiences in northwestern Zhejiang Province as they attempted to travel to the front lines.

[After a day of travel and meeting with Chinese military leaders] we were all eager for bed. But, as we were undressing, A. W. Kao came to announce that the "Anti-Japanese Corpse" of Siaofeng [Xiaofeng] had arrived to give us details of the Japanese atrocities in their town. So we struggled wearily into our clothes and went out to greet them—six men and a woman, all wearing their best clothes, and lined up, as Auden said, like a village choir.

Siaofeng had been occupied by the Japanese three times: in December, in February, and in March. When the regular Chinese troops had been forced to retire, the local anti-Japanese corps had remained. Apparently harmless farmers and peasants, they were, in reality, dangerous enemies of the invader. They had a highly-organized intelligence service, which co-operated with the Chinese General Staff. At night the Japanese were sniped at (for the irregulars had hidden stores of arms), bridges were blown up, cars were damaged. The Japanese, of course, had made terrible reprisals. Whole villages had been burnt. There had been mass-executions of men, women, and children. . . .

Walking and riding along the valley we reached Siaofeng. Outside the town the Mayor was waiting to receive us. The local ambulance corps lined the road and stood to attention as we passed. The Mayor led us through street after street of ruins; a wilderness of brick-heaps and rubbish, as hopeless as an unsolved jig-saw puzzle. The streets were crowded, now, to welcome our party, and everybody seemed lively and gay. Business was carried on as usual. All around the little town the fields were being cultivated; the fertile

countryside was in strange contrast to the desolation within. The Mayor told us that the Japanese had special burning-squads, who carried out their work carefully and systematically. Perhaps for this reason there were few actual signs of fire. The buildings simply looked smashed.

After a second breakfast we pushed on again along what looked like an unfinished motor-road, now overgrown with grass. At a booth near the city an old woman was selling food, tea, and cigarettes. T. Y. Liu warned us against a certain brand of cigarettes called *Pirates*. Some consignments of them were said to have been poisoned by the Japanese. Auden, the ever-inquisitive, immediately bought a packet. We both smoked them but neither suffered any bad results. (The poisoning story was probably nonsense, anyway. But we had already heard, on much better authority, that the Japanese had poisoned several junk-loads of salt, destined for a district near the southeastern front.)

Ti-pu, our next stopping place, was more badly damaged, even, than Siaofeng. Nevertheless, I was able to buy a pair of socks. My feet, by this time, were covered with blisters, and I was glad when my turn came to ride one of the fat, obstinate little horses. The horses knew what was before them, it seemed. Nothing would induce them to hurry. They were saving their strength.

Beyond Ti-pu the road shrank to a narrow flagged path winding through rice-fields and dense bamboo groves. Thin rain began to fall. Strings of peasants passed us in single file, heavily burdened with their household goods, making their slow way back to safety. Now and then we met wounded, carried on rough bamboo litters, who regarded us with bloodshot incurious eyes. We began to have that ominous, oppressive feeling experienced by travelers who are going alone in the wrong, unpopular direction—towards a glacier or a desert. I strained my ears for the first sound of the guns.

But we were still a long way from the lines. . . .

In 1942 and 1943, a devastating famine struck Henan Province in north-central China. Two renowned American journalists, Theodore White and Annalee Jacoby, who had been covering the revolutionary developments in China during the war years, turned their eyes to the famine in their book *Thunder out of China*. The famine was a tragedy brought and made worse by war. Making matters worse, Chiang Kai-shek's government responded slowly and with pathetically feeble support for the victims. The famine thus symbolized the Nationalist government's apparent blasé attitude toward the suffering of the masses, described in vivid detail by White and Jacoby. Indeed "thunder" was coming for Chiang and his regime, in large part because of episodes like this.

There were corpses on the road. A girl no more than seventeen, slim and pretty, lay on the damp earth, her lips blue with death; her eyes were open and the rain fell on them. People chipped at bark, pounded it by the roadside for food; vendors sold leaves for a dollar a bundle. A dog digging at a mound was exposing a human body. Ghostlike men were skimming the stagnant pools to eat the green slime of the waters. . . .

The people . . . were tearing up the roots of the new wheat; in other villages people were living on pounded peanut husks or refuse. Refugees on the road had been seen madly cramming soil

A Dirge

. . . the road leads us afar.
Slowly trudging on the road
Are the scattered shadows, all tired of walking,
All bending double, crawling along.
Why do they bend their heads low?
Look, the innocent souls,
Of those starved to death, frozen to death,
Or killed by the enemy,
Or simply wasted away by their hard life—
All who should be living today,
Our hearts carry the burden of life,
And the overweight burden of death.
This is a solemn hour,
Dark shadows float on the road—
What is that black thing on our shoulders?
Ai, it's a coffin we are carrying,
Containing a heavy corpse—
The humiliation and error of a people.
In this most solemn funeral procession,
The most devoted pallbearers
Sing in subdued voices the last dirge:
Bury it, bury it deep
Bury a destiny full of sighs
In the grave dug from a ravaged land,
Then say your good-by [sic] resolutely to
  yesterday.
Let new love belong to our hearts,
A new road to our footsteps,
And a new world to our shoulders.

—Poet Fang Jing, 1945

Starving people fill the streets to beg for food in Hunan Province. Famine was an ongoing scourge in many areas of China. The 1942–43 famine in Henan Province killed between 2 and 3 million people.

into their mouths to fill their bellies, and the missionary hospitals were stuffed with people suffering from terrible intestinal obstructions due to the filth they were eating . . .

In a fit of frenzy the parents of two little children had murdered them rather than hear them beg for something to eat. Some families sold all they had for one last big meal, then committed suicide.

By spring . . . the missionaries now reported something worse—cannibalism. A doctor told us of a woman caught boiling her baby: she was not molested, because she insisted that the child had died before she started to cook it. Another woman had been caught cutting off the legs of her dead husband for meat; this, too, was justified on the ground that he was already dead. In the mountain districts there were uglier tales of refugees caught on lonely roads and killed for their flesh . . . we heard the same tales too frequently, in too widely scattered places, to ignore the fact that in Henan human beings were eating their own kind.

Chapter Eight

Civil War

When World War II ended, the long-simmering hostility between the Nationalist and Communist parties was close to a boil. The Americans engineered a meeting between Chiang Kai-shek and Mao Zedong in Chongqing in August 1945. Talks lasted for six weeks and, on the surface, seemed quite successful; indeed, a photograph taken on October 10, 1945, shows the two men toasting each other in apparent good will. But it turned out to be only a façade.

In December 1945, the U.S. government dispatched World War II military hero George Marshall to defuse an increasingly tense situation and to try to head off open warfare. When he left thirteen months later, in January 1947, saying, in effect, "a plague on both your houses," there was nothing to prevent widespread civil war. Though Chiang's armies had all the advantages on paper—more men, materiel, and weapons—these advantages soon evaporated. With each battle, troops defected with their weapons and ammunition because of the increasingly promising fortunes of the Communists.

There were two deciding battles, the first in Manchuria and the second near the railroad center of Xuzhou in northwestern Jiangsu Province. In Manchuria, Chiang made the terrible decision to hold on to key cities even though Communist troops had surrounded them and cut off their supplies. That meant that cities had to be supplied through airlifts—an immensely expensive undertaking. For example, Chiang used the entire military budget for the last six months of 1948 to provide supplies for only one city for two months and four days. In the end, the Communists won easily in large-scale fighting in November 1948. With the defeat, Chiang lost almost half a million of his best troops plus a huge number of weapons and other equipment.

A month before the end of the fighting in Manchuria, the battle of Xuzhou began. With armies of 600,000 men on each side, this struggle was one of the largest battles in the world during the twentieth century. As in Manchuria, Chiang's strategy was faulty: here he made his stand where his troops were exposed on three sides, and he

Chinese Nationalist soldiers (walking toward the camera) pass wounded soldiers on stretchers in the vicinity of Suzhou. The wounded soldiers heading away from the camera make their way to first aid stations.

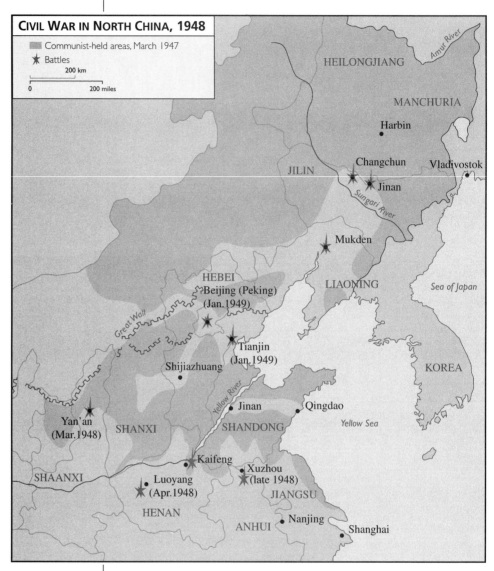

CIVIL WAR IN NORTH CHINA, 1948

Communist-held areas, March 1947
★ Battles

200 km
0   200 miles

insisted on personally directing the fight, though he was some two hundred miles from the battle.

The Communists won the two-month-long battle; and with this defeat Chiang again lost about half a million men and most of his mechanized troops. It was the war's decisive battle. Most of the nation's key cities fell between January and late fall 1949.

The question often raised is whether the outcome of the civil war was primarily a loss by Chiang Kai-shek or a win by the Communists. It was both; that is, Chiang made many mistakes that contributed to his defeat, while the Communists made positive decisions that contributed to their victory. Chiang's failure was not only military, but more notable, perhaps, political and especially economic. Politically, he refused to open his government up to those who did not subscribe either to the Nationalist Party or the Communist Party. There was a liberal "Third Force" called the Democratic League that Chiang simply did not trust; his policies drove most of them to the Communists. In addition, political scandal in the form of corruption dogged both his government and his family.

But it was the economy that eliminated any chance that Chiang had to succeed. Inflation was the culprit, a particularly vicious enemy that cut down the value of money and ruined lives. For example, prices in July 1948 were 3 million times higher than they had been in July 1937. At such an inflation rate, in a county seat in east central China the price for a picul (about 133 pounds) of rice in April 1949 cost more than 8 billion Chinese yuan (often called Chinese dollars). Such a staggering price meant that a single grain of rice cost about 2,500 Chinese dollars, whereas in 1937 that same grain of rice cost about .0003 cents. Such a reality turned almost everyone in society into a bitter critic and even a hater of Chiang's regime.

In December 1949, Chiang and his government fled to Taiwan. There he would undertake changes that he had been unwilling or unable to attempt in his twenty-one years of national leadership on the mainland.

Sources of Guomindang Defeat

In any account of the reasons for the defeat of Chiang Kai-shek's regime, inflation ranks near the top. Rising rates of inflation in 1947 and 1948 made Chinese currency eventually worthless. As inflation gutted money's value, it also eroded the confidence of citizens in their government, which should have been in charge of fending off this economic demon. In his memoir of the period, published in 1963, Chinese scholar A. Doak Barnett describes the scene firsthand in Shanghai in late 1947.

One cannot escape the inflation in Shanghai, any more than one can elsewhere in China. It is ever-present and all-important. A dollar is worth more today than it will be tomorrow; consequently, all money is "hot money." As a general rule, people spend money as soon as they get it, if they can. Printed notes are converted into more substantial commodities, such as silver dollars, foreign currencies, gold, cloth, fuel, land, or—in the case of the average person—more consumer goods. Despite the astronomical figures for

In this 1927 poem "One Sentence," Wen Yiduo asserts that the Chinese nation will one day stand up in unity to the threats and intimidations of outsiders. The line "the iron tree will bloom" comes from a Zen Buddhist koan, "conundrum," suggesting that something that seems impossible is possible.

There is one sentence that can light fire,
Or, when spoken, bring dire disasters.

Don't think that for five thousand years
  nobody has said it.
How can you be sure of a volcano's silence?
Perhaps one day, as if possessed by a spirit,
Suddenly out of the blue sky a thunder
            Will explode:
            "This is our China!"
How am I to say this today?
You may not believe that "the iron tree will
  bloom."
But there is one sentence you must hear!
Wait till the volcano can no longer be quiet,
Don't tremble, or shake you head, or stomp
  your feet,
Just wait till out of the blue sky a thunder
            Will explode:
            "This is our China!"

bank deposits, savings in currency are now much lower in real value than before the war. The manager of one of Shanghai's large private banks reports that the U.S. dollar value of savings deposits in his bank has been reduced from $20 million to $100,000. Insurance savings have been wiped out completely. A Chinese friend of mine, whose insurance policy was worth roughly U.S. $1,000 before the war, estimates that it is now worth U.S. $00.0064, less than a penny!

Prices continue to skyrocket. In the first three weeks of October, the wholesale community price index in Shanghai rose from 74,367 to 108,357 (1931=1). The current rate of interest for loans . . . is 16 percent per month and the bank does not make loans for period longer than a month. The free market exchange rate for U.S. dollars is now over 80,000:1, and the trend is steadily upward. The most important single cause of this inflationary situation is not difficult to define. With a civil war on its hands, the Chinese Nationalist Government is spending much more than it receives in revenue. The difference is being made up by the issuance of paper money.

From the beginning, Chiang Kai-shek's regime had been ready to repress those who dissented from the party line. On many occasions it used its secret police to silence its critics through terror and assassination. Wen Yiduo was a poet who had studied in the United States at the Art Institute of Chicago and Colorado College. In the late 1920s he became a professor of English and American literature at Nanjing University. When the war against Japan erupted, he went to Kunming in Yunnan Province to teach at South-West United University. He joined the Democratic League in 1946. On July 15, 1946, he gave the following address at a memorial service for Li Gongpu, a leading member of the Democratic League, who had been assassinated by Chiang's agents a few days earlier. Minutes after Wen spoke, he was gunned down on the street by Chiang's secret police.

A few days ago, as we are all aware, one of the most despicable and shameful events of history occurred here in Kunming. What crime did Mr. Li Gongpu commit that would cause him to be murdered in such a vicious way? He merely used his pen to write a few articles, he used his mouth to speak out, and what he said and wrote was nothing more than what any Chinese with a conscience would say. We all have pens and mouths. If there is a reason for it, why not speak out? Why should people be beaten, killed, or, even worse, killed in a devious way?

Are there any special agents here today? Stand up! If you are men, stand up! Come forward and speak? Why did you kill Mr. Li? You kill people but refuse to admit it and even circulate false rumors that the murder happened because of some sexual scandal or as the result of Communists killing other Communists. Shameless! Shameless! This is the shamelessness of the Guomindang, but the glory belongs to Mr. Li. . . .

Do you really think that if you hurt a few or kill a few, that you can intimidate the whole people? In fact, you cannot beat all the people or kill all of the people. For every Li Gongpu you kill, hundreds of millions of Li Gongpus will stand up! In the future you will lose the support of hundreds of millions of people.

The reactionaries believe that they can reduce the number of people participating in the democratic movement and destroy its power through the terror of assassination. But let me tell you, our power is great. . . .

The power of the people will win and truth will live forever! Throughout history, all who have opposed the people have been destroyed by the people! Didn't Hitler and Mussolini fall before the people? Chiang Kai-shek, you are so rabid, so reactionary, turn the pages of history, how many days do you think you have left? You're finished! It is over for you!

Bright days are coming for us. Look, the light is before us. Just as Mr. Li said as he was dying: "Daybreak is coming!" Now is that darkest moment before dawn. We have the power to break through this darkness and attain the light!

To attain democracy and peace, we must pay a price. We are not afraid of making sacrifices. Each of us should be like Mr. Li. When we step through the door, we must be prepared never to return.

With inflation eating up savings and destroying lives, panicky residents of Shanghai frantically struggle to get into a bank to withdraw their money before its value declines further. This financial desperation in December 1948 was crucial to the erosion of support for Chiang Kai-shek.

Evaluations of the Civil War

Zhu De, who as a young man had studied in Germany, was the founder of the Red Army in the late 1920s, and its commander from then on. In this speech to the CCP's Seventh

Congress in April 1945, Zhu argues that the CCP army is superior to that of the Nationalist army. The New Democracy he mentions was Mao's vision of a society where the four revolutionary classes—peasants, proletariat, national capitalists, and petty bourgeoisie—maintained a dictatorship over classes that were not part of the "people." At this stage of the revolution, in an effort to enlarge the appeal of the Communist movement, Mao included capitalists in the New Democracy; national capitalists were large businessmen and industrialists, and the petty bourgeoisie were small businessmen and shopkeepers. After the Communist victory in 1949, Mao's ultimate definition of the "people" would exclude these capitalist groups. The ambivalence of the Communists regarding the status of capitalists is shown in Zhu's speech where he includes capitalists along with the Guomindang and big landlords as making up an "anti-people's army."

The officers and soldiers of the people's army, whether it is the Eighth Route Army or the New Fourth Army, are recruited only in the sense that they join the army of their own accord. . . .

Since the army of the big landlords and capitalists works against the wishes of the people, it will not have any soldiers

Communist demonstrators march along the Pearl River waterfront in Canton (Guangzhou) carrying flags, banners, and signs with portraits of Stalin and Chinese Communist leaders. The flag with the large star and four smaller stars is the flag of the People's Republic of China.

unless it forces people to join it. The compulsory conscription as practiced by the Guomindang army is one of the worst systems imaginable, as young men are bought, kidnapped, or hoodwinked to join its ranks. Besides, the Guomindang recruiters, lawless and corrupt, are contemptuous of the lives of the draftees. The draftees are subject to inhuman treatment as they are tied up, beaten, imprisoned, or subject to the punishments of hunger and cold. They, in fact, do not even have the freedom of going to the bathroom whenever they wish. Those who have died are numerous; others who have managed to escape degenerate into bandits. The draftees who survive long enough to become regular army regulars constitute no more than twenty percent of the total.

Unlike the Guomindang, we in the Eighth Route Army and the New Fourth Army practice voluntarism in the recruitment of army personnel. People join us because they want to resist Japan and serve our country; they join us because they strive for the establishment of a new China based upon the principle of the New Democracy. Some of them are Communists, but the majority of them are not. . . .

The sources for supporting an anti-people's army come from exploitation—exploitation of the people as well as the soldiers. The sources for supporting a people's army, on the other hand, are derived from a mutual love between the army and the people. Needless to say, the Eighth Route Army and the New Fourth Army belong to the second category.

Invoking the saying that "the nation must support its army," the Guomindang reactionaries devise various ways to extort money from the people. When this source becomes inadequate, they invoke the name of China to borrow money from foreign countries. What do they do with all this money? They put it in their own pockets; the higher their positions are, the more they can pocket. Meanwhile, their soldiers have little to eat and few clothes to cover their emaciated bodies. In this regard the Kuomintang reactionaries are no different from the warlords; in fact, they are much worse. Most of the funds appropriated for military expenses wind up in their private accounts.

Now let us look at the Eighth Route Army and the New Fourth Army. Our soldiers are armed peasants, and our army is an amalgamation of armed peasants organized in a military fashion. They live no better or worse than other peasants; they work and rest in the same manner as other peasants. Their basic needs are always satisfied, though there are no luxuries; they are so well educated that they know why they have to fight Japan and why they must love the people. In other words, both their spiritual and material demands have been successfully met. . . .

To train its soldiers, the anti-people's army relies on a blind, compulsory method that leaves the soldiers uninformed and bewildered about its purpose. The people's army, on the other hand, first convinces its soldiers of the wisdom and importance of its training method before such a method is actually used, so that the soldiers will actively and enthusiastically participate in the training of their own accord. . . .

There are three elements in the training of a soldier, namely intelligence, physical strength, and military skill.

The most important of the three elements is intelligence, or an individual soldier's awareness of what a war is all about and why he must fight it. Without knowing the meaning and purpose of a war, a soldier will not be enthusiastic about the training for that war, let alone fighting it. . . .

Speaking of physical strength, let us remind ourselves that war itself is a contest of strength. The first priority in the improvement of a soldier's strength is that he must have enough to eat and enough clothing to keep his body warm. Then comes the strengthening of his body through physical exercise. . . .

As for military skill, we in the past made the mistake of de-emphasizing its importance by saying that the political awakening of a soldier was all that counted in winning a war. Yes, we have won many victories, but our victories would have been greater had we paid equal attention to the development of military skill and physical strength. This mistake, fortunately, has been corrected. . . .

Today our soldiers are brave and skillful warriors fighting gallantly on the front. Tomorrow, when the war ends with our victory over Japan, the same soldiers will become the backbone of our country's economic and cultural reconstruction. In other words, they are not now and will never be a burden to the people and the state.

In Chiang Kai-shek's 1957 book, _The Soviet Union in China_, written a mere eight years after he fled the mainland for Taiwan, Chiang searches for scapegoats for his loss in the civil war. Two of the three reasons Chiang gives for his loss to the Communists refer to external realities. The third reason is basically his mistake in not crushing the Communists earlier. On the whole, Chiang does not seem to recognize any faults or mistakes of his own regime. Perhaps this is too much to ask of a man who had come to see his own fate as synonymous

with that of China. Though he does not say it explicitly, his
anger with the role of the United States is clear.

What were the most serious mistakes we made in our anti-Communist struggle?

The first mistake, as generally assumed, was the conclusion of a treaty of friendship and alliance [1945] with the Soviet Union in accordance with the Yalta Agreement. In return for the Soviet promise to go to war against Japan, the United States concluded this secret document [Yalta Agreement] that was most damaging to China's sovereignty and territorial integrity as a nation. When we ourselves accepted the Yalta provisions and incorporated them in the Sino-Soviet treaty of friendship, we in effect provided the Soviet Union with a legal excuse to commit aggression against our Northeastern provinces and thus enabled the CCP to build a territorial base for its destructive activities against the nation and its people. This does not mean, however, that by signing the Sino-Soviet treaty of friendship and alliance we recognized the legality of the Yalta Agreement. The Republic of China did not participate in the Yalta Conference; nor did the United States consult us in advance. We, therefore, were not bound by the Yalta terms. We negotiated this treaty of friendship and alliance with the Soviet Union at the urging of the United States, though we ourselves also considered the necessity of taking this step. . . .

The second mistake, as generally assumed, was our acceptance of the American mediation in the Kuomintang-CCP conflict. From the CCP's point of view, the truce agreement was no more than a piece of paper to neutralize the United States in this conflict. It effectively prevented our mobilization and restricted severely our military operation, so much so that we sat still, while the enemy was making plans to attack us. Why did we accept the American mediation, sign the truce agreement, and thus tie up ourselves hand and foot? To answer this question, we must realize the most difficult situation we were then in. If we did not sign the Sino-Soviet treaty and if in the meantime we did not accept the American mediation, we would have been totally isolated internationally. . . .

The third mistake, as generally assumed, was the establishment of a constitutional government before the Communists were liquidated. To fight the Communists effectively, we needed unity of will and concentration of effort. Yet, as the constitutional government began, leaders of different occupations, nationalities, and religions became divided among themselves or even antagonistic toward one another, as they competed to be elected as officials at

The Yalta Conference

Held from February 4 to 12, 1945, the Yalta Conference was attended by U.S. President Roosevelt, British Prime Minister Churchill, and Soviet Premier Stalin. Chiang Kai-shek was not present, even though the other leaders made decisions that greatly affected China.

the various levels of the government. Contradictions emerged as opinions of different parties differed, and the organization and discipline of our own party were also adversely affected. The Communist bandits and their fellow travelers seized this opportunity and, under cover of such slogans as freedom and democracy, infiltrated different organizations and groups, set them up against one another, and spread defeatism for our anti-Communist cause. That is why we lost in our war against the Communists.

On July 30, 1949, U.S. Secretary of State Dean Acheson sent President Harry Truman a letter accompanying the *China White Paper*, which surveyed the U.S. role in China. The United States had played a major role aiding China during World War II. In the late 1940s, when fears of a spreading Communism had grown full-blown into the Cold War, the United States continued to aid Chiang Kai-shek. This letter reveals official U.S. thinking on what had happened and what was currently transpiring in China between the Nationalists and Communists. What the United States had most hoped to attain was a coalition government made up of both political parties.

In the spring of 1946 General Marshall attempted to restore peace. This effort lasted for months and during its course a seemingly endless series of proposals and counterproposals were made which had little effect upon the course of military activities and produced no military settlement. During these negotiations . . . [i]ncreasingly he became convinced, however, that twenty years of intermittent civil war between the two factions, during which the leading figures had remained the same, had created such deep personal bitterness and such irreconcilable differences that no agreement was possible. The suspicions and the lack of confidence were beyond remedy. He became convinced that both parties were merely sparring for time, jockeying for military position and catering temporarily to what they believed to be American desires. General Marshall concluded that there was no hope of accomplishing the objectives of his mission. . . .

In his farewell statement, General Marshall announced the termination of his efforts to assist the Chinese in restoring internal peace. He described the deep-seated mutual suspicion between the Kuomintang [Guomindang] and the Chinese Communist Party as the greatest obstacle to a settlement. He made clear that the salvation of China lay in the hands of the Chinese themselves and that, while the newly-adopted constitution provided the framework for the democratic China, practical measures of implementation by both sides would be the decisive test. He appealed for the assumption of leadership by liberals in and out of the Government as the road to unity and peace. . . .

[O]ur government . . . took the view, in light of the existing balance of forces in China, that peace could be established only if certain conditions were met. The Kuomintang would have to set its own house in order and both sides would have to make concessions so that the Government of China might become, in fact as well as name, the Government of all China and so that all parties might function within the constitutional system of the Government. . . .

None of these conditions has been realized. The distrust of the leaders of both the Nationalist and Communist Parties for each other proved too deep-seated to permit final agreement, notwithstanding temporary truces and apparently promising negotiations. The Nationalists, furthermore, embarked in 1946 on an over-ambitious military campaign in the face of warnings from General Marshall that it would not only fail but would plunge China into economic chaos and eventually destroy the Nationalist Government. General Marshall pointed out that although Nationalist armies could, for a period, capture Communist-held cities, they could not destroy the Communist armies. Thus every Nationalist advance would expose their communications to attack by Communist guerrillas and compel them to retreat or to surrender their armies together with the munitions which the United States has furnished them. No estimate of a military situation has ever been more completely confirmed by the facts.

In August 1945 Mao (left) flew to Chongqing for six weeks of talks with Chiang. They drank toasts to each other at the end of the discussions on Double Ten (October 10), the day commemorating the overthrow of the Manchu dynasty. Unfortunately, after these toasts, the trajectory of their relationship went increasingly downhill.

A. Doak Barnett, a political scientist in China at the time of the Communist victory, provides commentary on the CCP's success in his 1963 memoir of his time in China from 1947 to 1949. In the first quarter-century following the Communist victory, scholars often tried to isolate and focus on a few reasons as keys to the CCP's success. Researchers at the turn of the twenty-first century, however, generally contend that

When Chiang Kai-shek chose Nanjing, "southern capital," to be the capital in 1928, the name of Peking or Beijing, "northern capital," was changed to Peiping, "northern peace." It retained that name until the Communist victory in 1949.

the secret to the Communists' victory was their flexibility in adopting policies and approaches to appeal to the largest number of people possible. Barnett's description of their actions in newly conquered Beijing underscores that reality.

The Communist takeover of Peiping has been systematic, undramatic, and bloodless, without any of the violence and terror that often mark the accession to power of a revolutionary army. No violence was called for, because the city was plucked like a piece of ripe fruit. . . .

The Communists went about their takeover in a businesslike way, and the process was not unlike the reorganization of a bankrupt corporation. The old regime in Peiping had been placed in receivership. . . . The Military Control Commission acted as receiver and was the supreme local authority during bankruptcy proceedings. Its job was to take possession of the Nationalists' assets, and then to pass them on to the Peiping People's Government and other Communist administrative and governmental organs. . . .

The Communists' takeover of Peiping was obviously preceded by considerable thought and preparation. The process seemed slow at times, but it followed a definite and logical pattern. Probably because they did not have enough trained political workers to take over all the Nationalist organizations and institutions simultaneously, the Communists proceeded gradually, step by step, and took control of various bodies according to their priority rating.

The first organizations affected were the obvious instruments of power, thought control, and propaganda. On February 1 [1949], the *North China Daily News*, Central News Agency, and Central Broadcasting Station were transformed into the *People's Daily*, New China News Agency, and New China Broadcasting Station. With as little fuss as a chameleon changing color, these organizations abruptly changed their propaganda line and continued operation. . . .

During their first days in Peiping, the Communists not only began a takeover of key organizations, but also carried out an intensive sales promotion campaign. Once the garrison and police force were theirs, they had a monopoly of the instruments of force in the city, but in dealing with the population as a whole, they relied primarily on persuasion. They organized parades and mass meetings and used all the propaganda techniques at their disposal to sell themselves to the people.

The first big demonstration was held on February 3. The occasion was a monster victory parade, and it was a spectacular show. Thousands of people assembled in the square south of Chien Men, the front gate of the Tatar city. Hundreds waved colored paper pennants scrawled with slogans. Brass bands blared. Propaganda trucks crawled slowly through the crowd, distributing leaflets to everyone. Professional dancers wearing opera costumes and heavy make-up performed the Communist theme-dance, the Yangko, or Rice Transplanting Dance (a folk dance that combines elements of the Big Apple, the Charleston, and the Shag). Many non-professionals tried it too. Huge cloth banners with Communist slogans written in large black characters were hoisted above the crowd. Portraits of Mao Tse-tung [Mao Zedong] and other Chinese Communist leaders, some pasted against large red-paper stars, were prominently displayed. And the most brilliant touches of color, standing out against the drab grey mass of people, were several crimson Communist flags, each with the hammer and sickle emblem forming a yellow patch in the upper left-hand corner. . . .

The theme of the Communist takeover was "liberation"—from "Kuomintang reactionaries and American imperialists"—and the beginning of an era of "New Democracy." Many people who had been bitterly anti-Kuomintang did experience a sensation of political liberation. . . .

The parades and all the ballyhoo did not interrupt the less dramatic but more important tasks of taking over the city, however, and on February 4, General Yeh Chien-ying [Ye Jianying], the appointed Communist chief of both the Military Control Commission and the People's Government, walked casually into the municipal government building, made an informal speech, and assumed his job as new mayor. In his speech, Yeh said, "We've been living in the hills right along, and we know much less than you gentlemen about municipal government. Henceforth, we must learn from you." This sort of humility was characteristic of the Communists' line in taking over many organizations, but the Communists did not hesitate to start issuing orders, and soon began teaching as well as learning. The mildness of these first official contacts with the Communists, however, surprised and pleased many persons who had been apprehensive of the takeover, and in many respects, Peiping reacted like a small puppy which, when told to roll over, turns over meekly. During the first weeks of the takeover, there was almost no resistance on the part of non-Communists and almost no violence on the part of the Communists.

Peasants often told me: the [Communist] 8th Route Army [that took north China] is just like your own father and mother.
—Jack Belden commenting on how the Communist army nurtured the Chinese peasants like parents in *China Shakes the World*

Chapter Nine

The Mao Years

When Mao Zedong declared the founding of the People's Republic of China from atop the Gate of Heavenly Peace on October 1, 1949, China had not known long-lasting peace since 1911. Wars against Yuan Shikai, between warlords, between Nationalists and Communists, and between Japan and China had left a legacy of devastation. Now China had to be reconstructed, an immense task in itself. But because the new regime was determined to make a revolution that would completely remake Chinese society, the task was gargantuan. Mao and the CCP were remarkably successful in the first eight years of the regime.

Mao began by taming the out-of-control monetary inflation that had destroyed support for Chiang Kai-shek's regime. Following the Soviet model, he embarked on the first Five Year Plan, which emphasized building heavy industry, such as steel, machine tools, and trucks, that could serve as a base for further economic development. With Soviet aid and advice, China met and even surpassed most of the goals.

The heart of the revolution was land reform. The CCP had already begun this reform in some areas of North China during the civil war. Now the party set it into motion all over the country. The ultimate goal was to increase economic output so that China's industrialization could be built on the profits made in agriculture. The first step, "land to the tiller," was to get land into the hands of those who rented but did not own it. This was a bloody phase because landlords, whose lands were seized by local political leaders without compensation, were attacked by local peasants and often killed in struggle meetings. "Land to the tiller" was designed to give those who had not owned land in the past a stake in the system, but it was not meant to be permanent. Breaking up land to give small plots to farmers would not accomplish the goal of increased farm output. What was needed were larger plots that would make it feasible to introduce mechanized farming—with tractors, planters, and combines.

In this poster, entitled "The Glory of Mao's Ideologies Brightens up the New China," Mao stands in front of a red flag decorated with portraits of Stalin, Lenin, Engels, and Marx. The poster implies not only that Mao belongs in such august Communist company but, more important, that he stands out in front of all the others.

During land reform, many landlords faced struggle meetings held by their neighbors and led by Communist Party cadres. Often such meetings ended with the landlords, accused of unfair and exploitative treatment of their tenants, being beaten or killed. This landlord in Guangdong Province, on a leash in front of an armed guard, was condemned to death and executed.

The other phases of land reform, then, all dealt with joining farmers together, first into mutual aid teams, in which farmers joined voluntarily to help one another and perhaps share draft animals, and then into forced agricultural cooperatives. Small-scale co-ops were first, joining thirty to fifty families together. In these co-ops, farmers still owned their own land, but they contributed their land, animals, and equipment as capital shares to the co-op. In large-scale cooperatives (200 to 300 households), farmers lost the ownership of their land: the co-op owned all the land and paid the farmers for their labor. It was this last phase that led to discontent among many farmers, especially because the state became directly involved in agricultural planning and decision making—sometimes with disastrous consequences.

In the revolution, Mao made a considerable impact in two cultural arenas. The first was in family relations. In May 1950, the government announced the Marriage Law, which gave women equality with men, did away with arranged marriages, allowed women to divorce more easily, permitted women to inherit property and pass it on to their children, and protected children by outlawing infanticide. The second cultural aspect altered by Mao was people's view of themselves in the world. In traditional Chinese society, "fate" was a concept that dominated people's lives. One was fated to be male or female, to be born into a certain family of a certain social position, to have to marry this or that person, to be subject to this tragedy or to that trauma. Mao's contribution was to break down the hold that fate kept on people. Mao believed in the power of people's wills to change their world and the world around them—this was the core of the revolution. The land revolution showed, for example, that landless tenants were not fated to stay landless tenants. The absence of a bridge crossing the Yangzi River at Nanjing, for example, did not mean that fate had decreed it: no, the people could go and build that bridge. This change in the way of thinking had a tremendous impact on Chinese society and culture.

Mao mobilized the people to carry out government policies through mass political campaigns. In the first years of the regime, there were campaigns against corruption and waste among elites in party and government (Three-Anti Campaign) and against corruption in business and industry (Five-Anti Campaign). They were called "campaigns" because people were mobilized to campaign against the "evils" that were specified by the party. Mao launched a "Resist America, Aid Korea" campaign that struck out at those in Chinese society who were seen as political threats when China entered the Korean War in late 1950, out of fear that China would be attacked next.

Mao had done so well by 1956 that he even sponsored the Hundred Flowers Movement ("let a hundred flowers bloom") to allow intellectuals, whom he despised, to voice criticisms. He and other party leaders assumed that with all the regime's successes, criticisms would be mild, but the Hundred Flowers Movement brought heavy criticism of the party and its policies. In 1957, the party reined it in with a brutal Anti-Rightist Campaign that targeted for arrest and punishment (jail or heavy labor) so-called "rightists"—people opposed to the proper "leftist" Communist policies. Some 400,000 to 700,000 met that fate. Thus, by 1957, the early successes of the regime were starting to be overshadowed by the tyranny of what has often been called the party-state, in which party and state were practically identical.

In 1958, Mao launched the Great Leap Forward, a utopian campaign to mobilize the Chinese people to achieve the goal of rapid industrialization. To fund industrial programs the party would use profits from the agricultural sector, therefore the first priority was to increase agricultural output. That, in turn, meant full-fledged mechanization, something that would make sense only with larger plots of land, larger even than the large-scale cooperatives. In August 1958, the party began to establish "people's communes," each composed of around 5,500 households. Communes were to become the main local governmental units in charge of economic development, social services, education, and levying and collecting taxes.

Two features of the Great Leap Forward are notable. The first was that Mao believed that industrialization would succeed only if everyone had a stake in it, so each commune was to set up "backyard" steel furnaces. People contributed anything made of iron, from tools and implements to pots and pans to window frames, to be melted down to make a crude kind of iron. However, the iron they produced cracked easily and was completely worthless. In addition, to fuel the furnaces, many communes deforested hills and mountains, making soil erosion an increasingly serious problem.

The second notable feature of the Great Leap Forward was the huge mess halls where commune members had to eat. Because

This poster touts a ten-year production plan for Chinese agriculture. At the top, Mao chairs a meeting on the plan. Below, farmers hold a photograph of Mao and banners to celebrate the plan. At bottom are two rural scenes: farmers with vegetables and a horseman on the steppe.

both women and men worked in the fields, if each woman had to cook a family meal, it would take valuable time away from the central task of increasing agricultural output. But with the new arrangement, the traditional family ritual of farm life—the coming together of the family for shared meals—was gone.

The Great Leap Forward was really a gigantic step backward. Mao and the party tried to do too many things too fast. Instead of rising, agricultural production fell. To make matters worse, the government based the taxes it collected on crop estimates. Many communes exaggerated the amount their farms would produce so that their commune would excel above others. When the actual production turned out to be far less than the estimates, the government still took what had been estimated. The result was that many areas had very little grain left after the government had taken the taxes. People all over China's countryside began to go hungry. The rapid decline in grain production, in combination with floods, droughts, and insect problems, produced what is now considered the worst famine in human history. An estimated 30 million people perished between 1959 and 1962.

To make matters even worse, after years of deteriorating relations, the Soviet Union, on which China had relied for economic and technical advice in its effort to modernize, called all its advisors home in July 1960. This Soviet action was yet another blow on the heels of the disastrous Great Leap Forward and the deepening famine.

In the early 1960s Mao was increasingly agitated over the direction of the revolution; he railed against the so-called "revisionists," Liu Shaoqi and Deng Xiaoping, who allegedly revised Marxism-Leninism by sneaking capitalist practices into the economy. They favored spurring the output of workers with higher salaries, bonuses, and rewards; Mao thought that should be done just by appealing to national and individual ideals. They believed in the importance of having experts and professionals in charge; Mao thought that correct ideological thinking (political correctness) was more important. They believed in stable government and building bases for modernization slowly and methodically; Mao, obsessed with the ideal of class struggle, argued for continual revolution.

By the summer of 1966, Mao had had enough. He personally wrote a big-character poster with the title, "Bombard the headquarters," by which he meant the Communist Party. Mao was making war on the party that he had established and led. His soldiers were Red Guards, students from middle schools, high schools,

Farmers from a commune in Fujian Province read big character posters that strongly criticize the Gang of Four, who were blamed for many of the evils of the Cultural Revolution. These posters became a significant way for people to communicate political messages.

and universities, who came by the tens of thousands to Beijing to see Mao, whom they called their Red Sun. Mao called on them to destroy the "four olds": old ideas, habits, customs, and culture. The years from 1966 to 1968 were a period of almost total anarchy in China. Red Guards seized and humiliated—in some cases, beat to death—anyone allegedly linked with "feudal China." Many people committed suicide to escape such humiliation and torture. President Liu Shaoqi was tortured and sent off to die, ill, untreated, and alone; Deng Xiaoping was forced into exile. Irreplaceable cultural treasures were trashed. Red Guard actions gave rise to a conservative backlash, and there were pitched battles between supporters of the clashing ideological positions in cities across China. Mao, in the end, had to call out the People's Liberation Army to quell the chaos.

This violent phase of the Great Proletarian Cultural Revolution lasted until 1969. But the "revolution" itself continued until Mao's death in 1976 and the arrest of the most radical leaders, the Gang of Four, that fall. The Gang of Four, which included Mao's wife, Jiang Qing, continued to press for more radical policies through the early 1970s. But ultimately they failed. In a show trial in 1980–81, they were found guilty of persecuting 729,511 citizens and party cadres (officers) and of killing 34,800 people. All were sentenced to prison; Jiang committed suicide there in 1991.

A party resolution in 1981 criticized Mao for serious errors, but said that his contributions to modern China were far greater than the effects of his errors. One of the party-state's most important economic experts, Chen Yun, put it more trenchantly in the newspaper *Ming Pao* on January 15, 1979: "Had Chairman Mao died in 1956, there would have been no doubt that he was a great leader of the Chinese people. . . . Had he died in 1966, his meritorious achievements would have been somewhat tarnished, but his overall record was still very good. Since he actually died in 1976, there is nothing we can do about it."

Mao, the Leader

Dr. Li Zhusui, Mao's personal physician for twenty-two years recorded in his memoir, published in 1994, this description of Mao and activities at the founding of the People's Republic of China. It illustrates the excitement and great hope that many had in Mao's leading China into a new day.

On October 1, 1949, the whole population of the Fragrant Hills was awakened at five o'clock in the morning to the type of crisp, clear, and chilly day that makes autumn in Beijing the most magnificent season. We rode by truck from the Fragrant Hills and arrived in Tiananmen Square a little before seven, taking our places near the marble bridge just at the foot of the Gate of Heavenly Peace, which serves as the entrance to the Forbidden City. . . . When we arrived, the square was already swarming with people carefully chosen from all walks of life. I had a perfect view of the podium from which the leaders would proclaim the establishment of the People's Republic. Above the sea of people thousands of banners were unfurled, waving in the autumn breeze, their colors transforming the shabby city. The crowd was shouting slogans—"Long Live the People's Republic of China." "Long Live the Chinese Communist Party"—and singing revolutionary songs. . . .

At ten o'clock sharp, Mao Zedong and the other top leaders appeared on the podium overlooking the square. The effect was electric. Mao had been my hero since my brother first told me he was China's messiah, and this was my first glimpse of my savior. Even working in the Fragrant Hills, so close to Mao's residence, I had never seen him before. He was fifty-six years old then, tall and healthy and solid. His face was ruddy, his black hair thick, his forehead high, and broad. His voice was powerful and clear, his gestures decisive. He no longer wore the military uniform so familiar to us from his photographs. The founding of the new government was a state occasion and Mao officiated in his position as the chairman of the People's Republic of China, representing the central government rather than the party. He wore a dark brown Sun Yat-sen suit (only later would the style be referred to as the Mao suit) and a worker's cap for this civil occasion. . . .

Mao Zedong was the center of attention, but his manner was dignified, and there was an air of modesty about him, with no trace of arrogance. I had seen Chiang Kai-shek many times during the height of his power, and he had always been aloof, demanding subservience from everyone around him. The effect was invariably alienating.

Mao, though, was a truly magnetic force. Mao did not speak standard Mandarin. But the Hunan dialect he spoke is easy for Mandarin speakers to understand, and its rhythm and tones are pleasant to the ear. Mao's voice was soft, almost lilting, and the effect of his speech was riveting. "The Chinese people have stood up," he proclaimed, and the crowd went wild, thundering in applause, shouting over and over, "Long Live the People's Republic of China!" "Long Live the Chinese Communist Party!" I was so full of joy my heart nearly burst out of my throat, and tears welled up in my eyes. I was so proud of China, so full of hope, so happy that the exploitation and suffering, the aggression from foreigners would be gone forever.

Social Revolution

The May Fourth Movement had been the first round in the battle of the family, or more accurately in the struggle over power in the family. During the Jiangxi Soviet of the early 1930s, the Communists announced a marriage law, but at a time of struggle and outright war, the party called for the "filling of men's needs" (even so far as providing prostitutes for the Red Army). Later, the party insisted that anything resembling feminism be submerged in the struggle to bring forth a new nation.

Announced a mere seven months after the establishment of the People's Republic, the Marriage Law of 1950, at least on paper, looked like the answer to those female (and male) desires that had first been discussed during the May Fourth period.

Chapter 1: General Principles

Article 1. The feudal marriage system which is based on arbitrary and compulsory arrangement and the superiority of man over woman and ignores the children's interests shall be abolished.

結 婚 登 記

A HAPPY COUPLE VISIT THE REGISTRY OFFICE TO REGISTER THEIR FORTHCOMING MARRIAGE. THE OLD FEUDAL PRACTICE OF PARENTS CHOOSING THEIR CHILDREN'S MARRIAGE PARTNERS HAS BEEN ABOLISHED UNDER THE NEW MARRIAGE LAW.
Distributed by the FOREIGN LANGUAGE PRESS, Peking

The Marriage Law of 1950 allowed men and women to choose their own partners, ending the practice of childhood betrothal. In this poster, local Communist cadres discuss issues affecting the personal lives of its members. The presence of many bystanders points to the reality that the Chinese do not see privacy as important to their daily lives.

The New-Democratic marriage system, which is based on the free choice of partners, on monogamy, on equal rights for both sexes, and on the protection of the lawful interests of women and children, shall be put into effect.

Article 2. Bigamy, concubinage, child betrothal, interference with the remarriage of widows, and the exaction of money or gifts in connection with marriages, shall be prohibited.

Chapter 2: The Marriage Contract

Article 3. Marriage shall be based upon the complete willingness of the two partners. Neither party shall use compulsion and no third party shall be allowed to interfere.

Article 4. A marriage can be contracted only after the man has reached 20 years of age and the woman 18 years of age.

Chapter 3: Rights and Duties of Husband and Wife

Article 7. Husband and wife are companions living together and shall enjoy equal status in the home.

Article 8. Husband and wife are in duty bound to love, respect, assist, and look after each other, to live in harmony, to engage in productive work, to care for the children, and to strive jointly for the welfare of the family and for the building up of the new society.

Article 10. Both husband and wife shall have equal rights in the possession and management of family property.

The Persistence of Old Customs

A confidential study on the status of women and marriage . . . in 1980 discovered the persistence of other old customs which the Communists claimed to have eliminated. . . . In one commune in Shanxi, there were 146 girls under the age of five who were betrothed, accounting for 43 percent of their age group, the investigators found. Among those five to ten years old, 81 percent were engaged. In a county in Fujian, on the southeast coast, the investigators said that, because of the continued selling of child brides, parental interference in their daughters' marriages, and ill treatment of new brides there were four suicides by poisoning, four cases of nervous breakdown, and two attempted murders, all within the first five months of 1980.

—*New York Times* journalist Fox Butterfield, *China, Alive in the Bitter Sea,* 1982.

Article 11. Both husband and wife shall have the right to use his or her own family name.

Article 12. Both husband and wife shall have the right to inherit each other's property.

Chapter 4: Relations Between Parents and Children

Article 13. Parents have the duty to rear and educate their children; the children have the duty to support and assist their parents. Neither the parents or the children shall maltreat or desert one another.

The foregoing provision also applies to foster-parents and foster-children. Infanticide by drowning and similar criminal acts are strictly prohibited.

Article 14. Parents and children shall have the right to inherit one another's property.

Article 15. Children born out of wedlock shall enjoy the same rights as children born in lawful wedlock. No person shall be allowed to harm them or discriminate against them. . . .

Chapter 5: Divorce

Article 17. Divorce shall be granted when husband and wife both desire it. In the event of either the husband or the wife alone insisting upon divorce, it may be granted only when mediation by the district people's government and the judicial organ has failed to bring about reconciliation. . . .

Article 18. The husband shall not apply for a divorce when his wife is with child. He may apply for divorce only one year after the birth of a child. In the case of a woman applying for divorce, this restriction does not apply.

Article 19. The consent of a member of the revolutionary army on active service who maintains correspondence with his or her family must first be obtained before his or her spouse can apply for divorce.

Chapter 6: Maintenance and Education of Children
After Divorce

Article 20. The blood ties between parents and children do not end with the divorce of the parents. No matter whether the father or the mother acts as guardian of the children, they still remain the children of both parties. After divorce, both parents still have the duty to support and educate their children. After divorce, the guiding principle is to allow the mother to have custody of a baby still being breast-fed. After the weaning of the child, if a dispute arises between the parties over the guardianship and an agreement cannot be reached, the people's court shall render a decision in accordance with the interests of the child.

Article 21. If, after divorce, the mother is given custody of a child, the father shall be responsible for the whole or part of the necessary cost of the maintenance and education of the child. Both parties shall reach an agreement regarding the amount and duration of such maintenance and education. In the case where the two parties fail to reach an agreement, the people's court shall render a decision.

China's preeminent twentieth-century female author, Ding Ling, had been attacked during the years at Yan'an for writing essays and stories that pushed the goal of feminism. The CCP leadership argued that at a time of national crisis all literature should deal with the revolution and the drive to establish a strong state and must not focus on divisive topics like feminism. In *The Sun Shines over the Sanggan River*, published in 1948, Ding followed through with a novel on land reform that won the Soviet Union's Stalin Prize for literature in 1951. Here Ding depicts a struggle meeting against a landlord she calls "Schemer Qian." Struggle meetings were crucial elements in Mao's efforts to give people who had been subordinated a sense that they had the power to change their world.

Then three or four militiamen took Schemer Qian up to the platform. He was wearing a lined gown of grey silk and white trousers, his hands tied behind him. His head was slightly lowered, and his small beady eyes were screwed up, searching the crowd. . . .

For thousands of years the local despots had had power. They had oppressed generation after generation of peasants, and the peasants had bowed their necks under the yoke. Now abruptly they were confronted with this power standing before them with bound hands, and they felt bewildered, at a loss. Some who were particularly intimidated by his malevolent look recalled the days when they could only submit, and now, exposed to this blast, wavered again. So for the time being they were silent.

All this time Schemer Qian, standing on the stage gnawing his lips, was glancing round, wanting to quell these yokels, unwilling to admit defeat. . . .

At this point a man suddenly leapt out from the crowd. He had thick eyebrows and sparkling eyes. Rushing up to Schemer Qian, he cursed him: "You murderer! You trampled our village under your feet! You killed people from behind the scenes for money. Today we're going to settle all old scores, and do a thorough job of it. Do you hear that? Do you still want to frighten people? It's no use! There's no place for you to stand on this stage! Kneel down! Kneel to all the villagers!" He pushed Qian hard, while the crowd echoed: "Kneel down! Kneel down!" . . .

Peasants surged up to the stage shouting wildly: "Kill him!"•"A life for our lives!"

A group of villagers rushed to beat him. It was not clear who started, but one struck the first blow and others fought to get at him. . . .

One feeling animated them all—vengeance! They wanted vengeance. They wanted to give vent to their hatred, the sufferings of the oppressed since their ancestors' times, the hatred of thousands of years; all this resentment they directed against him. They would have liked to tear him with their teeth. . . .

"Bah! Killing's too good for him. Let's make him beg for death. Let's humble him for a few days, how about it?" Old Dong's face was red with excitement. He had started life as a hired laborer. Now that he saw peasants just like himself daring to speak out and act boldly, his heart was racing wildly with happiness.

The Great Leap Forward

In his 1994 memoir, Mao's doctor, Li Zhisui, described the phenomenon of the backyard steel furnaces and the changes they brought to the Chinese landscape.

Psychologists of mass behavior might have an explanation for what went wrong in China in the late summer of 1958. China was struck with a mass hysteria fed by Mao, who then fell victim himself. We returned to Beijing in time for the October first celebrations. Mao began believing the slogans, casting caution to the winds. Mini-steel mills were being set up even in Zhongnanhai, and at night the whole compound was a sea or red light. The idea had originated with the Central Bureau of Guards, but Mao did not oppose them, and soon everyone was stoking the fires— cadres, clerks, secretaries, doctors, nurses, and me. The rare voices of caution were being stilled. Everyone was hurrying to jump on the utopian bandwagon. Liu Shaoqi, Deng Xiaoping, Zhou Enlai, and Chen Yi, men who might once have reined the Chairman in, were speaking with a single voice, and that voice

Every revolution creates new words. The Chinese Revolution created a whole new vocabulary. A most important word in this vocabulary was fanshen (翻身). *Literally, it means "to turn the body," or "to turn over." To China's hundreds of millions of landless and land-poor peasants it meant to stand up, to throw off the landlord yoke, to gain land, stock, implements, and houses. . . . It meant to enter a new world.*

—Author and China scholar William Hinton, *Fanshen,* 1968

During the Great Leap Forward, Mao wanted all people to participate in industry and thus have a stake in its success. To this end, commune members built backyard steel smelters, such as this one at the Weixing Commune.

was Mao's. What those men really thought, we will never know. Everyone was caught in the grip of this utopian hysteria.

Incredibly after the October first celebrations, we set out again by train, heading south. The scene along the railroad tracks was incredible. Harvest time was approaching, and the crops were thriving. The fields were crowded with peasants at work, and they were all women and young girls dressed in reds and greens, gray-haired old men, or teenagers. All the able-bodied males, the real farmers of China, had been taken out of agricultural production to tend the backyard steel furnaces.

The backyard furnaces had transformed the rural landscape. They were everywhere, and we could see peasant men in a constant frenzy of activity, transporting fuel and raw materials, keeping the fires stoked. At night, the furnaces dotted the landscape as far as the eye could see, their fires lighting the skies.

The largest famine in world history, from 1959 to 1962, was produced by a combination of man-made and natural causes. The government policy of basing taxes on projected crop yields—which communes had trumped up in order lift their own revolutionary reputation—led to the government's taking almost all the grain from many localities. Floods and droughts only compounded the situation. In her memoir, *Wild Swans*, published in 1991, Jung Chang described the famine scene in Sichuan Province.

In Chengdu, the monthly food ration was reduced to 19 pounds of rice, a third of an ounce of cooking oil, and 3.5 ounces of meat when there was any. Scarcely anything else was available, not even cabbage. Many people were afflicted by edema, a condition in which fluid accumulates under the skin because of malnutrition. The patient turns yellow and swells up. The most popular remedy was eating chlorella, which was supposed to be rich in protein. Chlorella fed on human urine, so people stopped going to the toilet and peed into spittoons instead, then dropped the chlorella seed in; they grew into something looking like green fish roe in a couple of days, and were scooped out of the urine, washed, and cooked with rice. They were truly disgusting to eat, but did reduce the swelling.

The Cultural Revolution and After

Mao Zedong had called into being the Red Guards as the shock troops of his Cultural Revolution. As the movement unfolded, Red Guard organizations tended to factionalize, with each unit claiming to be closer to Mao and his thought. In many areas, physical struggles, leading to injury and death, erupted between factions. Perhaps the most notorious battles between student Red Guard units occurred at Qinghua University in Beijing, the most prestigious school of science and technology in China. As struggles developed on the university campus, the two key factions were called 4s and the Regiment, with the latter tending to be most radical and led by super-radical Kuai Dafu. American writer William Hinton recounted the Cultural Revolution at Qinghua in *Hundred Day War*, which first appeared as the July-August 1972 issue of *Monthly Review*. It underscores the violence and brutality of this revolution, in which each side seemed to fall into an evil irrationality.

A Regiment commander with one hundred "troops" occupied the Meeting Hall shortly after midnight on April 23. At dawn the Regiment loudspeakers blared forth the news that four hundred spears had been found, that the action had been taken in the nick of time, and that it had frustrated a major offensive planned by the 4s.

Thus began the violent fighting which lasted through July and steadily escalated from fists, sticks, and stones, through "cold"

One of the common ways of communicating political thoughts anonymously after the founding of the People's Republic was through wall posters, sometimes called "big character posters." These posters were often sharp in their criticism of the government and its policies. The poster translated here addresses the issue of starvation.

What does it mean when the Communists say they suffer so that the people may not suffer and that they let the people enjoy things before they do the same? What do they mean when they speak of suffering now in order to have a happy life late? These are lies. We ask: Is Chairman Mao, who enjoys the best things of life and passes the summer at Jinwangdao and spends his vacations at Yuquanshan, having a hard time? Are the starving peasants, with only a cup of spring water, enjoying the good life? In Yan'an was Chairman Mao, who had two dishes plus soup for every meal having a hard time? Were the peasants, who had nothing to eat but bitter vegetables, enjoying the good life? Everyone was told that Chairman Mao was leading a hard and simple life. That son of a bitch! A million shames on him!

weapons like swords and spears to "hot" weapons like revolvers, rifles, hand grenades, and rockets. . . .

At the end of May, Kuai and the regiment launched an all-out offensive against the 4s in order to finish them off. Many 4s were in a building called the Bathhouse.

Kuai concentrated his fighters at the north end of the building, where they tried once more to storm up ladders to the second-story windows. By concentrating a great hail of rock artillery on the windows, the Regiment fighters hoped to drive the defenders back and thus make entry possible. But their tactics failed again and again. One brave warrior fell or was pushed from the top of the ladder and landed head first on a rock, crushing his skull. He later died.

Unwilling to call off the attack, Kuai transferred his ambush contingent to the Bathhouse, leaving only twenty stalwarts to block the road against the 4s' uncommitted troops. When they saw this opening the 4s pushed forward with a formidable contingent of spear bearers behind a "tank." The tank was made out of a tractor welded over with steel plate. When the twenty Regiment fighters saw this monster coming, they formed a line across the road, but what could they do with spears against its steel plate? As the tank came close, they broke ranks and fled, only to be charged by the 4s' spearmen, who turned the retreat into a rout. One of the Regiment fighters, run through by a spear, bled to death.

To stop the 4s who were advancing from the south, Kuai ordered his "Flag" bow-and-arrow team into the fray. They fired a hail of arrows point blank at the opposition, killing one and wounding several.

The tank, invulnerable to arrows, kept going, but a little further down the road the Regiment defenders had buried what looked like a mine. "If you come any further, you'll be blown up," they shouted to the tank driver.

Not knowing whether the mine was real or not, the tank driver hesitated. Several Regiment fighters took advantage of this pause to rush forward and set the tank on fire with Molotov cocktails. Its crew had to abandon it before it blew up. One of them was so badly burned that three years later his face had still not healed.

With their tank out of action, with its crew scorched, with one man dead from an arrow and several other wounded, the 4s main force gave up the assault and retreated into an old dormitory

During the Cultural Revolution, people
singled out as counter-revolutionaries
were often paraded through the streets
wearing dunce caps, denounced, and
then tortured. Several such victims are
surrounded by their tormenters in this
1967 photograph.

During the Cultural Revolution, people
singled out as counter-revolutionaries
were often paraded through the streets
wearing dunce caps, denounced, and
then tortured. Several such victims are
surrounded by their tormenters in this
1967 photograph.

building to the west that had long been one of their strongholds.
There they took up defensive positions in the basement.

At this point Kuai became desperate. So many had been
wounded and several were already dead or dying on both sides,
yet nothing had been won. Far from taking power, it looked as if
the Regiment might even have to retreat. Kuai ordered his "rods"
to pour gasoline on the Bathhouse. Molotov cocktails were quickly made and thrown against the gas-soaked walls. Flames shot up
around the building. The 4s were trapped inside.

The defenders had had nothing to eat or drink since the night
before. With their throats parched and their clothes scorched,
they called out that they wanted to surrender. But Kuai would not
listen. Instead of putting out the fire, he ordered more fuel. When
the Haitien fire department arrived, he tried to prevent the fire-
men from going anywhere near the building,

This angered the peasants who had gathered from far and near
to watch the battle.

"Don't burn people to death! How can you go to such
extremes? Put up a ladder! Let the students out!" they shouted.

Finally Kuai relented.

As the scorched and suffocating 4s crawled down the rescue ladder, they were arrested as prisoners of war. The 4s lost a major fighting force—over thirty of their best people, the main troops of the Generator Building fighting team.

After Mao had to rein in the Red Guards when they turned China into a battleground, he sent them down to the countryside to learn about life from the peasants. Many youth were sent to poverty-stricken areas deep in China's interior, where they spent years of their lives. In his book *Blood Red Sunset*, published in 1988, Ma Bo describes the hardships of life as a sent-down youth in the Mongolian grasslands.

September 1, 1970
Sweltering.

Spent the day making adobe bricks, stripped to the waist and working as far from camp as possible, stopping only to eat and relieve myself. I don't dare take a break, not even to catch my breath, since I'm probably being watched. Working alone all the time wipes all thoughts right out of your head.

Blood blisters on the palms of my hands, and my feet ache.

September 14, 1970
For over a week I've been mixing mud for two squads making adobe blocks. It's impossible to keep up with them. . . .

Since my hands are in the mud all day, they're covered with sores. I look like a leper. I've got open sores on the soles of my feet where straw gets embedded. The pain is terrible. I go to bed without washing the mud off my arms because removing it hurts too much.

October 1, 1970
National Day
Snow is falling lightly under a dark sky. Freezing winds knife through the gaping door and windows as I huddle under my sheepskin coat and enjoy a rare break from work, the first in over a month. Lying here without moving is heavenly. I've been in this position all day, reflecting on the past month; slaving away, driving myself mad, wearing myself out digging and mixing clay. Ten hours a day of backbreaking labor, which leaves every joint in my body swollen and painful. All to make a good impression and not give anyone a reason to find fault with me.

Chapter Ten: Picture Essay

The Cult of Mao Zedong

In a Communist state where the watchword supposedly is "equality," it would seem that the rise of a leader to the status of a demigod would not be possible. Yet such a rise did happen during the Cultural Revolution, and the demigod was Mao Zedong. What was the recipe that gave the Chinese their Red Sun? One ingredient that propelled Mao to cult status was the fact that he was already seen by his countrymen as the hero of the Communist revolution. He had led most of the Long March; his forces had fought the Japanese; he had led his troops to victory in the civil war; and, during the first eight years of his rule, he had brought economic successes and a huge increase in pride about the new China. Mao lusted for power and was resentful of any challenge. His megalomania was rooted in his sense that he (and sometimes he alone) possessed the Truth. Mao could rationalize his becoming a demigod by pointing to Joseph Stalin, who developed his own cult following in the Soviet Union. And he could rely on his supporters, especially defense minister Lin Biao and the People's Liberation Army, and later the Gang of Four, to keep the Mao fever hot.

The cult grew to absured levels. Workers and students stopped each day to read the Little Red Book. Everyone was to report to Mao whatever he or she did every day, and because Mao was thought to be omnipotent and omnipresent, this could be done through thought alone. Once a day everyone—stewardesses on airplanes, workers in the fields, and children in school—was supposed to dance the Victory Dance in Mao's honor. Almost twenty years after his death, a huge Mao "theme park" opened across from the Mao family home in Shaoshan, Hunan Province. The park, according to its publicity brochure, was both educational and entertaining. Park visitors "are likely to experience the revolutionary process in China for themselves by walking down the revolutionary road and 'reading' of the life and form of the revolution in this history book without words."

Just before launching the Cultural Revolution, Mao swims in the Yangzi River on July 16, 1966, to show the country his vigor and that he was a leader to be taken seriously. All over China people began to throw themselves into rivers to try to emulate the Great Helmsman. According to "official records," the seventy-two-year-old swam four times faster than the world record.

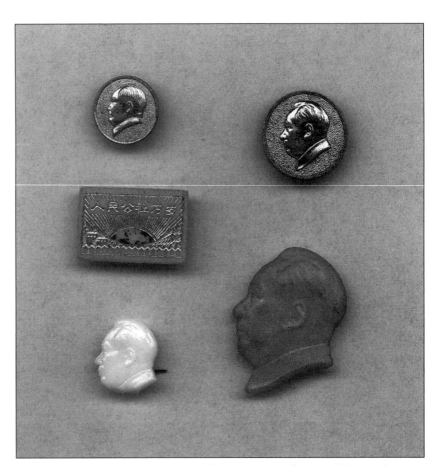

Mao badges come in all sizes and designs, but most are red and round, and feature a headshot of Mao. The first Mao badge appeared in Yan'an in 1948; the government produced almost 5 billion badges during the Cultural Revolution. There was a nostalgic rebirth of interest in them in the 1990s. During the Cultural Revolution, the badge pointed to the wearer's revolutionary credentials.

Street vendors still sell the red cigarette lighter with Mao's image, and it remains a popular souvenir into the twenty-first century. When it is opened, it plays "The East Is Red" or "Jingle Bells." It joins countless other items that attest to the Mao cult: Mao watches, tie clips, pendants, cuff links, brooches, shopping bags, and yo-yos. Taxi drivers often hang these objects from their rearview mirrors to serve as amulets.

Two-year-old Ding Hongbing leads her family as they sing a Mao quotation set to music. The Ding family were poor peasants, but they were able to build their own home after Liberation. They became obsessed with promoting Mao. All family members, except for youngest, Hongbing, memorized three of Mao's essays and more than a hundred of his quotations.

During the Cultural Revolution, the government printed millions of copies of the Little Red Book, whose proper title was *Quotations from Chairman Mao*. First printed by the political department of the army, it was promoted by defense minister Lin Biao, who made preposterous claims about the extraordinary power of Mao's thought. Red Guards and properly revolutionary masses waved the book; people studied and memorized it at work and at home around the country. Some even ascribed magical properties to it.

Farm workers at a commmune in Dazhai take a study break from their manual labor to discuss quotations in the Little Red Book in 1969. During the Cultural Revolution, Mao touted Dazhai as a model production brigade. Only after Mao's death did authorities find that the brigade had falsified production statistics and was involved in many financial irregularities.

Kindergarten children in Beijing in 1968 wave the Little Red Book. Kindergarten and elementary classes were filled with propaganda that popularized the Cultural Revolution. Mao believed that students were never too young to be taught the reality of class struggle.

In propaganda posters, Mao appears most clearly as a demigod. Here beams of light radiate from Mao's head, which appears literally as the Red Sun. Its rays of light shine beneficently onto the masses, made up of farmers, the army, and ethnic groups. They march under revolutionary banners, carry oversized books of Mao's writings, and hold aloft bouquets of flowers. Designed by the Central Academy of Industrial Arts in 1968, this poster bears the title, "Advance victoriously while following Chairman Mao's revolutionary line in literature and the arts."

Chapter Eleven

"To Get Rich Is Glorious"

The Reforms of Deng Xiaoping and Jiang Zemin

V isitors going through Mao's mausoleum at Tiananmen Square in Beijing exit through a gift shop to be greeted by hawkers outside competing to sell an array of cheap Mao memorabilia—from cigarette lighters to badges to clocks and watches. Such a flagrant display of capitalism so close to Mao's body is high irony. It is clear that Mao's brand of socialism differed greatly from that of his successors. When Deng Xiaoping emerged as China's leader in the late 1970s, he set out to remake the face of China by embarking on a bold program of economic liberalization, specifically the introduction of widespread capitalism. By the time of Deng's death in 1997, someone living in Mao's China would not have recognized the economic and social face of China.

Between 1979 and 1984, the party-state abolished the centerpiece of Mao's China, the rural commune. By 1984, 98 percent of Chinese farm households were participating instead in what was known as the "responsibility system." Though farmers did not own their land (they leased it from the collective), it could be bought, sold, and inherited. After the farmer paid the required tax to the state, he could keep the profits made on the sale of his crops—a far cry from the commune system in which farmers could not even have garden plots and lived only on the wages paid by the commune. Many farmers, in order to make as much money as possible, shifted to cash crops that would bring more on the market. The results were astounding. Between 1978 and 1984 the per capita income in the countryside almost doubled. People purchased more consumer goods, built new homes, and ate a

Deng Xiaoping (with arm raised) and Jiang Zemin, together in the Great Hall of the People in Beijing, were determined economic-reform leaders. They moved China well beyond its Communist ideology, to capitalism—or, as Deng preferred to call it, "socialism with Chinese characteristics."

This silk factory worker in Wuxi (in the Lower Yangzi region) culls silk cocoons.

better diet, all of which indicates a higher living standard. Part of the rural wealth came from township and village enterprises that produced, for example, fertilizers, pesticides, and machine tools.

In urban areas, the government introduced the "market model" in 1979. Here the market, not government planning, regulated the production and distribution of goods. Individual businesses could operate fairly autonomously, and they could make a profit. In larger enterprises, factory managers could hire and fire their employees, a major shift in policy, because under the previous system what was known as the "iron rice bowl" or lifetime job security, meant workers could never be fired. The government set in place an industrial responsibility system that allowed an enterprise to keep half its profits after paying the state the other half in taxes. Price controls were gradually lifted. As in the countryside, this more liberal policy brought growing wealth. Between 1979 and 1989, the real wages of urban workers more than doubled.

During the late 1980s and following the political turmoil in the spring of 1989, there was a constant battle between those who wanted to continue economic liberalization and those who wanted a slower approach or even an end to liberalization. Deng, however, gave his firm blessing to liberalizing in early 1992. Leading the way were so-called special economic zones along China's southeast coast, where incentives such as low tax rates encouraged foreign investment. One opponent of reform described these zones as "savagely capitalist." The effect of these thriving zones spilled out beyond the zones themselves, transforming surrounding areas and making coastal China from Hong Kong to Shanghai increasingly modern.

Jiang Zemin, chair of the party, head of state, and head of the Military Commission in the 1990s, continued Deng's bold economic moves. The boldest was to begin to turn state enterprises into private ones. The huge majority of these enterprises, which produced up to 40 percent of China's total industrial product, lost money year after year and had to be subsidized by the government. The boldness of the effort to move toward privatization came in part from the fact that once enterprises went private, they would be driven by the bottom line—profits. Without the iron rice bowl, many workers were in danger of losing their jobs. Another impact of privatization was ideological. In socialism the state owns and controls industry. Once companies became private and worked for individual company profits, there was no way the new Chinese system could remain socialist. The official party-state line became "socialism with Chinese characteristics," clearly a euphemism for capitalism.

In national terms China enjoyed a spectacular economic boom in the 1990s; indeed, China's economy quadrupled between 1980 and 2000. For Chinese families and individuals, this explosion of wealth had both positive and negative effects. On the positive side it allowed the Chinese masses to go on a consumer spending spree, purchasing color televisions, washing machines, air conditioners, refrigerators, stereo tape recorders, and sewing machines. With money to spend on such items, individual choice increased.

But all the results were not so happy. Under the old system workers did not have to pay for medical care or put money into pension funds. Beginning in the 1990s, they had to do both, in addition to contributing co-payments for insurance. Under the traditional system, workers were assigned positions and then could not be fired. Under the reforms, workers could choose their own jobs (if jobs were even available) and could be fired. In addition, there was a growing disparity of income between cities and countryside, within cities, between coastal China and the interior, and between workers at state enterprises and private ones. This gave rise to considerable jealousy (called the "red-eye" disease) and social grumbling.

There were many unhappy results of the reforms for the nation as well. The reforms changed some regions remarkably while doing very little for others. Coastal areas prospered while interior regions languished. Rural areas lagged far behind cities. Many people left rural areas for presumably better jobs and lives in cities. But once they got there, most found no permanent or satisfying jobs. Without work or home, they took to living in train stations, under overpasses, or on the streets: they were tagged the "floating population" and were a potential threat to social order.

An unfortunate offshoot of reform was corruption. The goal in life was to get rich, and many came to believe that anything one did to reach that goal was legitimate. Therefore, on every level of government and in all areas of private society, anything went: embezzlement, bribery, extortion, smuggling, fraud, deception, kickbacks, nepotism, stock manipulation, and illegal business transactions, among others. Criticisms grew that life under the reforms had transformed China into a money-mad culture without any redeeming moral values; some critics charged that China had lost its soul. Indeed, at the beginning of the twenty-first century, while thriving economically in many areas, China appeared to be drifting morally and culturally.

Reforms of Deng Xiaoping

In his capacity as special assistant to party General Secretary Hu Yaobang, Ruan Ming helped direct agricultural reform in the early 1980s. In this memoir published in 1992, he notes some of the consequences of the reform.

The rapid spread of the family responsibility system in the countryside and disappearance of the People's Communes emancipated the peasants and the forces of agricultural production. The outlook of the rural population was fundamentally changed. As a first consequence, harvests were bountiful four years in a row, from 1980 to 1984. In five years' time, the total output of grain increased by 100 billion kilograms and cotton production by 3.8 million tons. The old problem of the nourishment and basic clothing of the Chinese peasants was at last resolved. After 1984, stagnant agricultural production had a lot to do with the stagnation in the guiding ideology of reform. . . .

The second consequence of the rural reform was that the market economy made great strides in the countryside. The most profound economic change induced by reform was that it put an end to the combination of the self-reliant and semi-self-reliant natural economy that has dominated China for thousands of years and that was joined after 1953 to a barter economy under the protection of the state. But the Chinese economy was nevertheless entering a new era. Despite the many frustrations of the ten-year reform, the development of the rural commercial economy is irreversible. More than 65 percent of the rural economy was converted into a market economy. More than 100 million people formed rural enterprises that produced one trillion yuan worth of merchandise. The production value of Chinese rural industries surpassed that of rural agricultural production and so brought an end to the old view of Chinese villages as places where "eight hundred million shift for themselves to feed themselves." Not only do they now shift for themselves to feed themselves, but they throw themselves into animal husbandry, forestry, and fishing;

they are entrepreneurs in industry, commerce, and transportation or other services sectors. This great upheaval has made altogether impossible a return to the old economy based on People's Communes and the state grain monopoly.

Finally, the third consequence of rural reform: The farmers constitute the greatest force for reform in China and a powerful new independent force. Land reform in the early 1950s freed them the first time, as a class, from the landlords. In theory they were the masters of the country, but in reality they lived as prisoners of the People's Communes and state planning. This time, now that they are emancipated, they truly want to influence the nation's destiny.

Their power is first of all manifested in the economic realm: Rural merchandise has flooded the Chinese market, and some has even penetrated the global economy. The independent economic status of China's farmers has truly increased. At the same time, the emancipation of agricultural production forces has led more and more free rural people to quit the land to enter industry, commerce, and service areas or to install themselves in cities, where they have become the motivating factor behind urban reforms. That was the big picture of the great reform carried out from 1979 to 1980: The countryside had overwhelmed the cities.

This Shanghai street scene is noteworthy for its sophisticated cosmetics advertisements, for having many more cars than bicycles, and for the American fast-food restaurants Pizza Hut and KFC. This scene is now more the norm than the exception in many Chinese cities.

The great strides of the market economy in the countryside and the motivating role that the farmers play characterize the Chinese reform. There reside its advantages (compared to Gorbachev's reforms in the USSR). There also reside its weaknesses. The market has no coherence, and its mechanisms are incomplete. The coexistence of two systems of price setting—by the market and by the state—allows an abuse of power and a sabotage of market mechanisms. Cultural and technical backwardness or rural enterprise has created a huge waste of natural resources and labor as well as environmental pollution. The reform launched in the countryside must be relieved. It needs the support of workers and intellectuals from the cities to help the farmers transform this rural market economy, backward and partially developed, into an advanced and fully developed one. But this second phase has not been realized. And that is the source of the tragic fate of reform in China.

After the late 1980s, when the rate of inflation suggested that the economy might be in trouble and the severe political turmoil in 1989 suggested that openness brought by the reforms might be destabilizing, the future of reforms seemed much in question. On a trip in early 1992 to the special economic zones, especially Shenzhen very near to Hong Kong, eighty-eight-year-old Deng Xiaoping encouraged more rapid expansion of the reforms rather than cutting back as the conservatives would have wished. His remarks to local officials in effect said "full steam ahead" for China to continue to liberalize its economic policy. His statement takes on the issue of whether the reforms were capitalist or socialist, but he dances around the issue without much of a satisfying conclusion.

It doesn't matter if the cat is white or black, so long as it catches rats.

—Deng Xiaoping, in Beijing in the early 1960s, opposing Mao Zedong's emphasis on ideological correctness

We should be bolder in carrying out reforms and opening up to the outside world and in making experimentations; we should not act like a woman with bound feet. For what we regard as correct, just try it and go ahead daringly. Shenzhen's experience means daring to break through. One just cannot blaze a trail, a new trail, and accomplish a new undertaking without a spirit of daring to break through, the spirit of taking a risk, and without some spirit and vigor. Who can say that everything is 100 percent sure of success with no risk at all? One should not consider one always in the right—there is no such thing. I never think so myself. Leaders should sum up experiences every year. They should persist in what

Small electronics shops, such as this one in the city of Chengdu, in Sichuan Province in far western China, are ubiquitous in Chinese towns and cities.

is right and promptly correct what is not. New problems should be immediately solved whenever they emerge. It may take thirty more years for us to institute a whole set of more mature and complete systems in various fields. Under this set of systems, our principles and policies will fall more into a pattern. Now we are better experienced with each passing day in building socialism of the Chinese type. . . .

Failing to take bigger steps and break through in carrying our reforms and opening to the outside world is essentially for fear that there may be too much capitalism or that the capitalist road is followed. The question of whether a move is socialist or capitalist is crucial. The criterion for judging this can only be whether or not a move is conducive to developing the productive forces in socialist society, increasing the comprehensive strength of the country, and improving the people's living standards. There were differing views on setting up special economic zones from the beginning, and people feared that they might involve the practice of capitalism. The achievements made in the construction of Shenzhen provide clear answers to people with various misgivings. The special economic zones are socialist, not capitalist. Judging from Shenzhen's situation, public ownership is the main system of ownership, and the investment by foreign businessmen accounts for only one-fourth of the total amount of investment in the zone. As for foreign investment, we can also benefit from it through taxation and by providing labor services. . . .

Whether the emphasis is on planning or market is not the essential distinction between socialism and capitalism. A planned economy is not socialism—there is planning under capitalism too; and a market economy is not capitalism—there is market regulation under socialism, too. Planning and market are both economic means. The essence of socialism is to liberate and develop productive forces, to eliminate exploitation and polarization, and to finally realize common prosperity. . . .

In short, in order to win a relative edge of socialism over capitalism, we must boldly absorb and draw on all fruits of civilization created by the society of mankind, as well as all advanced management and operational methods and modes reflecting the law on modern socialized production in various countries of the world today, including developed capitalist countries.

Impact of Reform

Deng Xiaoping's reforms brought nothing less than a consumer revolution. Between 1978 and 1990, the per-capita income doubled, and from 1990 to 1994 it soared another 50 percent. A poll of 461 people taken in the city of Guangzhou in 1994 showed that about 80 percent applauded the availability of consumer items. Even in areas far from the coastal regions where the changes were most marked, there was a rise in households purchasing refrigerators, washing machines, and color TVs.

But the reality as time passed was that the economy of coastal regions flourished and pulled further ahead of the economy of the interior. It produced a regionalization of the haves and have-nots. This 1993 analysis from a Hong Kong newspaper underscores the widening gap between eastern China and other regions.

The gap in economic development between China's eastern region and the central and western regions, whose area comprises 88.6 percent of the country's total and whose population accounts for 63.1 percent of the country's total, is visibly widening with every passing year. An Agriculture Ministry official has pointed out that if this state of affairs is allowed to continue, it will be disadvantageous to China's economic development and political stability. . . .

A quantitative analysis shows that the gap between the eastern region and the central and western regions can be seen through the rural population's per capita agricultural product, the output value of township enterprises, [and] the per capita income of the rural population. . . .

According to information provided by the Agriculture Ministry, the per capita agricultural product of the rural population in 1985 was 1,450 yuan [U.S. $254] in the eastern region and 716 and 630 yuan [$125, $110] respectively in the central and western regions. In 1990, the figure rose to 2,929 yuan, 1,382 yuan, and 976 yuan, [$513, $242, and $171] respectively. In other words, the gap between the eastern region and the central and western regions grew wider by 110 and 150 percent.

Of the total output value of township enterprises in 1991, the eastern region accounted for 65 percent; the central, 30 percent; and the west, only 4.2 percent. Moreover, while the three eastern region provinces of Jiangsu, Zhejiang, and Shandong had a total output value of over 100 billion yuan [$18 billion], nine provinces and autonomous regions in the western region produced a total output value of less than 10 billion yuan [$1.8 billion].

In 1985, per capita income of the rural population was 497 yuan [$87] in the eastern region and 343 and 355 yuan, respectively [$60, $62] in the central and western regions. In 1990, the figure rose to 812, 538, and 497 yuan [$142, $94, $87]. In other words, the gap between the eastern region and the central and western regions grew wider by 80 and 120 percent.

One of the major social problems facing the regime at the turn of the century was the huge "floating population." Composed of millions of rural people who fled the countryside, lured by the hope of wealth or at the least a decent job, the floating population was—and still is—often unemployed or working only temporarily or in fly-by-night operations. Homeless and without any sort of social safety net, they live a mostly hand-to-mouth existence and potentially pose a threat to social order. As such, the local populations see them as potentially dangerous. These brief summaries of interviews provide reasons why people chose to become a part of the floating population. The first two interviews were completed by two Chinese scholars in 1990 in their study of the problem; the remainder were conducted by U.S. political scientist Dorothy Solinger as part of a research project in the summer of 1992.

A village construction team from Wusheng County, Sichuan, composed of thirty-one people, now working in Haikou, Hainan.

People who leave the countryside for opportunities in cities are called the floating population. When they get to the city, most have no shelter, no job, and no connections to those who might help them. Often, they end up like this man, sleeping on the sidewalk in Guangzhou in 1990.

Their leader said the produce at home is plentiful, eating is no problem, but because people are many and land is scarce, the average per capita arable is only half a *mu* (1/12 of an acre). If the wife and kids till it, that's enough. Young, strong people have nothing to do at home; only can go out to work and don't care how much they earn, if they can save a little, that's fine.

In a township of Dongguan, Guangdong, there are 540 Sichuan girls from the far suburbs of Chengdu; because their spirit is very strong, local people call them "Sichuan peppery misses." Three came to chat with the reporters; are junior and senior high graduates, working in processing enterprises. . . . Speaking of their future plans, these lively young girls at once change to being at a loss: "On the one hand, go on as we are, on the other hand look around; wherever we end up, we'll figure it out there."

A scrap-paper collector in Nanjing, twenty years old, . . . has a wife and nine-month-old child who have already gone back home. He's attained just five years of primary school education. Why is he here, I asked? "We have 2.5 *mu* (.4 acre) to till, which is rather a lot." "But," he complained, ". . . tilling the fields is meaningless . . . if it isn't drought, then it's floods."

A twenty-two-year-old female from Huai'an in Subei [northern Jiangsu Province], now a restaurant worker in Nanjing, is paid 80 yuan (U.S.$9.60) a month and gets her meals free, with no rent to pay. She sleeps in the restaurant, on a chair; works 5:15 a.m. to 10 p.m., with no days off. The job is unsuitable, she laments, and she wants to go back home. But there's nothing to do there. Her older sister, unmarried, sits at home, completely idle.

An eighteen-year-old shoe repairer from Zhejiang left home after primary school and came directly to Tianjin, five years ago. He came to make money, since he can't make any tending the fields. I asked, "Why come so far?" "The further the better," was his rejoinder. "Why not go on to Tibet, if that's the case?" I wondered. He ran out of travel money, was his only excuse. Does he have future plans? "Live one day, write off one day," he quips.

As China entered the twenty-first century, it swam in an ever-expanding sea of consumerism. In such a society there was a risk of everything being seen as a commodity, including relationships with others. In the description of the Chinese version of Monopoly (called "Entrepreneur" in Chinese), taken from blurbs on the game box, it is apparent that under the contemporary conditions in China even this game can be instructive. The Chinese underneath the drawing of the entrepreneur reads, "Popular around the world; suitable for old and young alike."

In the game of skill, "Entrepreneur," the basic elements of the original American edition have been altered in accordance with our country's national situation. Part of the rules have also been altered to make the game easier to learn, and therefore more popular.

In 1987 and early 1990, we launched the first and second editions of the game and received widespread accolades from consumers. This is because it is a leisure item that can be enjoyed by old and young alike, but it has particular social benefits in that it fosters the intelligence of young students. Furthermore, it is not merely a game for whiling away the hours, for by playing this game, you will learn a little correct business knowledge and sharpen your judgment and bold enterprising spirit, as well as the enterprising spirit of "Entrepreneur." Because of this, its benefits to the market economy and society are incomparable.

The following account of the lifestyle of a rich entrepreneur by American journalists James and Ann Tyson in their 1995 book, *Chinese Awakenings*, reveals the nature of entrepreneurship in contemporary China at a time of great economic flux.

Gazing at the red earth of his native land from the penthouse balcony of his headquarters, Zhang does not seem inspired by the heroics of Mao and other Communist insurgents. Instead, the short, bald, and bubbly millionaire raises a snifter of cognac toward the fiery sun as it sets between Nanchang and Jinggang Mountain [in the province of Jiangxi] and toasts a different sort of idol. "In the future I will face a lot of political and financial difficulties, but if I bravely face these challenges then I will be a real man—like Lee Iacocca [former CEO of Chrysler Corporation]," he said. . . .

As the youngest of seven children from a poor farming family, Zhang shows how China's speedy development is driven by the obsessive desire of Chinese to escape centuries of penury and frequent famine. Zhang's story is woven with political satire worthy of Gogol: He has mastered the absurd task of justifying his riches in a totalitarian state that was founded on the ideal of equal wealth for all. . . .

Zhang is one of thousands of go-getters who have amassed millions since senior leader Deng Xiaoping checked the powers of bureaucrats and allowed the market to animate the economy. But few people in China are as rich as Zhang. . . .

The Tysons go on to explain how Zhang came into his wealth and the hoops he had to jump through to start his business. In the 1970s Zhang set up a wooden-products company specializing in intricate woodcarvings. With cash from the sale of his uncle's home, he built a workshop; with sheer determination and considerable charisma, he gathered a workforce and enlisted master-carvers to train them. He then had to get approval from local authorities by calling it a "collective enterprise."

In his rural backwater, Zhang constantly had to face down petty officials and Maoist fanatics. Officials hindered Zhang's supply of wood. They routinely shut off his electricity. They denied him financing. They withheld rail transport to Shanghai. . . . In April 1974 a leading party official of Yujiang county criticized Zhang before 1,000 Maoist devotees as a "new-born, bourgeois thing" and "a capitalist wearing a red hat. . . ."

In 1982, after investigating the market and manufacturers for Buddhist shrines in Tokyo and Osaka, Zhang realized he had enough highly skilled carvers to challenge his competitors from Taiwan and South Korea. He had already launched more than thirty carving workshops in Yujiang and Dongyang and upgraded the quality of his craftsmanship. His lower labor costs enabled him to underprice his rivals. Moreover, through wily negotiating he engineered an arrangement by which he became the sole supplier to three Japanese shrine manufacturers. . . . Later, he invested 12 million yen in a joint venture with an Osaka firm to produce detailed black and gold lacquerware shrines that sell in Japan for more than $10,000 each.

Commanding a large chunk of the Japanese market and the political support of Beijing, Zhang's company took off. From 1982 until 1988, the profits of the Yinghai Wooden Products Trade Company annually rocketed an average of 143 percent. Still local leftists continued to badger him. The Jiangxi Province party secretary accused him of profiteering and other alleged illegalities in June 1985. . . . An investigation, however, turned up no evidence. . . .

The . . . pretentiousness of Zhang [is] typical of the nouveaux riches. There are more than 5,000 other millionaires throughout China [as of 1995]. . . . Some 70 percent of these upstart vulgarians are illiterate or semi-literate, according to official figures. These *da kuan*, "big bucks," flaunt their cash with a crude and comical ostentation.

A modern apartment building looms behind an old courtyard in Beijing. As China modernizes, contrasts such as this are commonplace. In the face of urban development, the old alleyways of Beijing, which once led to homes grouped around courtyards, are disappearing.

Since Zhang first struck his fortune, his lifestyle has always had a plutocratic glint. He hunts for wild boar and pheasant in nearby hills and plays billiards in his penthouse. He sent his oldest child to Shanghai for schooling and owns eight cars. He asked the province for permission to purchase a helicopter and at one time owned several homes in cities throughout China decked out with the newest electronic hardware. He also planned to lay out his own golf course and acquire a jet. At first he indulged in his little excesses with a wide-eyed, gee-whiz innocence and endearing self-deprecation. But now he increasingly goes about such pastimes with a jaded air.

Zhang reveals his new haughtiness in subtle ways. Before Zhang quit smoking on May 1, 1992, he switched from Marlboros to 555s, an upscale British brand. He has put risers in his shoes. He has grown long nails on his little fingers that preclude carving and other manual labor; the nails have traditionally been a badge in China of affluence and leisure. . . .

[On Shenzhen Bay] . . . he has built an $800,000 "holiday home." The three-story Spanish-style house overlooks a beach. . . .

Zhang shows off his Shenzhen house with his typical swashbuckler bearing. It is decorated in a hybrid of Italian baroque and Cantonese kitsch. Parquet woodwork in rich brown hues spreads across the floors to every corner. Chandeliers dangle like large globs of glass firing a rainbow, carnival dazzle. Heavy pleated fabric of plush red surrounds the windows in a buxom display. Gigantic specimens of finely detailed woodwork—phoenixes, dragons, and demure fleeing maidens—lunge and leap across tabletops and up the walls. . . .

Outside, a patio overlooks a fountain, a row of manicured hedges, and lush, close-clipped grass. Off to the side, across a white marble wall, a marble dragon's head gapes from a marble bas-relief of two dragons bearing a pearl. The head of the mythical beast spews water into a swimming pool.

One of the offshoots of the reforms was the creation of a widespread mania to get rich. This craze for money and a better lifestyle produced corruption at many levels of society. Some believed that China lost its moral standards and was culturally adrift. This radio report about a December 1990 meeting on "building a spiritual civilization" in Nanjing reveals this growing concern. The CCP speaker, Shen Daren, never defines what he means by "spiritual civilization," itself an indication that the Chinese are uncertain about which ideas and values are most important for the new China. As would a skillful politician, the speaker avoids specifics and speaks only in generalities.

A four-day meeting on building spiritual civilization and antipornography work in the province ended in Nanjing on the afternoon of December 10. Shen Daren, secretary of the provincial CCP committee, delivered an important speech at the meeting.

He pointed out: The key to furthering the building of spiritual civilization and antipornography work lies in the full implementation of relevant policies. Shen Daren said: It is our unswerving principle to pay equal attention to persisting in building both socialist material and spiritual civilizations. When pursuing our socialist modernization drive, we must persist in making economic construction our central task and strive to develop social productive forces. Making economic construction our central task, however, does not mean we can be lax about building spiritual civilization. The building of spiritual civilization will guarantee that we take the correct direction in building material civilization. The development of material civilization requires spiritual and intellectual support from spiritual civilization. . . .

First, we must formulate a good plan for building spiritual civilization and include it in the overall scheme of the Eighth Five-Year Plan [1991–95] and the ten-year strategy for economic and social development. Second, we must pay particular attention to doing well in ideological and moral education. Third, we should organize well the activities for launching the building of spiritual civilization among the masses, continue proven methods for activities, constantly enlarge the scope of activities, and improve the forms of activities. Fourth, we must continuously do a good job in antipornography work. Great efforts should be made to effect a thriving socialist culture.

Chapter Twelve

Political Authoritarianism

If the Deng Xiaoping and Jiang Zemin regimes identified themselves with and fostered liberal economic reforms, they just as clearly identified themselves with political authoritarianism. As the Communist regime aged, its concern focused ever more fixedly on keeping itself in power.

Deng came to power in 1978. Perhaps to separate himself from the Maoist political record, he opted to allow comments on the party-state. He reportedly said, "The masses should be allowed to vent their grievances." Deng apparently—and naively—believed that criticisms would remain within the limits that the party considered acceptably mild. Posters with criticisms of the party-state went up on a wall near Tiananmen Square; it was promptly dubbed Democracy Wall. The level of criticism rose quickly. The poster-writer who became most outspoken was Wei Jingsheng, an electrician in his late 20s. Deng had earlier called for the Four Modernizations—in agriculture, industry, national defense, and science and technology. Wei now called for a Fifth Modernization: democracy. Deng and the party felt that the growing attacks could not continue. The government began arresting poster-writers, including Wei, in late March 1979. Wei was convicted and sent to prison for fifteen years. Democracy Wall was closed.

As the party-state undertook economic reforms, it opened its doors to the outside world. Foreign firms could invest in China's special economic zones. Opening a window to the modern world also made it easier to acquire the computers and high technology necessary for developing the country. Spokesmen for the government said that mosquitoes and flies (that is, unwanted ideas) might come in this open window, but they declared that bad elements could easily be swatted down. The government launched two campaigns in the early 1980s. The first, the Campaign against Bourgeois Liberalization in

In an act of bravery and daring, a single man blocks a tank column in Beijing on June 4, 1989, after a night of pro-democracy student protests. After stopping the column for a few minutes, he was whisked away by friends.

1981, was primarily an attack on writers and intellectuals, accusing them of upholding capitalist values. Specifically suspect were any Western political values that might inch their way into the Chinese political system. Without fail, conservatives used "pornography" as the name under which they attacked bourgeois values. The second, the Campaign against Spiritual Pollution in 1983, was almost a carbon copy of the first. Conservatives ranted that the reforms were leading to pornography and "box office" values—derived from the entertainment world—in literature and art. In the end, the top party and government leaders stopped the conservatives out of fear that foreigners might stop investing in China in the face of such anti-foreign rhetoric.

Late in 1986, student demonstrations erupted on campuses across China, calling for reforms both at the colleges themselves and in the government. The protests were halted, but they claimed a victim: CCP General Secretary Hu Yaobang, who had been a supporter of some student demands and a spokesman for general political reform, was ousted. Hu's sudden death in April 1989 became the stimulus for the extraordinary events of April through June, often called the Beijing Spring, though the events spread far beyond the capital.

Citizens inspect an armored vehicle that was destroyed during the overnight fighting between the civilians and the military in June of 1989.

The huge demonstrations that began in late April came in the name of "democracy," though exactly what the demonstrators meant by that term is rather hard to determine. The protests erupted from many social and political developments, including the economic problems of inflation, declining wages, and increasing unemployment; growing awareness of governmental corruption; and the government's resistance to political reforms. Tens of thousands of students marched to Tiananmen Square. The party's condemnation of their actions as "turmoil" only heightened the determination of students and they began to set up their own autonomous associations. When student interest seemed to wane in mid-May, student leaders called a hunger strike. From this point, the students occupied the square, living there around the clock. The hunger strike brought the movement much support and the increasing participation of workers, professional groups, and general citizens. It also helped stimulate nationwide interest: by the end of May, 3 million people outside of Beijing had demonstrated in support of the students.

For the government, the demonstrations and protests were a sickening nightmare. The Soviet Union's President Mikhail Gorbachev arrived on May 15 to begin normal diplomatic relations with China. Because the demonstrations upstaged the normalization, the episode was a huge humiliation for Deng Xiaoping. The regime's last major supporter of student interests, CCP chairman Zhao Ziyang, was ousted from the Politburo in late May. Early on the morning of June 4, the People's Liberation Army cleared the streets and the square, killing many people as it approached the square. The world watched with horror as brutal military force crushed the movement.

During the 1990s the Chinese leadership, the object of deep criticism around the world, played on-again, off-again repression. Dissidents were rounded up and jailed. Some were released at times when their release might serve as gestures to the Western nations who condemned China for its violations of the political rights of its citizens; then some were picked up and jailed once again. In 1999 about 10,000 members of the Falun Gong, "the Buddhist Law Sect," demonstrated in front of the CCP compound, Zhongnanhai, because of the treatment of their leader in the press. This action frightened the Communist leadership, for it was the first large protest since 1989, and millions of people in China adhered to this sect.

Western nations hoped that China's continuing economic liberalization would lead to more liberal political institutions. In Western political history that is what happened. The question remains whether this kind of pattern is peculiar to the West and might not apply in the non-Western world. Whatever the case, China's increasing involvement on the world stage means that its treatment of the issue of human rights will be all more evident and important.

Political Dissent

In this essay, dissident Wei Jingsheng pointedly attacks the policies of Deng Xiaoping. This essay was part of the prosecution's case against Wei in 1979; the state argued that it was evidence of his "counter-revolutionary agitation and propaganda" and his "incitement to overthrow the dictatorship of

the proletariat." It was first published in March 1979 in the journal *Tanguo* [Explorations].

Everyone in China knows that the Chinese social system is not democratic, and that this lack of democracy has severely stunted every aspect of the country's social development over the past thirty years. In the face of this hard fact, there are two choices before the Chinese people. Either to reform the social system if they want to develop their society and seek a swift increase in prosperity and economic resources; or, if they are content with a continuation of the Mao Zedong brand of proletarian dictatorship, then they cannot even talk of democracy, nor will they be able to realize the modernization of their lives and resources.

Where is China heading and in what sort of society do the people hope to live and work? The answer can be seen in the mood of the majority. It is this mood that brought about the present democratic movement. With the denial of Mao Zedong's style of dictatorship as its very prerequisite, the aim of this movement is to reform the social system and thereby enable the Chinese people to increase production and develop their lives to the full in a democratic social environment. This aim is not just the aim of a few isolated individuals but represents a whole trend in the development of Chinese society. . . .

Does Deng Xiaoping want democracy? No, he does not. He is unwilling to comprehend the misery of the common people. He is unwilling to allow the people to regain those powers usurped by ambitious careerists. He describes the struggle for democratic rights—a movement launched spontaneously by the people—as the actions of troublemakers who must be repressed. To resort to such measures to deal with people who criticize mistaken policies and demand social development shows that the government is very afraid of this popular movement. . . .

After [Deng] was reinstated in 1975, it seemed he was unwilling to follow Mao Zedong's dictatorial system and would instead care for the interests of the people. So the people eagerly looked up to him in the hope that he would realize their aspirations. . . . But was such support vested in his person alone? Certainly not. If he now wants to discard his mask and take steps to suppress the democratic movement then he certainly does not merit the people's trust and support. From his behavior it is clear that he is neither concerned with democracy nor does he any longer protect the people's interests. By deceiving the people to win their confidence he is following the path to dictatorship.

With the Gate of Heavenly Peace and the Goddess of Democracy (modeled after the Statue of Liberty) in the background, students encamped in tents cover Tiananmen Square in May 1989. After six weeks of protest, trash and garbage in the square created squalid living conditions.

It has been demonstrated countless times throughout China's history that once the confidence of the people has been gained by deception, the dictators work without restraint—for as the ancients said, "He who can win the people's minds, can win the empire." Once masters of the nation, their private interests inevitably conflict with those of the people, and they must use repression against those who are struggling for the interests of the people themselves. So the crux of the matter is not who becomes master of the nation, but rather that the people must maintain firm control over their own nation, for this is the very essence of democracy. . . .

Furthering reforms within the social system and moving Chinese politics toward democracy are prerequisites for solving the social and economic problems that confront China today. Only through elections can the leadership gain the people's voluntary cooperation and bring their initiative into play. Only when the people enjoy complete freedom and expression can they help their leaders to analyze and solve problems. Cooperation, together with the policies formulated and carried out by the people, are necessary for the highest degree of working efficiency and the achievement of ideal results.

This is the only road along which China can make progress. Under present-day conditions, it is an extremely difficult path.

Opposition to party corruption became an increasingly common theme in writings about political realities in the 1980s and 1990s. "General, You Can't Do This," a poem written by Ye Wenfu in 1979, was a reaction against an actual event: an old general who had an outstanding revolutionary résumé ordered the destruction of a kindergarten in order to build a mansion on its site. This picture of how revolutionary leadership had lost the essence of what "revolutionary" meant was publicly attacked by none other than Deng Xiaoping himself. The government forbade Ye to publish the poem and imprisoned him in a dwelling where wintertime temperatures fell to below zero.

My high and mighty General,
You rode in battle for decades.
What was it ultimately for?
Ignoring people's sufferings,
You!
Is not the conscience of a Communist
Rebuked by truth?
Could it be that you firmly believe
That the law
Is but a card in your hand,

Wei Jingsheng, a Democracy Wall dissident during the 1970s, was jailed for fourteen years. In 1995, when this picture captured him in court, he was being sentenced to another term. In 1998 he was released and left for the United States.

Or at most
A gentle breeze on a summer night?
Could it be that
All the pores of your body
Are now impermeable to even a drop
Of Premier Zhou's virtue?
For your own Modernization
The kindergarten was torn down
The children forsaken!
Snowy-haired one
How many more years of comfort can you have?
Tomorrow is the children's.

What right do you have
To brazenly squander
The blood of martyrs
The people's faith in the party
The hardworking sweat of the laborers?!
Must the Four Modernizations,
Solemnly proclaimed
By Premier Zhou,
The Four Modernizations for which
The party and the people,
Enduring ten years' wounds,
Are sweating and bleeding
In front of furnaces,
In the fields,
Be the greasy crumbs
And
Spittle,
That you,
Belching,
Casually toss to us.

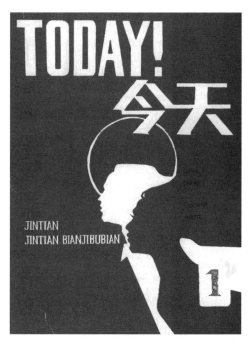

Focusing on the Democracy Wall, Jintian [Today] was one of the smaller magazines published during the brief period of political openness between 1978 and 1979.

During and immediately following the events of Beijing Spring, most people in and outside of China believed that the only conflicts were between the students (and their allies) and the government. Later it became clear that both "sides"—students and government—were divided among themselves as well. In the government, hardliners not willing to give an inch fought and overwhelmed those who early on had counseled moderation in dealing with the students. Among the students, there were those who were willing to

Many people criticized the unwillingness of some student leaders to compromise in order to achieve at least some of what they desired. Much of the criticism of Chai Ling's zealotry was leveled at her in the documentary film The Gate of Heavenly Peace. *The film was produced by Carma Hinton, the daughter of an American, William Hinton, long known for his friendship with party leaders and support of the Communist movement, at least in its early days. Chai's defensive reaction in June 1995 was published in the journal* Tiananmen.

Certain individuals have, for the sake of gaining the approval of the authorities, racked their brains for ways and means to come up with policies for them. And there is another person with a pro-Communist history [Carma Hinton] who has been hawking [her] documentary film for crude commercial gain by taking things out of context and trying to reveal something new, unreasonably turning history on its head and calling black white.

Premier Li Peng speaks with student protest leader Wang Dan at a meeting that Li called in the Great Hall of the People to defuse the tension between government and protestors. If anything, the meeting was counterproductive, as students disrespectfully lectured Li, angering him further.

negotiate and compromise with the government officials as long as the students earned some some concessions. But they were opposed by hardliners among the student ranks, zealots whose position is perhaps best put forward by revolutionary Chai Ling. Because of the power of these hardliners, several government initiatives to negotiate an end the standoff came to nothing. This interview, which Chai Ling gave to Philip Cunningham, an American journalist, was recorded in a Beijing hotel room on May 28, 1989, and reveals the depth of her revolutionary feelings.

Chai Ling: My fellow students keep asking me, "What should we do next? What can we accomplish?" I feel so sad, because how can I tell them that what we are actually hoping for is bloodshed, the moment when the government is ready to butcher the people brazenly? Only when the square is awash with blood will the people of China open their eyes. Only then will they really be united. But how can I explain any of this to my fellow students?

And what is truly sad is that some students, and famous, well-connected people, are working hard to help the government, to prevent it from taking such measures. For the sake of their selfish interests and their private dealings, they are trying to cause our movement to disintegrate and get us out of the square before the government becomes so desperate that it takes action. . . .

That's why I feel so sad, because I can't say all this to my fellow students. I can't tell them straight out that we must use our blood and our lives to wake up the people. Of course, they will be willing. But they are still so young

(cries). . . .

Interviewer: Are you going to stay in the square yourself?

Chai Ling: No.

Interviewer: Why?

Chai Ling: Because my situation is different. My name is on the government's blacklist. I'm not going to be destroyed by this government. I want to live. Anyway, that's how I feel about it. I don't know whether people will say I'm selfish. I believe people have to continue the work I started. A democracy movement can't succeed with only one person. I hope you don't report what I've just said for the time being, OK?

Hou Dejian was a pop music star in Taiwan from the early 1980s on. In 1983, he left Taiwan for the mainland, where he retained his superstar status. He also became known as a critic of the state and was joined in that role by China's most famous rock star, Cui Jian. Hou became a participant in the events at Tiananmen Square shortly before the crackdown. The government forced Hou back to Taiwan in the middle of 1990, where he both wrote and performed the songs "Heirs of the Dragon" and "Carry On."

"Heirs of the Dragon," was heard so often in the 1980s that it became almost a pop national anthem. Hou changed the last stanza on the night of June 3, before the troops struck.

In the far-off East flows a river called the Yangtze.
In the far-off East flows the Yellow River too.
I've never seen the beauty of the Yangtze
Though often have sailed it in my dreams.
And while I've never heard the roar of the Yellow River.
It pounds against its shores in my dreams.

In the ancient East there is a dragon;
China is its name.
In the ancient East there lives a people,
The dragon's heirs every one.
Under the claws of this mighty dragon I grew up
And its heir I have become.
Like it or not—
Once and forever, an heir of the dragon.

It was a hundred years ago on a quiet night,
The deep dark night shattered by gunfire.
Enemies on all sides, the sword of the dictator.
For how many years did those gunshots resound?
So many years and so many years more.
Mighty dragon, open your eyes
For now and evermore, open your eyes.

Hou sang the second song, "Carry On," in August 1989 at the Australian embassy in Beijing.

We must carry on.
Go on living.
Do it well.

What's the sound of life?
The melody of age?
I cannot sing an illness,
I'm not willing to die.

I'm afraid.
Is there really a God above?
I doubt it.
Does anybody believe in anything anymore?
Why is life so unfair?
Why can't things work out the way we'd like?

I'm sick of that ancient and boring game.
I love you, more than anyone else.
But there's just one thing—I love myself even more.
I can't help loving myself more.

What are the melodies of love?
The acoustics of anger?
I cannot sing my grief,
I forgot long ago what happiness is.

We played too many games these past few years
We only just discovered that someone else made up the rules.
I protest against the unfair rules
I refuse to play a game I'll never win.

To carry on is my last remaining right.
Don't tell me to give it up.
No matter what others have to say,
We must carry on.

We must carry on,
And not bring grief upon ourselves again.
We must go on living,
We must carry on.

The Falun Gong

Near the end of April 1999, more than ten thousand members of the Falun Gong staged a sit-in on the streets outside the compound where Chinese leaders live. They were protesting the negative treatment in the Chinese press of their leader, Li Hongzhi, who is seen as a cult leader by the

Falun Gong members practice meditation and exercise outside the National Theater in Taipei, Taiwan. China still sees members as dangerous to the state and therefore set out to control the movement through intimidation and mass arrests.

Chinese authorities. It was the first large act of civil disobedience since the tragic events in the spring of 1989, and it frightened party leaders. Falun Gong, which was not founded until 1992, had grown explosively. It is based on traditional Chinese ideas about *qigong,* "energy." The goal is to heighten one's energy level in order to increase individual well-being through meditation and exercise. The government itself estimated there were 2 million members, while Falun Gong claimed up to 10 million. Li Hongzhi describes the general goals of his teaching in his 2001 book *Falun Gong*.

Falun Gong is a special cultivation practice in the Buddha School. Its uniqueness distinguishes itself from other regular cultivation methods of the Buddha School. Falun Gong is an advanced cultivation system. In the past, it served as an intensive cultivation method that required practitioners with extremely high *Xinxing,* "mind-nature," or great inborn quality. For this reason, this cultivation practice is hard to popularize. However, in order for more practitioners to improve their levels, to know about this cultivation system, and also to meet the demands of numerous devoted practitioners, I have compiled a set of cultivation exercises suitable for the public. In spite of the modifications, these exercises still far exceed average cultivation systems in terms of what they offer and the levels at which they can be practiced.

Falun Gong practitioners not only can quickly develop their energy potency and supernormal capabilities, but also can acquire a *Falun*, "law wheel," that is incomparable in power in a very short period of time. Once formed, the Falun rotates automatically in a practitioner's lower abdomen at all times. It incessantly collects energy from the universe and transforms it into *Gong*, "cultivation energy," in a practitioner's *Benti*, "true being". Thus, the goal of "the *Fa*, 'law,' refines the practitioner" will be achieved.

Falun Gong consists of five sets of movements, which are Buddha Showing A Thousand Hands Exercise, Falun Standing Stance Exercise, Penetrating the Two Cosmic Extremes Exercise, Falun Heavenly Circulation Exercise, and Way of Strengthening Divine Powers Exercise.

Well aware that through the centuries several Chinese dynasties had been brought down by sects similar to the Falun Gong, the government began a crackdown that continued through at least 2003. In July 1999, it banned the organization, alleging that it had participated in illegal activities (one being that it was not properly registered with the government). It also claimed that Falun Gong was promoting superstitions, inciting disturbances, and risking social stability.

The government made much use of stories of people who allegedly rejected or did not seek medical advice because of their allegiance to the sect and then died; the government thus claimed that the sect was destructive to people and Chinese society. The government intended to stem the interest in the growing movement through its use of anti-sect propaganda. These accounts appeared in 1999 in the official English language periodical, *Beijing Review.*

Some Cases of Sickness, Handicap, and Death Resulting from Falun Gong Practice

Oil Worker Ma Jianmin Committed Hara-Kiri

Ma Jianmin, 54, a retired worker from the North China oilfield.

According to his family, Ma was often in a trance and became distraught after two years of practicing Falun Gong. He insisted that he had a "Dharma Wheel" (Falun) in his stomach. On September 4, 1998, Ma died at home after cutting open his abdomen with a pair of scissors to look for it.

Gao Encheng Leapt to His Death from Building

Gao, 42, a [member of the] staff of the Industrial and Commercial Agency of Tianbai Township of Kaixian county, Chongqing Municipality, and also a person-in-charge of a Falun Gong practice group.

In November 1997, Gao and his wife (Li Xiaofen, 25 and jobless) began to practice Falun Gong. They bought related books and practiced every morning and night. From then on, Gao, who used to be strong and tough, turned quiet and unsociable, often practicing alone at home. Gao held a strong belief in Li Hongzhi's promise that, after reaching a certain level, he would become immortal.

On November 2, 1998, Gao drew out all his bank savings and gave 1800 yuan to his daughter born by his ex-wife, saying he had become immortal. Later, he gave some money to his parents and mother-in-law. On the night of November 5, Gao told another person-in-charge he dreamed the night before his wife had been a poisonous snake in the former life. He then cried at home for most of the night. At 10:00 the next morning, Gao announced at his work unit's meeting: "Man's nature is good at birth. You all can't understand it. But my thought has reached such a zenith after only one year's practice of Falun Gong." Hearing his colleagues refutation, Gao said, "I don't speak to you mortals. Only my son, Gao Xiong, can read my mind." After returning home, Gao practiced Falun Gong first, then he jumped from the fourth floor of a building while holding his son in his arms. His colleagues immediately called for the doctor, but Gao's wife refused to allow any treatment, saying, "Li Hongzhi will protect him." Although their son was saved, Gao died due to lack of treatment.

Wu Deqiao of Jiangsu Province Killed His Wife

Wu Deqiao, 36, a clerk of a supply and marketing cooperative of Wujiang City.

Wu began to practice Falun Gong in February 1998. On the night of February 25, while he was practicing, he felt somebody was going to murder him, so he shouted wildly "earthquake, earthquake." He even ran to the local police substation shouting these words. He was later sent to a mental hospital by his family. The next night Wu again practiced Falun Gong at home, believing he had become a Buddha. When his wife, Shen Yuzhen, tried to stop him, Wu felt that having a woman around would affect his practice. So, he chopped her to death with a kitchen knife.

Chapter Thirteen

China and the World at the Turn of the Century

There was jubilation in the streets after the news that Beijing had been selected as the site for the summer Olympic games in 2008. That joy overcame the bitterness that had festered since the International Olympic Committee had turned China down for the games in 2000, a loss that many Chinese blamed on the United States. The Olympic stakes were high for China because they symbolized the present and future of China's role in the world.

China's experience with imperialism—the nineteenth-century wars against various Western nations and Japan, culminating in the ignominious Boxer uprising and consequent foreign invasion—had humiliated the Central Kingdom, as China had called itself at times of power in the past. Indeed, after the Twenty-One Demands in 1915, China had annually commemorated the date as one of national humiliation. China's twentieth-century history in relation to the world was a story, first, of China's throwing out the Western nations that had taken advantage of its weakness, and, second, of China's efforts to emerge on the world stage as a respected leader among the world's foremost nations.

We can discuss China's relations with other parts of the world by looking at four different regions. The first region is actually inside China: non-Han Chinese ethnic groups who live in what are called autonomous regions. The largest autonomous regions are Tibet, or Xizang, as it is known by many in China, and far-western China's

Chinese President Jiang Zemin speaks in Hong Kong during ceremonies marking Hong Kong's return to Chinese rule. The agreements between the PRC and Great Britain specified that Hong Kong could retain its own political system for fifty years.

Xinjiang Province, which is the home to the Uighurs, a traditionally Muslim ethnic group with a population of more than 1 million. China has claimed authority in Tibet since the eighteenth century. In the early twentieth century, because of pressure from Great Britain, China had lost the control it had wielded. But throughout the turbulence of the warlord years, the Sino-Japanese War and the Civil War, all major Chinese political leaders and both major parties were determined to reassert control over the Himalayan country. China secured control in 1950–51, and its power was solidified in 1959, when the Chinese crushed a rebellion and Tibet's religious and political leader, the Dalai Lama, fled to India. In Xinjiang the threat of Muslim separatists loomed ever more serious during the 1980s and 1990s, punctuated with sporadic outbursts of bombings and assassinations. The future of Chinese and Muslim relations there is obviously troubled.

Moving outward, the second region of the world interacting with China includes what has been called "greater China"—Hong

Citizens celebrate in Tiananmen Square on learning of the decision of the International Olympic Committee to award the 2008 Summer Olympics to the PRC.

Kong, Macao, and Taiwan. Though Hong Kong became a part of China in 1997 and Macao in 1999, the issue of Taiwan remains the chief focus in Chinese foreign policy. Fear that Taiwan might declare its independence from China has led to harsh verbal condemnations of the Taiwanese leadership and to several episodes of war games off the Taiwan coast. The fact that President Chen Shuibian, elected in 2000, belonged to a political party that called for independence only increased Beijing's unease and fear about the Taiwan situation.

The third region is China's East Asian neighbors—Japan, Korea, and Vietnam, those nations that traditionally formed China's cultural sphere of action. By the turn of the century, China had closest relationships with the two Koreas. North Korea had been an important ally of China's since China entered the Korean War in late 1950; their ideological similarities had generally been as close as their geographical proximity. In the 1990s South Korea became an important trade partner and its companies became significant investors in economic development in China's Shandong Province. Although China's relationship with Japan was marked by substantial trade and investment, especially in southern Manchuria, the nightmare of Japan's actions in China during World War II remained very much in Chinese minds. Outrage erupted in China over Japanese textbook revisions that downplayed Japan's role during the war and over Japanese political leaders' visits to Japanese shrines where war dead, including those convicted of war crimes, are buried. Relations with Vietnam were the coldest. China's 1979 invasion of Vietnam to "teach it a lesson" after it took over Cambodia (a Chinese ally) put relations into the deep freeze, where they remained.

The fourth region encompasses the powers beyond—the rest of the countries of the world. Most important are the United States and Russia. Relations between China and Russia have been cordial since 1989, with trade increasing and the Russians' promising assistance in the building of the colossal Three Gorges Dam. The extraordinarily long border that the two nations share suggests that this relationship will remain an important one. However, it is the relationship between China and the United States that is pivotal. The Chinese distrust of the United States stems not so much from fear of outright imperialism as it does from the almost unanimously held belief among the Chinese that the United States does not want to see China emerge to take its rightful place among the community of nations. China blamed pressure from the United States for its losing out to Sydney for the 2000 Olympic games. Though it was in a NATO-led campaign, China blamed the United States for intentionally bombing the Chinese embassy in Belgrade, Yugoslavia, in 1999 during the war over Kosovo. In 2001 a U.S. spy plane conducting surveillance along the Chinese coast landed on Hainan Island after it was damaged by a mid-air collision with a Chinese plane; China held the crew for interrogation for ten days. Incidents like these have only increased animosity between the two nations; and as a result, relations have run hot and cold. Taiwan remains the sticking point in the relationship because leaders in the United States have both treaty and moral commitments to Taiwan. Any military attack by Beijing on the island would almost certainly bring a military response by the United States.

The United States has continually cried out against China's human rights record. U.S. spokesmen railed against Chinese repression of dissidents, the use of torture to extract confessions in criminal cases, and the lack of civil liberties (freedom of assembly, freedom of the press, and political rights). The Chinese responded that "human rights" includes much more than political rights, that economic livelihood and opportunity and other concerns also fall within the rubric of human rights.

Ending the Imperialist Era: The Retrocession of Hong Kong

Hong Kong was composed of three parts: Hong Kong Island and Kowloon, which were ceded to Great Britain in the mid-nineteenth century, and the New Territories, which had been leased by Britain in 1898 for a period of ninety-nine years. Negotiating with Britain in the early 1980s, the Chinese insisted on the return of all three parts of Hong Kong, not just the New Territories. Britain agreed, though the thirteen years between the agreement and the Chinese takeover were filled with more than a little tension. The Chinese were irritated that the British Governor Chris Patten tried to cause trouble by democratizing the Hong Kong government more than Britain had done in its all its 130 years of control.

Hong Kong residents were wary and afraid about what would happen when the Chinese at last took over. When the Chinese took control on July 1, 1997, perhaps the greatest symbol of China as the prey of imperialist powers was gone.

A junk sails from the Kowloon peninsula toward Hong Kong island. The peninsula, island, and the New Territories that made up Hong Kong reverted to the control of the People's Republic on July 1, 1997.

The last such symbol, the peninsula of Macao west of Hong Kong, returned to Chinese control on December 20, 1999.

Signed in Beijing, the 1984 agreement between China and Great Britain on the ceding of Hong Kong to China spells out the conditions for the return.

(1) The Government of the People's Republic of China declares that to recover the Hong Kong area (including Hong Kong Island, Kowloon, and the New Territories, herein after referred to as Hong Kong) is the common aspiration of the entire Chinese people and that it has decided to resume the exercise of sovereignty over Hong Kong with effect from 1 July 1997.

(2) The Government of the United Kingdom declares that it will restore Hong Kong to the People's Republic of China with effect from 1 July 1997.

(3) The Government of the People's Republic of China declares that the basic policies of the People's Republic of China regarding Hong Kong are as follows:

(1) Upholding national unity and territorial integrity and taking account of the history of Hong Kong and its realities, the People's Republic of China has decided to establish . . . a Hong Kong Special Administrative Region. . . .

(2) The Hong Kong Special Administrative Region will enjoy a high degree of autonomy except in foreign and defense affairs, which are the responsibility of the Central People's Government.

(3) The laws currently in force in Hong Kong will remain basically unchanged.

(4) The Government of the Hong Kong Special Administrative Region will be composed of local inhabitants. Their chief executive will be appointed by the Central People's Government on the basis of the results of elections or consultations to be held locally.

(5) The current social and economic systems in Hong Kong will remain unchanged, and so will the lifestyle. Rights and freedoms, including those of the person, of speech, of the press, of assembly, of association, of travel, of movement, of correspondence, of strike, of choice of occupation, of academic research and of religious belief will be insured by law in the Hong Kong Special Administrative Region. Private property, ownership of enterprises, legitimate right of inheritance and foreign investment will be protected by law.

(6) The Hong Kong Special Administrative Region will retain the status of free port and a separate customs territory.

(7) The Hong Kong Special Administrative Region will retain the status of an international financial center, and its markets for foreign exchange, gold, securities and futures will continue. . . .

(8) The Hong Kong Special Administrative Region will have independent finances. The Central People's Government will not levy taxes on the Hong Kong Special Administrative Region.

(11) The maintenance of public order in the Hong Kong Special Administrative Region will be the responsibility of the government of the Hong Kong Special Administrative Region.

(12) The above-stated policies of the People's Republic of China regarding Hong Kong . . . will remain unchanged for fifty years.

Language and Flag
In addition to Chinese, English may also be used in organs of government and in the courts in the Hong Kong Special Administrative Region.

Apart from displaying the national flag and national emblem of the People's Republic of China, the Hong Kong Special Administrative Region may use a regional flag and emblem of its own.

Charges and countercharges between China and Great Britain marked the years between the agreement and the transfer of power. This newspaper report from the *South China Morning Post* on December 4, 1992, notes British fears

Chinese troops arrive in the vicinity of Hong Kong just before China took control of Hong Kong in 1997.

about the extent China would go to block any British efforts to institute democratic changes in Hong Kong.

Britain's former China policy chief yesterday warned that Beijing was ready to wreck the economy of Hong Kong rather than back down in its battle to block democratic reforms.

Whoever won the battle of wills between China and Britain, Hong Kong would suffer, he said.

In a major BBC television interview, . . . Sir Percy Craddock, foreign policy advisor to two prime ministers before his retirement this year, said Sino-British tensions over Hong Kong were worse than at any time since the Cultural Revolution.

In grim remarks that contributed to the stock market's devastating 433-point plunge, Sir Percy dismissed as an "economic fallacy" the belief that China would put prosperity above politics in its clash with Britain.

"We encountered it a lot in the main negotiations in 1983–84— the view that economic considerations come first. The Chinese made it abundantly clear that politics comes first," he said.

China was resentful and bitter over the British effort to increase the number of elected seats on the Legislative Council of Hong Kong (LEGCO). Here the Chinese news agency Xinhua reacts to the British efforts in an article published in 1994.

After the seventeenth round of the Sino-British talks on the arrangements for the 1994–95 election in Hong Kong was held, the British side walked away first from the negotiating table and submitted the electoral bill to the Legco despite the earlier statement made by the Chinese side, thus terminating the talks.

Even so, we made it clear repeatedly that for the Chinese side the door for negotiations was open under the prerequisite that the British side must withdraw the submitted partial bill from the Legco. However, the British side has ignored this and clung obstinately to its own course. It has not only had the partial bill passed at the Legco, but also decided unilaterally to make public the contents of the seventeen rounds of the Sino-British talks and to submit the rest of the electoral bill to the Legco, thus closing completely the door for resuming talks. Therefore, the British side should be held fully responsible for ruining the talks.

Taiwan and Tibet

Though both the People's Republic of China (PRC) and the Republic of China (ROC), recognized formally that the civil war had ended and started having cross-strait relations in 1993, the nature of the final settlement between the two entities was far from clear. In Taiwan the decline of the Guomindang (Nationalist Party) and the rise of the Democratic Progressive Party, which called for an independent Taiwan, made Beijing anxious and defensively aggressive. In a radio broadcast on January 31, 1995, Chairman Jiang Zemin set forth the problem from Beijing's perspective.

Taiwan is an integral part of China. A hundred years ago on 17th April 1895, the Japanese imperialists, by waging a war against the corrupt government of the Qing dynasty, forced the latter to sign the Shimonoseki Treaty of national betrayal and humiliation. Under the treaty, Japan seized Taiwan and the Penghu islands, subjecting the people of Taiwan to its colonial rule for half a century. The Chinese people will never forget this humiliating chapter of their history. Fifty years ago, together with the people of other countries, the Chinese people defeated the Japanese imperialists. October 25th 1945 saw the return of Taiwan and the Penghu islands to China and the end of Japan's colonial rule over our compatriots in Taiwan. However, for reasons everybody knows, Taiwan has been severed from the Chinese mainland since

1949. It remains the sacred mission and lofty goal of the entire Chinese people to achieve the reunification of the motherland and promote the all-around revitalization of the Chinese nation.

Since the Standing Committee of the National People's Congress issued its "Message to the Taiwan Compatriots" in January 1979, we have formulated the basic principles of peaceful reunification and "one country, two systems" and a series of policies towards Taiwan. Comrade Deng Xiaoping, the chief architect of China's reform and opening to the outside world, is also the inventor of the great concept of "one country, two systems." With foresight and seeking truth from facts, he put forward a series of important theories and ideas concerning the settlement of the Taiwan question which reflect the distinct features of the times, and defined the guiding principles for the peaceful reunification of the motherland.

Comrade Deng Xiaoping has pointed out that the most important issue is the reunification of the motherland. All descendants of the Chinese nation wish to see China reunified. It is against the will of the Chinese nation to see it divided. There is only one China, and Taiwan is a part of China. We will never allow there to be "two Chinas" or "one China, one Taiwan." We firmly oppose the "independence of Taiwan." There are only two ways to settle the Taiwan question: One is by peaceful means and the other is by non-peaceful means. The way the Taiwan question is to be settled is China's internal affairs [sic], and brooks no foreign interference. We consistently stand for achieving reunification by peaceful means and through negotiations. But we shall not undertake not to use force. Such commitment would only make it impossible to achieve peaceful reunification and could not but lead to the eventual settlement of the question by the use of force. After Taiwan is reunified with the mainland, China will pursue the policy of "one country, two systems." The main part of the country will stick to the socialist system, while Taiwan will retain its current system. "Reunification does not mean that the mainland will swallow up Taiwan, nor does it mean that Taiwan will swallow up the mainland." After Taiwan's reunification with the mainland, its social and economic systems will not change, nor will its way of life and its non-governmental relations with foreign countries, which means that foreign investments in Taiwan and the non-governmental exchanges between Taiwan and other countries will not be affected. As a special administrative region, Taiwan will exercise a high degree of autonomy and enjoy legislative and independent judicial

Much of our experience in Taiwan should be readily understood by people on the mainland. Taking a serious look at Taiwan, they ought to realize the fundamental and serious contradictions inherent in the course their government is pursuing. The "Taiwan experience," or the "Taiwan model," is not for the people of Taiwan alone but for all of China. It will be an essential model for the reunified China. . . . We therefore cannot assent to the one-China formula that is so high-handedly upheld by the PRC authorities.

—President Lee Tung-hui, in *The Road to Democracy: Taiwan's Pursuit of Identity*

This recorded exchange between Mao Zedong and Henry Kissinger in October 1975 reflects the centrality of the role of Taiwan in U.S.-China relations.

Mao: I am going to heaven soon. . . . And when I . . . see God, I'll tell him it's better to have Taiwan under the care of the United States now.

Kissinger: He'll be very astonished to hear that from the Chairman.

Mao: No, because God blesses you, not us. God does not like us because I am a militant warlord, also a communist. That's why he doesn't like me. He likes you.

Kissinger: I've never had the pleasure of meeting him, so I don't know.

We understand that in principle you will not renounce the right to use force. We want you to understand that we will defend Taiwan. Period.

—Speaker of the U.S. House of Representatives Newt Gingrich in Shanghai, March 1997

power, including that of final adjudication. It may also retain its armed forces and administer its party, governmental, and military systems by itself. The central government will not station troops or send administrative personnel there. What is more, a number of posts in the central government will be made available to Taiwan.

From 1949 until 1972 there were few contacts between the United States and China; ambassadorial talks in Warsaw, Poland, took place only sporadically. President Nixon's overtures to Beijing and its receptiveness led to Nixon's trip to China and the signing of the Shanghai Communiqué in 1972. This agreement set forth the U.S. position on China and Taiwan that was maintained into the twenty-first century. Even given Nixon's initiative, it took the United States another seven years, then under President Carter, to recognize the existence of the PRC. Comparing this communiqué with Jiang Zemin's 1995 message to Taiwan makes clear that China's basic position on Taiwan did not change from 1972 through 1995.

There are essential differences between China and the United States in their social systems and foreign policies. However, the two sides agreed that countries regardless of their social systems should conduct their relations on the principle of respect for the sovereignty and territorial integrity of all states, non-aggression against other states, equality and mutual benefit, and peaceful coexistence. International disputes should be settled on this basis, without resorting to the use or threat of force. . . .

The two sides reviewed the long-standing serious disputes between China and the United States. The Chinese side reaffirmed its position: The Taiwan question is the crucial question obstructing the normalization of relations between China and the United States; the Government of the People's Republic of China is the sole legal government of China; Taiwan is a province of China which has long been returned to the motherland; the liberation of Taiwan is China's internal affair in which no other country has the right to interfere; and all U.S. Forces and military installations must be withdrawn from Taiwan. The Chinese Government firmly opposes any activities which aim at the creation of "one China, one Taiwan," "one China, two governments," "two Chinas," an "independent Taiwan" or advocate that the "status of Taiwan remains to be determined."

Chairman Mao Zedong talks with President Richard Nixon in February 1972. Nixon's pathbreaking visit to China was the first step toward the United States's diplomatic recognition of the most populous country in the world.

The U.S. side declared: The United States acknowledges that all Chinese on either side of the Taiwan Strait maintain there is but one China and that Taiwan is a part of China. The United States Government does not challenge that position. It reaffirms its interest in a peaceful settlement of the Taiwan question by the Chinese themselves. With this prospect in mind, it affirms the ultimate objective of the withdrawal of all U.S. Forces and military installations from Taiwan. In the meantime, it will progressively reduce its forces and military installations on Taiwan as the tension in the area diminishes.

When the United States recognized the People's Republic of China in 1979, the U.S. Congress passed the Taiwan Relations Act. The act makes clear that a military effort by the PRC to bring Taiwan into "one China" could lead to a wider war.

[The United States would] consider any effort to determine the future of Taiwan by other than peaceful means . . . a threat to the peace and security of the Western Pacific area and of grave concern to the United States; to provide Taiwan with arms of a defensive character; [and] to maintain the capacity of the United States to resist any resort to force or other forms of coercion that would jeopardize the security or social and economic system of the people of Taiwan.

Although there was a general relaxation of Chinese controls over Tibet from 1979 to 1987, the Chinese grasp was never loose. From China's perspective, retaining control over Tibet was an essential element in maintaining the Chinese nation. Demonstrations in 1987 and 1989 led to the Chinese declaring martial law, but social outbursts continued into the 1990s. The stature of the Dalai Lama grew during these times. He made his case before the world with the lecture he gave up on receiving the Nobel Peace Prize in December 1989, months after the 1989 demonstrations led to the killing or wounding of hundreds of Tibetan protesters.

The awarding of the Nobel Prize to me, a simple monk from faraway Tibet, here in Norway, also fills Tibetans with hope. It means that, despite the fact that we have not drawn attention to our plight by means of violence, we have not been forgotten. . . .

As you know, Tibet has, for forty years, been under foreign occupation. Today, more than a quarter of a million of Chinese troops are stationed in Tibet. Some sources estimate the occupation army to be twice this strength. During this time, Tibetans have been deprived of their most basic human rights, including the right to life, movement, speech, worship, only to mention a few. More than one sixth of Tibet's population of six million died as a direct result of the Chinese invasion and occupation. Even before the Cultural Revolution started, many of Tibet's monasteries, temples, and historic buildings were destroyed. Almost everything that remained was destroyed during the Cultural Revolution. I do not wish to dwell on this point, which is well documented. What is important to realize, however, is that despite the limited freedom granted after 1979 to rebuild parts of some monasteries and other such tokens of liberalization, the fundamental human rights of the Tibetan people are still today being systematically violated. . . .

If it were not for our community in exile, so generously sheltered and supported by the government and people of India and helped by organizations and individuals from many parts of the world, our nation would today be little more than a shattered remnant of a people. Our culture, religion, and national identity would have been effectively eliminated. As it is, we have built

State and spiritual leader of the Tibetan people, the Dalai Lama fled Tibet in 1959. He won the Nobel Peace Prize in 1989, and he has remained a potent symbol of Tibetan opposition to Chinese control.

schools and monasteries in exile and have created democratic institutions to serve our people and preserve the seeds or our civilization. With this experience, we intend to implement full democracy in a future free Tibet. . . .

The issue of most urgent concern at this time is the massive influx of Chinese settlers into Tibet. Although in the first decades of occupation a considerable number of Chinese were transferred into the eastern parts of Tibet . . . since 1983 an unprecedented number of Chinese have been encouraged by their government to migrate to all parts of Tibet, . . . Tibetans are rapidly being reduced to an insignificant minority in their own country. This development, which threatens the very survival of the Tibetan nation, its culture and spiritual heritage, can still be stopped and reversed. But this must be done now before it is too late.

It was against the background of this worsening situation and in order to prevent further bloodshed, that I proposed what is generally referred to as the Five Point Peace Plan. . . .

The Five Point Peace Plan . . . calls for (1) Transformation of the whole of Tibet, including the eastern provinces of Kham and

Amdo, into a Zone of *Ahimsa*, "non-violence"; (2) Abolition of China's population transfer policy; (3) Respect for the people's fundamental human rights and democratic freedoms; (4) Restoration and protection of Tibet's natural environment; and (5) Commencement of earnest negotiations on the future status of Tibet and of relations between the Tibetan and Chinese peoples.

The United States and China

Traditionally, the United States has viewed its role in China as one of benevolence and humanitarianism in trying to assist China in entering the modern world. That view is set forth by Pearl Buck, daughter of American missionaries, writing about her life in China in the wake of the Boxer Rebellion. She was eight years old when the events that she is describing occurred.

In the year of 1900, however, throughout the spring, the beautiful springtime of the Yangtse [Yangzi] River Valley, I felt my world splitting unexpectedly into its parts. The stream of visitors thinned and sometimes days passed without a single Chinese friend appearing before our gates. My playmates were often silent, they did not play with the usual joy, and at last they too ceased to climb the hill from the valley. Even my schoolmates did not clamor to share my desk seat. I was a child spoiled by love and gifts and at first I was bewildered and then sorely wounded, and when my mother saw this, she explained to me as best she could what was happening. It had nothing to do with Americans, she said, for surely we had never been cruel to the Chinese nor had we taken their land or their river ports. Other white people had done the evil, and our friends, she promised me, understood this and did not hate us. Indeed, they felt as warmly to us as before, only they did not dare to show their feelings, since they would be blamed. At last I comprehended that all of us who were foreigners were being lumped together in the cruel fashion that people can adopt sometimes, for particular and temporary reasons, which are no real reasons but merely vents for old hatreds. . . . I could not understand why we, who were still ourselves and unchanged, should be lumped with unknown white men from unknown countries who had been what we were not, robbers and plunderers. . . . I was innocent. . . .

In direct contrast to the views of Pearl Buck are those of Wang Jisi, the director of the Institute of American Studies at the Chinese Academy of Social Sciences in Beijing. In this journal article titled "A Role of the United States as a Global Pacific Power: A View from China" published in 1997, Wang sees U.S. policy to China as sinister and hostile.

In the People's Republic of China (PRC), textbook interpretations describe the history of the United States as a world power in negative terms. Toward the end of the nineteenth century, the United States as a leading imperialist country joined major European powers . . . in a worldwide contest for hegemony. It soon began to play a significant role in Asia by pronouncing the "Open Door" doctrine in 1899 and 1900, which was designed to dominate China by squeezing out the other imperialist powers.

Political observers and educators in the PRC have never accepted the American textbook cliché that the United States has been inspired by its revolutionary tradition. . . . Although there are some variations and moderation of this line, no one of political weight in China would actually portray the United States as playing a generally constructive role in maintaining world peace. . . . In the bilateral relationship, U.S. hostility toward the PRC is manifested in an incessant effort since 1949 to separate Taiwan from other parts of China. A more sinister American plan has been to sabotage the Communist regime by encouraging political dissension and promoting Western-type democracy within China. This plan is referred to as the "strategy of peaceful evolution."

John K. Fairbank, the father of modern China studies in the United States, presents a more balanced view of U.S.-China relations in his 1971 book *The United Sates and China*.

Unfortunately for us, a proud people when weak do not enjoy receiving help. The American attitude toward China during the century of the unequal treaties was consciously acquisitive but also benevolent. . . . We were proud of our record, indeed a bit patronizing toward the imperialist powers of lesser virtue. Inevitably, however, the Chinese experience of Sino-American relations was different from the American experience. We found our contact with China adventurous, exhilarating, rewarding in material or spiritual terms. Americans who did not like it could avoid it. China,

The police lead a suspect away by his hair in Guangzhou Province. Many Westerners remain highly critical of what they perceive as human rights abuses in the PRC.

on the other hand, found this contact forced upon her. It was a foreign invasion, humiliating, disruptive, and in the end catastrophic. . . . Out of the mix of past-Sino-American relations, Chinese today can stress American imperialism [or its late-twentieth-century cousin, hegemony] where we see mainly our philanthropy, exploitation where we see American aid to the Chinese people.

Human Rights

In 1948, the United Nations adopted the Universal Declaration of Human Rights, which guaranteed numerous rights to all people.

. . . every person's right to life, free from arbitrary killing, and to physical and psychological integrity, free from torture or mistreatment; to freedom from slavery, and from arbitrary arrest, detention, or other physical restraint; to fair trial in the criminal process; to freedom of residence and movement within one's country, including the right to leave any country, as well as the right to return to one's own country; to freedom of conscience and religion, expression, and association; to participation in government; to the equal protection of the law; as well as, and not least, a claim to have basic human needs satisfied—food, shelter, health care, an adequate standard of living for oneself and one's family, education, work, and leisure.

When China entered the United Nations in 1971, it was required to respect the goals of the Declaration of Human Rights. Many times since then, especially in dealing with dissidents and Tibetans, China has been charged with violating many of these principles, specifically supporting and condoning torture, arbitrary arrests, and unfair trials and by not allowing freedom of religion, expression, and association.

China's response has been that "rights" are culture-specific. It points out that traditionally Chinese did not have a concept of individual "rights" but instead the emphasis was placed on individual responsibilities to the group. Thus, to push "rights" today is using a concept from another cultural tradition to force down the throats of Chinese, and indeed other Asians as well. In 1993, before the U.N. World Conference on Human Rights, Asian nations met to set forth their view of human rights in the Bangkok Declaration. The Chinese view on the issue is clear and forceful in the document.

The concept of human rights is a product of historical development. It is closely associated with specific social, political, and economic conditions and the specific history, culture, and values of a particular country. Different historical development stages have different human requirements. . . . Thus, one should not and cannot think of the human rights standards and models of certain countries as the only proper ones and demand all other countries to comply with them. . . . For the vast number of developing countries, to respect and protect human rights is first and foremost to ensure the full realization of the rights to subsistence and development. . . . To wantonly accuse another country of abuse of human rights and impose the human rights criteria of one's own country or region on other countries or regions are tantamount to an infringement upon the sovereignty of other countries and interference in the latter's internal affairs. . . . State sovereignty is the basis for the realization of citizen's human rights. If the sovereignty of a state is not safeguarded, the human rights of its citizens are out of the question, like a castle in the air.

The United States maintains a triple standard. For their own human rights problems they shut their eyes. For some other countries' human rights questions, they open one eye and shut the other. And for China, they open both eyes and stare.
—Chinese Finance Minister Liu Zhongli, March 20, 1994

In other villages, probing ineptly for the peasants' conception of human rights, I had sometimes asked whether there was anything they felt was absolutely their right and something they deserve to have. The answer often came quickly and without hesitation: "Yes, roads."
—Writer Ann Thurston, *Muddling toward Democracy,* 1998

Timeline

1898–1900
The Boxer uprising

1901
Boxer Protocol

1905
The Qing government abolishes civil service system; Sun Yat-sen's forms Revolutionary Alliance in Tokyo

1906
Manchu court promises constitutional system

1908
Cixi and the Guangfu Emperor die

1911
Revolution breaks out in central China

1912
Manchus abdicate; Republic of China is established

1912–16
Presidency of Yuan Shikai

1915
Japan presents the Twenty-One Demands; publication of *New Youth* inaugurates May Fourth Movement

1919
May Fourth demonstration

1921
Founding of the Chinese Communist Party

1924
First Congress of the Nationalist Party (Guomindang)

1925
Sun Yat-sen dies; May Thirtieth Movement

1926–28
Northern Expedition

1927–28
Chiang Kai-shek unleashes White Terror

1930–34
Chiang launches "Extermination Campaigns" against the Communists

1931
Establishment of the Chinese Soviet Republic (Jiangxi Soviet); Manchurian incident

1932
The Communist Party announces Jiangxi Soviet Land Law

1934
Chiang Kai-shek launches New Life Movement

1934–35
Long March

1936
Xi'an Incident

1937–45
Sino-Japanese War

1937
Rape of Nanjing

1942
Yan'an Forum on Art and Literature

1945–47
Marshall mission

1946–48
Land reform campaign in northern China

1947–49
Civil War between the Nationalists and Communists

1949
Establishment of the People's Republic of China; Chiang Kai-shek retreats to Taiwan

1950
Marriage Law announced; China enters Korean War

1951
China seizes Tibet

1957
Hundred Flowers Movement; Anti-Rightist Campaign

1958
Establishment of the first People's Commune

1958–61
Great Leap Forward

1959–62
Great famine

1960
Sino-Soviet split

1966–76
Great Proletarian Cultural Revolution

1971
United Nations admits PRC

1972
President Richard Nixon visits China; United States and China issue Shanghai Communiqué

1975
Chiang Kai-shek dies

1976
Tangshan earthquake; Mao Zedong dies

1978–79
Democracy Wall open

1979
United States establishes diplomatic relations with the PRC

1979–84
Deng Xiaoping launches economic reforms

1989
Pro-democracy demonstrations and government crackdown

1992
Deng Xiaoping gives go-ahead for more economic reforms

1993
Bangkok Declaration on Human Rights

1997
Deng Xiaoping dies; Hong Kong reverts to Chinese control

1999
Macao reverts to Chinese control; Government begins repression of the Falun Gong

2000
Guomindang loses control in Taiwan

Chinese Pronunciations

The following is a list of common people and place names with their Pinyin spelling and phonetic pronunciations.

People

Pinyin	Phonetic
Ai Qing	eye ching
Chen Duxiu	chun doosheeoh
Chen Shuibian	chun shway bee-en
Chiang Kai-shek	jee-ahng kai shek
Cui Jian	tsway jee-en
Deng Yingchao	dung ing chow
Empress Dowager Cixi	tsi she
H. H. Kung	gung
Hou Dejian	hoe duh jee-en
Hu Feng	who fung
Hu Yaobang	who yao bahng
Huang Shaoxiong	hwahng shaow sheeong
Jiang Qing	jee-ahng ching
Jiang Zemin	jee-ahng dzi-mean
Lee Tung-hui	lee dung hway
Li Dazhao	lee dah jao
Li Hongzhi	lee hung jer
Li Zongren	lee dzung ren
Lin Yutang	lin you tahng
Liu Shaoqi	lee-o shaow chee
Lu Xun	lu shwun
Mao Zedong	mao dzi dung
Peng Zhen	pung jun
Qiu Jin	chee-oh jeen

Pinyin	Phonetic
Qu Qiubai	chew chee-oh by
Shen Congwen	shun tsong one
Shen Dingyi	shun deeng ee
Song Jiaoren	soong jee-ow ren
Soong Meiling	soong may ling
Sun Yat-sen	suhn yat sen
Wang Jingwei	wahng jeeng way
Wang Shiwei	wahng sher way
Wei Jingsheng	way jeeng shung
Wen Yiduo	one yee dwo
Wu Peifu	woo pay foo
Xu Xilin	shu she lin
Ye Jianying	yeh jee-en yeeng
Ye Wenfu	yeh one foo
Yuan Shikai	yu-en sher kai
Zeng Guofan	dzung guo-fahn
Zhang Xueliang	jahng shweh leeahng
Zhang Zongchang	jahng dzung chahng
Zhao Ziyang	jao dzi yahng
Zhou Enlai	jo en lai
Zhu De	joo duh
Zou Rong	dzoh ruong

Places

Pinyin	Phonetic	Pinyin	Phonetic
Anhui	ahn hway	Ningbo	neeng bwo
Changsha	chahng sha	Peiping	bay ping
Chengdu	chung doo	Penglai	pung lie
Chongqing	chong ching	Qingdao	ching dao
Dagu	dah goo	Quzhou	chew jo
Dairen	die ren	Rehe	ruh huh
Dongbei	dong bay	Shaanxi	shen she
Fujian	foo jee-en	Shandong	shahn dung
Gansu	gahn su	Shanxi	shahn she
Guangdong	gwahng dung	Shaoxing	shao shing
Guangxi	gwahng she	Shenyang	shun yahng
Guangzhou	gwahng jo	Shenzhen	shun jun
Guizhou	gway jo	Sichuan	si chew-ahn
Hainan	high nahn	Subei	soobay
Hangzhou	hahng jo	Tianjin	tee-en jeen
Heilongjiang	hay lowng jeeahng	Wuchang	woo chahng
Hunan	who nahn	Wuhan	woo hahn
Jiangsu	jeeahng su	Xi'an	she ahn
Jiangxi	jeeahng she	Xinjiang	sheen jee-ahng
Jilin	jee lin	Xunwu	shwun woo
Kunming	kwun meeng	Xuzhou	shoo jo
Liaodong	lee-ow dung	Yan'an	yen ahn
Liaoning	lee-ow neeng	Yunnan	yuwn nahn
Loyang	lwo yahng	Zhejiang	juh jeeahng
Nanjing	nahn jing	Zhili	jer lee
		Zhongnanhai	jong nahn high

Further Reading

Chinese History

Goldman, Merle, and Andrew Gordon, eds. *Historical Perspectives on Contemporary East Asia*. Cambridge: Harvard University Press, 2000.

Schoppa, R. Keith. *The Columbia Guide to Modern Chinese History*. New York: Columbia University Press, 2000.

———. *Revolution and Its Past*. Upper Saddle River, N.J.: Prentice Hall, 2002.

Spence, Jonathan. *The Gate of Heavenly Peace*. New York: Viking Penguin, 1981.

———. *The Search for Modern China*. New York: Norton, 1999.

Chinese Culture

Barme, Geremie. *In the Red: On Contemporary Chinese Culture*. New York: Columbia University Press, 1999.

Butterfield, Fox. *Alive in the Bitter Sea*. New York: Times Books, 1982.

Chang, Jung. *Wild Swans: Three Daughters of China*. New York: Simon & Schuster, 1991.

Cohen, Paul. *History in Three Keys: The Boxers as Event, Experience, and Myth*. New York: Columbia University Press, 1997.

Dutton, Michael. *Streetlife China*. Cambridge: Cambridge University Press, 1998.

Fei Xiaotong. *From the Soil: The Foundations of Chinese Society*. Berkeley: University of California Press, 1992.

Ko, Dorothy. *Every Step a Lotus: Shoes for Bound Feet*. Berekely: University of California Press, 2001.

Kristof, Nicholas, and Sheryl WuDunn. *China Wakes: The Struggle for the Soul of a Rising Power*. New York: Times Books, 1994.

Schoppa, R. Keith. *Song Full of Tears*. Boulder, Colo.: Westview Press, 2002.

Tyson, James and Ann. *Chinese Awakenings: Life Stories from the Unofficial China*. Boulder, Colo.: Westview, 1995.

Zha, Jianying. *China Pop: How Soap Operas, Tabloids, and Bestsellers Are Transforming a Culture*. New York: New Press, 1995.

The Mao Years

Belden, Jack. *China Shakes the World*. New York: Monthly Review Press, 1970.

Hinton, William. *Fanshen: A Documentary of Revolution in a Chinese Village*. New York: Monthly Review Press, 1966.

Li, Zhisui. *The Private Life of Chairman Mao*. New York: Random House, 1994.

Short, Philip. *Mao, A Life*. New York: Henry Holt, 1999.

Snow, Edgar. *Red Star over China*. New York: Random House, 1937.

Wu, Ningkun, with Yikai Wu. *A Single Tear: A Family's Persecution, Love, and Endurance in Communist China*. Boston: Little, Brown and Company, 1993.

Yang, Rae. *Spider Eaters: A Memoir*. Berkeley: University of California Press, 1997.

Post-Mao Years

Baum, Richard. *Burying Mao*. Princeton, N.J.: Princeton University Press, 1994.

Goodman, David S. G. *Deng Xiaoping and the Chinese Revolution: A Political Biography*. New York: Routledge, 1994.

Lieberthal, Kenneth. *Governing China: From Revolution through Reform*. New York: Norton, 1995.

Ogden, Suzanne, Kathleen Hartford, Lawrence Sullivan, and David Zweig, eds. *China's Search for Democracy: The Students and Mass Movement of 1989*. Armonk, N.Y.: M. E. Sharpe, 1992.

Salzman, Mark. *Iron and Silk*. New York: Random House, 1986.

The Republic

Bergere, Marie-Claire. *Sun Yat-sen*. Trans. Janet Lloyd. Stanford, Calif.: Stanford University Press, 1998.

Cochran, Sherman, Andrew C. K. Hsieh, and Janis Cochran, eds. *One Day in China: May 21, 1936*. New Haven: Yale University Press, 1983.

Heresy, John. *The Call*. New York: Knopf, 1985.

Lu, Xun. *Selected Stories of Lu Xun*. San Francisco: China Books, 1994.

Mo, Yan. *Red Sorghum: A Novel of China.* Trans. Howard Goldblatt. New York: Viking, 1993.

Peck, Graham. *Two Kinds of Time.* Boston: Houghton Mifflin, 1950.

Schoppa, R. Keith. *Blood Road.* Berkeley: University of California Press, 1995.

White, Theodore H., and Annalee Jacoby. *Thunder out of China.* New York: William Sloane Associates, 1946.

Wilbur, C. Martin, and Julie Lien-ying How. *Missionaries of Revolution: Soviet Advisors and Nationalist China, 1920–1927.* Cambridge: Harvard University Press, 1989.

The United States and China

Cohen, Warren. *America's Response to China: An Interpretive History of Sino-American Relations.* New York: Columbia University Press, 1990.

Mann, James. *About Face: A History of America's Curious Relationship with China, from Nixon to Clinton.* New York: Alfred A. Knopf, 1998.

Schaller, Michael. *The United States and China in the Twentieth Century.* New York: Oxford University Press, 1990.

Shambaugh, David. *Beautiful Imperialist: China Perceives America, 1972–1990.* Princeton, N.J.: Princeton University Press, 1991.

Primary Source Collections

Benton, Gregor, and Alan Hunter, eds. *Wild Lily, Prairie Fire: China's Road to Democracy, Yan'an to Tian'anmen.* Princeton, N.J.: Princeton University Press, 1995.

Cheng, Pei-kai, and Michael Lestz, eds., with Jonathan Spence. *The Search for Modern China: A Documentary Collection.* New York: Norton, 1999.

Gentzler, J. Mason. *Changing China: Readings in the History of China from the Opium War to the Present.* New York: Praeger, 1977.

Han, Minchu, and Hua Sheng, eds. *Cries for Democracy in China: Writings and Speeches from the 1989 Chinese Democracy Movement.* Princeton, N.J.: Princeton University Press, 1990.

Li, Dun J., ed. *Modern China: From Mandarin to Commissar.* New York: Scribner, 1978.

———. *The Road to Communism: China Since 1912.* New York: Van Nostrand Reinhold, 1969.

Saich, Tony, ed. *The Rise to Power of the Chinese Communist Party: Documents and Analysis, 1920–1949.* Armonk, N.Y.: M. E. Sharpe, 1994.

Websites

China the Beautiful
www.chinapage.com/main2.html

A wide range of information on historical and contemporary China.

The Chinese Embassy, Washington D.C.
www.china-embassy.org

Organized into more than twenty broad categories, this guide includes press releases and political, economic, and cultural information.

Inside China Today
www.insidechina.com

An English-language newspaper in the PRC.

China Times
www.chinatimes.com.tw/english/english.htm

An English-language newspaper in Taiwan.

Harvard Yenching Library
Hcl.harvard.edu/harvard-yenching

The main website of the Yenching library at Harvard University provides information about its holdings of Chinese, Japanese, Korean, and Western materials.

John Fairbank Memorial Chinese History Virtual Library
www.cnd.org/fairbank

Virtual bookshelf of the *China News Digest,* holding links to titles of important works dealing with twentieth century China.

Text Credits

Main Text

17–19: Mark Twain, "To the Person Sitting in Darkness," *North American Review* vol. 531 (February 1901): 162–64.

19–22: *The Boxer Protocol.* W. W. Malloy, ed. *Treaties, Conventions, International Acts, Protocols and Agreements between the United States of America and other Powers, 1776–1909.* Washington, D.C.: Government Printing Office, 1910, vol. 2, pp. 2,006–12. Quoted in R. Keith Schoppa, *The Columbia Guide to Modern Chinese History.* New York: Columbia University Press, 2000, 275–77. © 2000 Columbia University Press. Reprinted with the permission of the publisher.

22–23: Cartoon entitled "The Open Door that China Needs," *Brooklyn Eagle,* July 14, 1900. Reprinted in Paul Cohen, *History in Three Keys,* New York: Columbia University Press, 1997, 236; and cartoon entitled "National Humiliation Picture," *Anhui Common Speech Journal,* October 1905. Reprinted in Paul Cohen, *History in Three Keys,* 242.

27–28: Wolfgang Franke, *The Reform and Abolition of the Traditional Examination System.* Cambridge, Mass.: Harvard University Press, 1968, 59–64.Reproduced by permission of Harvard University Asia Center.

28–29: The Revolutionary Alliance Manifesto. *Zhougshan quanshu* [The Complete Works of Sun Yatsen]. n.p., 1905. Quoted in Schoppa, *The Columbia Guide to Modern Chinese History,* 278–79. © 2000 Columbia University Press. Reprinted with the permission of the publisher.

30–31: Edward J. M. Rhoads, "The Assassination of Governor Enming and Its Effect on Manchu-Han Relations in Late Qing China," in *China's Republican Revolution* ed. Eto Shinkichi and Harold Z. Schiffrin. Tokyo: University of Tokyo Press, 1994, 6–7.

31–33: Ono Shinji, "A Deliberate Rumor: National Anxiety in China on the Eve of the Xinhai Revolution," in Eto Shinkichi and Harold Z. Schiffrin, eds., *China's Republican Revolution.* Tokyo, Japan: University of Tokyo Press, 1994, pp. 6–7.

34: *Qiu Jin ji* [The Writings of Qui Jin]. Beijing, 1960, 4–5. Quoted in Jonathan Spence, *The Gate of Heavenly Peace.* New York: Viking, 1981, 51.

34–35: Pei-kai Cheng and Michael Lestz with Jonathan Spence, *The Search for Modern China: A Documentary Collection.* New York: W.W. Norton, 1999, 211–12.© 1999 by W.W. Norton & Company, Inc. Used by permission.

37–39: Ernest Young, "Politics in the Aftermath of Revolution: The Era of Yuan Shih-k'ai" in *The Cambridge History of China, Vol. 12, Republican China 1912–1949, Part 1.* Cambridge: Cambridge University Press, 1983, 243. Reprinted with the permission of Cambridge University Press.

40–43: Pei-kai Cheng and Michael Lestz with Jonathan Spence, *The Search for Modern China, A Documentary Collection.* New York: Norton, 1999, pp. 217–20. © 1999 by W.W. Norton & Company, Inc. Used by permission.

43–44: Edgar Snow, *Living China.* Westport, Conn.: Hyperion, 1937, 222–25.

45: Odoric Y. K. Wou, "The Military and Nationalism: The Political Thinking of Wu P'ei-fu," in *China in the 1920s, Nationalism and Revolution,* ed. F. Gilbert Chan and Thomas Etzold. New York: New Viewpoints, 1976, 120. All rights reserved. Reprinted by permission of Franklin Watts, an imprint of Scholastic Library Publishing, Inc.

46–47: Diana Lary, *Warlord Soldiers.* Cambridge: Cambridge University Press, 1985, 149–52. Reprinted by permission of Cambridge University Press.

53: Ssu-yu Teng and John K. Fairbank, *China's Response to the West: A Documentary Survey, 1839–1923.* Cambridge, Mass.: Harvard University Press, 1954, 240–46. © 1954, 1979 by the President and Fellows of Harvard College. Copyright renewed 1982 by Ssu-yu Teng and John King Fairbank.

54–56: Deng Yingchao, "My Experience with the May Fourth Movement," in *Modern China: From Mandarin to Commissar,* trans. Dun J. Li. New York: Scribner's, 1978, 154–57.

56–57: Ssu-yu Teng and John Fairbank, *China's Response to the West: A Documentary Survey, 1839–1923.* Cambridge: Harvard University Press, 1954, pp. 240–46.

58–59: Lu Hsun [Xun], *Selected Stories of Lu Hsun.* San Francisco: China Books and Periodicals, 1994, 2–5.

59: Chow Tse-tsung, *The May Fourth Movement.* Stanford, Calif.: Stanford University Press, 1960, 184.

60–61: Li Dazhao, "The Victory of Bolshevism," *New Youth,* November 15, 1918. Reprinted in Ssu-yu Teng and John K. Fairbank, *China's Response to the West.* Cambridge, Mass.: Harvard University Press, 1954, 246–49.

66: *Shenbao,* June 6, 1927, September 23, 1927.

66–68: Speech delivered by Sun Yat-sen, 1924. Quoted in Schoppa, *The Columbia Guide to Modern Chinese History,* 282–84.

68: Wang Jingwei, political testament signed by Sun Yat-sen, March 11, 1925. Quoted in Marie-Claire Bergere, *Sun Yat-sen.* Stanford, Calif.: Stanford University Press, 1998, 406.

69: Marie-Claire Bergere, *Sun Yat-sen.* Stanford, Calif.: Stanford University Press, 1998, p. 406.

70–72: Mao Zedong, *Report to the Central Committee of the Chinese Communist Party,* March 1927. Reprinted in J. Mason Gentzler, *Changing China: Readings in the History of China from the Opium War to the Present.* New York: Praeger, 1977, 217–22.

72–75: Li, *Modern China: From Mandarin to Commissar,* 230–36.

79–81: Madame Chiang Kai-shek, *General Chiang Kai-shek and the Communist Crisis.* Shanghai: China Weekly Review Press, 1935. Reprinted in Cheng and Lestzwith Spence, *The Search for Modern China: A Documentary Collection,* 295–97.

81–83: Kang Yimin, *Zhongguo diyiri* [One day in China]. Shanghai, n.p., 1936. Quoted in *One Day in China: May 21, 1936,* ed. Sherman Cochran, Andrew C. K. Hsieh, and Janis Cochran. New Haven, Conn.: Yale University Press, 1983, 101–4. © Yale University Press.

83–84: Xi, *Zhongguo diyiri* [One day in China]. Shanghai, n.p., 1936. Quoted in *One Day in China: May 21, 1936,* ed. Cochran, Hsieh, and Cochran, 130–37.

85–87: Speech delivered by Chiang Kai-shek in Nanchang, Jiangxi, May 8, 1933. Reprinted in Li, *Modern China: From Mandarin to Commissar,* 256–57.

88–89: Chiang Kai-shek, *The Soviet Union in China.* Taipei: Central Cultural Supplies, 1956. Quoted in Li, *Modern China: From Mandarin to Commissar,* 238–40.

89–91: Speech delivered by Zhang Xueliang at Xi'an, December 13, 1936. Reprinted in Li, *Modern China: From Mandarin to Commissar,* 240–42.

96–98: The Soviet Land Law. *Gongfei tudi zhengze zhongyao wenxian huibian* [Important documents on the CCP land policies]. Shanghai: Zhonglian Publishers, 1937. Reprinted in Schoppa, *The Columbia Guide to Modern Chinese History,* 288–90.

98–100: Edgar Snow, *Red Star over China.* New York: Random House, 1937, 215–17. © 1938, 1944 by Random House; copyright © 1968 by Edgar Snow. Used by permission of Grove/Atlantic, Inc.

100: Speech by Mao Zedong at the Yan'an Forum on Art and Literature, May 23, 1942. Reprinted in Schoppa, *The Columbia Guide to Modern Chinese History,* 290–91. © 2000 Columbia University Press. Reprinted with the permission of the publisher.

102–4: Wang Shiwei, "Wild Lily," *Liberation Daily,* March 13 and 24, 1942. Reprinted in *Wild Lily, Prairie Fire,* ed. Gregor Benton and Alan Hunter. Princeton, N.J.: Princeton University Press, 1995, 70–75. © 1995 by Princeton University Press. Reprinted by permission of Princeton University Press.

105–5: Ding Ling, "Thoughts on March 8 (Women's Day)," 1942. Reprinted in *Wild Lily, Prairie Fire,* ed. Benton and Hunter, 78–82.

110: Konoye Fumimaro, "New Order in East Asia," speech given in Tokyo, November 3, 1938. Wu Tieting, *Kang Ri huashi* [The war of resistance against Japan]. Hong Kong: Xiandai Publishers, 1970, 133–34.

110–11: Chiang Kai-shek, December 1936. Chang Chi-yun, ed., *Chiang Tsung-tung chi* [Works of President Chiang]. Taipei: Research Institute of National Defense, 1968, vol. 1, 1083-89. Reprinted in Li, *Modern China: From Mandarin to Commissar,* 271–75.

112–13: "Radio address by Mr. Wang Ching-wei, President of the Chinese Executive Yuan," June 24, 1941. *Tokyo Gazette,* vol. 5, no. 2. Tokyo, August 1941, 82–88.

113–14: Verdict by the Military Tribunal for the Trial of War Criminals at Tokyo, March 10, 1947. Reprinted in Dun J. Li, *The Road to Communism: China Since 1912*, New York: Van Nostrand Reinhold, 1969, 208–9.

115–16: *Quzhou shizhi* [Gazetteer of Quzhou city]. Hangzhou: Zhejiang People's Press, 1994, 1155–56, and *Rijun qinlue Zhejiang shilu* [A record of aggression by the Japanese army in Zhejiang.] Beijing: Chinese Communist Party Publishing House, 1995, 784.

118–19: W. H. Auden and Christopher Isherwood, *Journey to a War*. New York: Random House, 1939, 216–20.

116–18: Theodore White and Annalee Jacoby, *Thunder out of China*. New York: William Sloane, 1946, 169–72.

123–24: A. Doak Barnett, *China on the Eve of the Communist Takeover*. New York: Praeger, 1963, 20.

124–25: Speech by Wen Yiduo at memorial service for Li Gongpu, July 15, 1946. Reprinted in Cheng and Lestz with Spence, *The Search for Modern China: A Documentary Collection*, 337–38. © 1999 by W.W. & Company, Inc. Used by permission.

126–28: Speech by Zhu Deu to the CCP's Seventh Congress, April 25, 1945. Reprinted in Li, *Modern China: From Mandarin to Commissar*, 291–96.

129–30: Chiang Kai-shek, *The Soviet Union in China*. Taipei: Central Cultural Supplies, 1957. Reprinted in Li, *Modern China: From Mandarin to Commissar*, 313–15.

130–31: *The China White Paper*, Stanford, Calif.: Stanford University Press, 1967, xii–xv.

132–33: Barnett, *China on the Eve of the Communist Takeover*, 339–44.

141–42: Li Zhusui, *The Private Life of Chairman Mao*. New York: Random House, 1994, 51–52. © 1995 by Dr. Zhi-Sui Li. Used by permission of Random House, Inc.

142–45: J. Mason Gentzler, *Changing China: Readings in the History of China from the Opium War to the Present*. New York: Praeger, 1977, 268–72.

145–46: Ding Ling, *The Sun Shines over the Sanggan River*. Beijing: Foreign Languages Press, 1984, 309–15.

146–47: Li, *The Private Life of Chairman Mao*, 277.

148: Jung Chang, *Wild Swans*. New York: Simon and Schuster, 1991, 231–32. © Simon and Schuster.

148–51: William Hinton, "Hundred Day War," *Monthly Review*, vol. 24, 3. July/August 1972, *154*, *160–61*. © *1972 by Montly Review Press*.

151: Ma Bo, *Blood Red Sunset*. New York: Viking, 1995, 158, 161, 165.

162–64: Ruan Ming, *Deng Xiaoping: Chronicle of an Empire*, trans. Nancy Liu, Peter Rand, and Lawrence R. Sullivan. Boulder, Colo.: Westview, 1992, 73–74.

164–66: Speech by Deng Xiaoping in Wuchang, Shenzhen, Zhuhai, and Shanghai, January 18 to February 21, 1992. Reprinted in *China Since*

Tiananmen: Political, Economic, and Social Conflicts, ed. Lawrence R. Sullivan. Armonk, N.Y.: M. E. Sharpe, 1995, 151–53.

166–67: *Zhongguo tongxun she* [China News Agency], "Gap between Eastern, Other Regions 'Widening,'" April 1, 1993. Translated in *China Since Tiananmen: Political, Economic, and Social Conflicts*, ed. Sullivan, 189–90.

167–69: Dorothy Solinger, *Contesting Citizenship in Urban China*. Berkeley: University of California Press, 1999, 156–57. © 1999 by The Regents of the University of California.

170: Michael Dutton, *Streetlife China*. Cambridge: Cambridge University Press, 1998, 279. Reprinted with the permission of Cambridge University Press

170–72: James and Ann Tyson, *Chinese Awakenings*. Boulder, Colo.: Westview, 1995, 40–60.

173: Radio report in Nanjing, December 1990. *Shen Daren*, "On Building Spiritual Civilization," December 11, 1990. Reprinted in *China Since Tiananmen: Political, Economic, and Social Conflicts*, ed. Sullivan, 211–12.

178–80: Wei Jingsheng, "Do We Want Democracy or a New Dictatorship?" *Explorations*, March 1979, 192–96. Reprinted in *Wild Lily, Prairie Fire*, ed. Benton and Hunter, 180–84. © 1995 by Princeton University Press. Reprinted by permission.

180–81: Ye Wenfu, "General, You Can't Do This," *Shikan* [Poetry], 1979. Reprinted in *Mao's Harvest*, ed. Helen F. Siu and Zelda Stern. New York: Oxford University Press, 1983, 163–64.

182: Geremie Barmé, *In the Red*. New York: Columbia University Press, 1999, 329–30. ©1999 Columbia University Press. Reprinted with the permission of the publisher.

183–84: Geremie Barmé and Linda Jairin, eds., *New Ghosts, Old Dreams*. New York: Times Books, 1992, 153–54. © 1992 by Geremie Barme and Linda Jaivin. Used by permission of Times Books, a division of Random House, Inc.

185–86: Li Hongzhi, *Falun Gong*, April 2001. *www.falundafa.org/book/eng/flg.htm*.

186–87: "Some Cases of Sickness, Handicap, and Death Resulting from Falun Gong Practice," *Beijing Review*. August 9, 1999: 11–12.

193–94: Agreement between China and Great Britain, September 26, 1984. Reprinted in Cheng and Lestz with Spence, *The Search for Modern China: A Documentary Collection*, 476–79.

195: Jonathan Braude, "UK's Craddock: PRC Prepared to 'Wreck' Hong Kong Economy," *South China Morning Post*, December 4, 1992, 1. Reprinted in *China Since Tiananmen*, ed. Sullivan , 129–30.

196: Press release, "PRC Office Reacts to Legco's Adoption of Electoral Bill," Xinhua News Agency, Beijing, February 24, 1994. Reprinted in *China Since Tiananmen* ed. Sullivan, 131.

196–98: Radio broadcast delivered by Jiang Zemin, January 31, 1995. Reprinted in Cheng and Lestz with Spence, *The Search for Modern China: A*

Documentary Collection, 516–17.

198–99: The Shanghai Communiqué. *Peking Review*, 9: March 3, 1972, 4–5. Reprinted in Cheng and Lestz with Spence, *The Search for Modern China: A Documentary Collection*, 438–39.

200–2: Nobel Peace Prize speech delivered by the Dalai Lama in Helsinki, December 1989. Reprinted in Cheng and Lestz with Spence, *The Search for Modern China: A Documentary Collection*, 508–10.

202: Pearl Buck, *My Several Worlds: A Personal Record*. New York: John Day, 1954, 37–38. Quoted in Benson Lee Grayson, *The American Image of China*. New York: Frederick Ungar, 1979, 150–51.

203: "The Role of the United States as a Global Pacific Power: A View from China," *Pacific Review* 10, no. 1, 1997, 2–3.

203–4: John K. Fairbank, *The United States and China*, 3rd ed. Cambridge, Mass.: Harvard University Press, 1971, 402–3. Reprinted in David Lampton, *Same Bed, Different Dreams*. Berkeley: University of California Press, 2001, 252–54.

204: Universal Declaration of Human Rights. Quoted in Louis Henken, "The Human Rights Idea in Contemporary China: A Comparative Perspective," in *Human Rights in Contemporary China*, ed. R. Randle Edwards, Louis Henken, and Andrew Nathan. New York: Columbia University Press, 1986, 9.

205: Speech by Li Huagiu in Vienna on June 15, 1993. Quoted in Michael Davis, "Chinese Perspectives on Human Rights," in Michael C. Davis, *Human Rights and Chinese Values*. Hong Kong: Oxford University Press, 1995, 17.

Sidebars

17: Letter from D. Z. Sheffield to Judson Smith, March 26, 1901, American Board of Commissioners for Foreign Missions Archives, vol. 29, no. 17.

19: George Lynch, *The War of Civilizations, Being a Record of a "Foreign Devil's" Experience with the Allies in China*. London: Longmans Green, 1901, 84.

29: Zou Rong, *Gemingjuan* [The Revolutionary Army]. Shanghai, 1903. Quoted in Spence, *The Gate of Heavenly Peace*, 47–48.

30: Qiu Jin, *Collected Works of Qiu Jin*, Beijing, 1960. Quoted in Jonathan Spence, *The Gate of Heavenly Peace*, 50–51.

38: John Dewey and Alice Chapman Dewey, *Letters from China and Japan*. New York: E. Dutton, 1920, 216–17.

43: Gong Yao, et al., "Huoguo yangmin tanwu canbao zhi Zhang Zongzhang," [The cruelty and greediness of Zhang Zhanzhang harms the country and its people]. *Yijing* [Unorthodox classics], 6: May 20, 1936, 316–20.

16: Shen Congwen, "Staff Adviser," *Wenxue*, [Literary studies] vol. 7, no. 1, 1935: 96–101. Translated in *Imperfect Paradise*, ed. Jeffrey Kinkley. Honolulu: University of Hawaii Press, 1995, 173.

49: Alan Baumler, ed., *Modern China and Opium: A Reader.* Ann Arbor: University of Michigan Press, 2001, 111. © University of Michigan Press.

53: Qu Qiubai, *Wenji*, vol. 1. Beijing: Renmin Wenxui Chubanshe, 1954, 23. Quoted in Joanna Waley-Cohen, *The Sextants of Beijing.* New York: Norton, 1999, 216.

54: Lu Xun, *Lu Xun xuanji* [Complete works of Lu Xun]. Beijing: Renmin Wenxui Chubanshe, 1963. Quoted in Gladys Yang, tr., *Silent Chinese.* Oxford: Oxford University Press, 1973, 137–47. Used by permission of Oxford University Press.

56: Lu Xun, *Lu Xun xuanji,* [Complete works of Lu Xun], 196. Quoted in "On Expressing an Opinion," in Yang, *Silent China,* 126.

55: Lu Xun, *Lu Xun xuanji* [Complete works of Lu Xun]. Quoted in Yang, *Silent China,* 140–41.

59: Lu Xun, *Lu Xun xuanji* [Complete works of Lu Xun]. Quoted in Yang, *Silent China,* 148, 150–51.

60: Shi Cuntong, *Wusi shigi de shetuan* [Associational organizations of the May Fourth period]. Edited by Zhang Yunhou, Yin Xuyi, Hong Qing xiang, and Wang Yunkai. Vol. 3, Beijing: Shenghuo, dushu, xinzhi sanlian sudian, 135.

66: Shen Dingyi, "Huibo" (Ripples), *Xingqi pinglun* [Weekly review]. June 6, 1920: 1.

67: R. Keith Schoppa, *Blood Road.* Berkeley, Calif.: University of California Press, 1995, p. 101. © 1995 by the Regents of the University of California.

80: New Life Promotion Society of Nanchang, *What Must Be Known about New Life.* Nanjing: n.p., 1935, 216–20. Reprinted in Cheng and Lestz with Spence, *The Search for Modern China: A Documentary Collection,* 298–300.

85: Parks Coble, *Facing Japan.* Cambridge, Mass.: Harvard University Press, 1991, 295.

101: *Jiefang Ribao* [Liberation daily], June 28 and 29, 1942. Quoted in Tony Saich, *The Rise to Power of the Chinese Communist Party.* Armonk, N.Y.: M. E. Sharpe, 1996, 1120.

111: Tian Jian, "To Those Who Fight," [Zhonghua xin shi xuan,] ed. Zang Kojia. Beijing, 1956, 148–60. Translated in *Twentieth Century Chinese Poetry,* ed. Hsu Kaiyu. Garden City, N.Y.: Doubleday, 1964, 322–23. © 1963 by Kai-yu Hsu. Used by permission of Doubleday, a division of Random House, Inc.

113: Meng Wei. Quoted in *One Day in China: May 21, 1936,* ed. Cochran, Hsieh, and Cochran, 207–8.

118: Fang Jing, "A Dirge," *The Songs of a Stroller.* Shanghai: n.p., 1948, 62–64. Translated in *Twentieth Century Chinese Poetry,* ed. Kaiyu Hsu, 387–88.

124: Wen Yiduo, "One Sentence," *The Complete Works of Wen Yiduo.* Shanghai: n.p., 1948, 23–24. Reprinted in *The Columbia Anthology of Modern Chinese Literature,* ed. Joseph S. M. Lau and Howard Goldblatt. New York: Columbia University Press, 1995, 507–8. © 1995 Columbia University Press. Reprinted by permission of the publisher.

133: Jack Belden, *China Shakes the World.* New York: Harper, 1949, p. 469.

144: Fox Butterfield, *China: Alive in the Bitter Sea.* New York: Times Books, 1982, 167.

146: William Hinton, *Fanshen.* New York: Random House, 1968, vii.

148: *Wild Lily, Prairie Fire,* ed. Benton and Hunter, 99–100. © 1995 by Princeton University Press. Reprinted by permission of the publisher.

164: Richard Baum, *Burying Mao.* Princeton, N.J.: Princeton University Press, 1994, p. 29. © 1995 by Princeton University Press. Reprinted by permission of the publisher.

182: Chai Ling, "Qing zunzhong lishi," *Tiananmen* 1, 1: June 1995, 4. Quoted in Geremie Barme, *In the Red.* New York: Columbia University Press, 1999, 330–31. © 1999 Columbia University Press. Reprinted with the permission of the publisher.

197: Lee Tung-hui, *The Road to Democracy: Taiwan's Pursuit of Identity.* New York: Dell, 1999, pp. 124–25.

198: "Word for Word/Kissinger Transcripts," *New York Times,* January 10, 1999. Steven Mufson, "Gingrich Tells China: 'We'd Defend Taiwan.'" *Washington Post,* March 31, 1997, 1. Reprinted in David Lampton, *Same Bed, Different Dreams.* Berkeley: University of California Press, 2001, 204–5. © 2001 by The Regents of the University of California.

205: Lampton, *Same Bed, Different Dreams.* Berkeley: University of California Press, 2001, 111. Anne F. Thurston, *Mudling toward Decomcracy.* Washington D.C.: U.S. Institute of Peace.

Picture Credits

Adrian Bradshaw-Imaginechina: 163, 168; Alan Chin/Sovfoto: 179; Associated Press, AP Photographer JEFF WIDENER, Staff: 174; By Permission of The British Library. Shelfmark: Or.5896: 18, 62; ChinaStock: 28, 176; Cixi, Empress Dowager of China, 1835-1908 Photographs. David Rose / Panos Pictures: 195; Freer Gallery of Art and Arthur M. Sackler Gallery Archives. Smithsonian Institution, Washington, D.C.: Purchase. Photographer: Xunling, negative number SC-GR 255: 24; CNS - Imaginechina: 199; Courtesy of the Falun Dafa Information Center: 185; Dewey Webster/Sovfoto: 172; Feng Zikai: 12; Image take from *History in Three Keys: The Boxers as Event, Experience, and Myth* by Paul Cohen ©1997 Columbia University Press. Reprinted with the permission of the publisher.: 22, 23; Hedda Morrison Collection, Harvard-Yenching Library, Harvard University.: 39, 76, 82; Hoover Institution Archives: 26, 42, 57, 99, 112, 117, 143, 179, 181, 156; IISH Stefan R. Landsberger Collection, *www.iisg.nl/~landsberger:* 57; Image courtesy of Ira Toff: 160; Imaginechina: 36, 60; Jim Steinhart of *www.PlanetWare.com:* cover, 2, 3, 165, 193; Kautz Family YMCA Archives, University of Minnesota Libraries, Minneapolis, MN: 50; Li Wei - Imaginechina: 190; Library of Congress: 21, 30, 32, 44, 54, 68, 72, 79, 86, 89, 92, 105, 109, 119, 120, 126, 134, 136, 138, 150, 169; Long Bow Group, Inc.: 155, 54, 56, 157; Lu Houmin/ChinaStock: 152; Mark Henley / Panos Pictures: 204; Michael Collopy: 201; National Archives: 14, 114; Courtesy Dept. of Library Services American Museum of Natural History: 19; © 1936 *New York Times:* 91; Photograph courtesy of the Imperial War Museum, London. Negative # NYP 57283: 106; Renchenming - Imaginechina: 188; S&R Greenhill: 140; Shen Bao June 24, 1927: 66; *Shen Bao,* June 6, 1927:65; Sovfoto/Eastfoto: 147; The Sidney D. Gamble Foundation for Chinese Studies: 48; Xinhua/Sovfoto: 180, 182; Xinxiue News Agency: 103, 125, 131; Zhengruide - Imaginechina: 158.

Index

About the Author

R. Keith Schoppa holds the Doehler Chair in Asian History at Loyola College in Maryland. He is the author of *Blood Road: The Mystery of Shen Dingyi in Revolutionary China*, *Xiang Lake: Nine Centuries of Chinese Life*, *Chinese Elites and Political Change*, *Revolution and Its Past*, and *The Columbia Guide to Modern Chinese History*.